Poltergeist over Scotland

Geoff Holder

As the word poltergeist is German
(*poltern*, noisy, *geist*, ghost), it seems appropriate
to tip the titfer to the legends of *kosmische musik*:
Amon Düül II, Can, Cluster, Embryo, Faust,
Neu!, Popol Vuh, Klaus Schulze and Tangerine
Dream. Thanks for the wig-outs, chaps.

First published 2013
The History Press
The Mill, Brimscombe Port
Stroud, Gloucestershire, GL5 2QG
www.thehistorypress.co.uk

© Geoff Holder, 2013

The right of Geoff Holder to be identified as the Author
of this work has been asserted in accordance with the
Copyrights, Designs and Patents Act 1988.
All rights reserved. No part of this book may be reprinted
or reproduced or utilised in any form or by any electronic,
mechanical or other means, now known or hereafter invented,
including photocopying and recording, or in any information
storage or retrieval system, without the permission in writing
from the Publishers.
British Library Cataloguing in Publication Data.
A catalogue record for this book is available from the British Library.

ISBN 978 0 7524 8283 5

Typesetting and origination by The History Press
Printed in Great Britain

Contents

	Acknowledgements	4
	Introduction	5
Chapter One:	The Seventeenth Century	11
Chapter Two:	The Eighteenth Century	49
Chapter Three:	The Nineteenth Century	59
Chapter Four:	The Twentieth Century, Part I: 1900-1949	102
Chapter Five:	The Twentieth Century, Part II: 1950-1975	129
Chapter Six:	The Twentieth Century, Part III: 1976-1999	167
Chapter Seven:	The Twenty-First Century (to 2012)	195
	Bibliography	215
	Index	223

Acknowledgements

Many thanks to: the AK Bell Library, Perth; the Burns Monument Centre, Kilmarnock; Edinburgh Libraries, the National Records of Scotland, the National Library of Scotland and the Advocates Library, Edinburgh; Aberdeen Library Local Studies; the Mitchell Library, Glasgow; Shetland Archives; and Shetland Library. I would also like to express my appreciation to the various organisations that responded to my Freedom of Information requests.

I wish to extend my gratitude to: Alan Murdie of The Ghost Club; Julian Drewett of The Churches' Fellowship for Psychical and Spiritual Studies; the Revd Angus Haddow; Tim Prevett; Dr John Holliday; Lachie Campbell; Tricia Robertson of the Scottish Society for Psychical Research; Melvyn Willin of the SPR; Professor Peter Jánosi of the University of Vienna; the late Norman Adams; Jamie Cook; Dane Love; Ron Halliday; Dr Peter McCue; Archibald Lawrie; Jenni Wilson for designing the maps; and, *bien sûr*, Ségolène 'Cactus' Dupuy. All sins of commission and omission are of course the author's.

Geoff Holder manifests mysteriously at www.geoffholder.com.

Introduction

'The annoyances appear rather like the tricks of a mischievous imp.
I refer to what the Germans call the Poltergeist, or racketing spectre,
for the phenomenon is known in all countries, and has been known
in all ages.'

Catherine Crowe, *The Night-Side of Nature*, 1848.
This book introduced the word 'poltergeist' into the English language.

This is the first-ever history of Scottish poltergeists. It covers 134 cases, from the 1630s to the present day. Herein, furniture flies, objects move, electricity goes haywire, fires and floods flourish, terrifying noises bluster and bang, skin is scratched, blood and maggots ooze, and foul stenches pervade.

Enjoy.

WHAT ARE POLTERGEISTS?

The late John Peel (1939-2004) once described his favourite group, The Fall, as 'always different, always the same'. And so it is with poltergeists, whose cantrips are as similar – and as bafflingly pointless – today as they were many centuries ago.

As with other paranormal episodes, poltergeist cases tend to have two parts: the 'description of phenomena' (i.e. the experiences, as described by the participants or commentators) and the 'interpretation', which is an entirely different kettle of aquatic vertebrates. For example, two people can experience being overwhelmed by a mysterious bright light, and one will interpret it as a UFO/alien experience, while the other will ascribe to it a religious interpretation (angel/saint/vision of God). Interpretation of poltergeist experiences depends in part on the social and religious context of the time, and the belief system of the individual.

In 1691 the Revd Robert Kirk of Aberfoyle, in what was then Highland Perthshire, wrote *The Secret Commonwealth of Elves, Fauns & Fairies*, in which he had this to say of the fairies: 'The invisible Wights which haunt Houses… throw great Stones, Pieces of Earth and Wood, at the Inhabitants, [but] they hurt them not at all.' This notion, that poltergeists were fairies, brownies, or household spirits such as kobolds or follets, was widely circulated in Europe during the Early Modern Period (Claude Lecouteux's *The Secret History of Poltergeists and Haunted Houses* gives numerous examples) – but I suspect it would find few adherents today. Kirk also wrote of the belief that 'those creatures that move invisibly in a house, and cast huge great stones, but do no much hurt' were 'souls that have not attained their rest'. The 'survival hypothesis', the idea that poltergeists are the ghosts of the restless dead, remains popular, at least with journalists and Spiritualists (whose religion is founded on the reality of communications with the dead).

Intriguingly enough, however, we do not find this belief expressed in the earliest Scottish cases – but post-Reformation Protestant theology had removed the Catholic doctrine of Purgatory (a kind of unpleasant holding-area for souls, perhaps akin to the waiting room at Birmingham Coach Station), and so could conceive of no mechanism by which a soul could escape from Heaven or Hell for a day-visit to Earth. Therefore, any time a ghost appeared, it could only be one thing: a demon, often taking on the disguise of a deceased person so as to lead the living

Introduction

into sin. The notion that poltergeists are demons or unclean/evil spirits is as potent today as it was in the seventeenth century. A subset of the 'polt as demon' trope is the idea that poltergeists are invoked by witches; and as case 100 shows, this interpretation has also persisted into modern times.

By the nineteenth century we find a rationalistic insistence on the mundane reality of poltergeists: they were either the result of misperception or simply tricks employed by cunning fraudsters (and indeed, a small number of Scottish cases definitely fall into this category). The post-Freudian twentieth century brought us the concept of the poltergeist as externalized distress – the idea that some people, known as 'focal persons', can manifest their internal unhappiness by unconsciously projecting it into the world beyond their body. This notion – now named Recurrent Spontaneous Psycho-Kinesis or RSPK – remains the favourite hypothesis with parapsychologists. Statistical studies showed that most RSPK cases centred on a young person, often female, who was usually suffering from some form of stress (puberty, problems with family, school or relationships, and so on). The 'troubled young girl' has become something of a default position, but many cases (both in this book and elsewhere) show that the 'focus' can be a middle-aged man, a menopausal woman, or two siblings, or even several people consecutively or simultaneously. In other words, anyone can be a poltergeist focus – although why (and how) only a few of the millions of people under stress actually generate RSPK still remains a mystery – if, of course, RSPK is the actual agency. Like other attempts at explaining poltergeists, it is at best a hypothesis.

The post-war period also saw the rise of alternative explanations for poltergeists: earth tremors or changes in subterranean water pressure; ley-lines or 'earth energy'; and electromagnetic fields or atmospheric conditions. In recent years the pages of august journals such as that published by the Society for Psychical Research have suggested that some poltergeist activity may be directed by 'discarnate intelligences' – that is, non-corporeal entities. Here we see the resurgence of the idea of ghosts, demons or spirits, only without the religious baggage. Who knows, perhaps in the next few years the pendulum may swing towards fairies and kobolds again.

Personally, my considered opinion on the nature of poltergeists is very simple: I have absolutely no idea what they are.

POLTERGEISTS AND HAUNTINGS

There is a great deal of overlap between what are thought of as traditional hauntings (which principally feature apparitions, voices, noises, temperature changes, etc.) and poltergeist cases. Many hauntings encompass minor poltergeist activity, and apparitions number among the reported phenomena in a significant minority of poltergeist outbreaks. The two categories are not distinct and may well be part of the same spectrum of phenomena. There is also the popular notion that hauntings are 'place-based' while poltergeists are 'person-based'; but several cases in this book (for example, 15, 64 and 79) would appear to contradict that notion. In fact, the totality of the cases as a whole contradict any standard notion, any set belief – poltergeists challenge expectations; their reality often trumps theory.

WHERE DO POLTERGEISTS MANIFEST?

The overwhelming majority of the polts within this book (111, or 82.8 per cent) appear where people live. Of these, twenty-one of sixty-six cases before the Second World War centred on farms or crofts (31.8 per cent of the pre-war total, 15.7 per cent of the full list); twelve took place in council houses (18 per cent of the post-war cases, 9 per cent of the full total); while seven castles or mansions appear (5.2 per cent), closely followed by six manses and rectories (4.5 per cent). Meanwhile, pubs, clubs or hotels feature in nine (6.7 per cent) cases, with other workplaces taking up twelve (9 per cent) of the total. Only a tiny number of episodes occur in uninhabited locations.

▲ **Introduction** ▲

PHENOMENA

Here are the elements that characterise the Scottish cases, by frequency.

1. **Objects/furniture moved**: 96 of 134 cases (71.6 per cent).
2. **Noises** (taps, knocks, bangs, cries etc.): 88 (65.7 per cent).
3. **Apparitions** (including shadows and 'mists'): 36 (26.9 per cent).
4. **Displacement** (an item vanishes from one place to be found elsewhere): 33 (24.6 per cent).
5. **Doors locked/unlocked/opened/closed**: 31 (23.1 per cent).
6. **Damage to objects/furniture/fixtures**: 28 (20.9 per c ent).
7. **Lithobolia (throwing of stones etc.)**: 24 (17.9 per cent).
8. **Electrical effects**: 22 (16.4 per cent; as electrical products only became available from the 1890s, the more accurate percentage is 22 out of 83, or 26.5 per cent).
9. **Assaults** (punches, shoves, scratches, etc.): 19 (14.2 per cent).
10. **Voices**: 19 (14.2 per cent).
11. **Fire or smoke**: 16 (11.9 per cent).
12. **Witchcraft/magic**: 14 (10.5 per cent).
13. **Sense of presence**: 12 (9 per cent).
14. **Apports** (objects that appear 'out of nowhere'): 9 (6.7 per cent).
15. **Conversations**: 9 (6.7 per cent).
16. **Food interfered with**: 9 (6.7 per cent).
17. **Invisible hands etc.**: 9 (6.7 per cent).
18. **Temperature effects**: 9 (6.7 per cent).
19. **Water**: 9 (6.7 per cent).
20. **Writing**: 9 (6.7 per cent).
21. **Demons/Satan**: 9 (6.7 per cent).
22. **Smells**: 8 (6 per cent).
23. **Miniature beings/fairies**: 7 (5.2 per cent).
24. **Hoax** (at least in part): 6 (4.5 per cent).
25. **Names** (poltergeist names itself or responds to suggested names): 6 (4.5 per cent).
26. **Attacks on religious visitors/objects**: 6 (4.5 per cent).
27. **Levitation of persons**: 6 (4.5 per cent).

28. **Luminous effects**: 6 (4.5 per cent).
29. **Music/tunes**: 5 (3.7 per cent).
30. **Animals interfered with**: 4 (3 per cent).
31. **Clothes etc. cut/slashed**: 4 (3 per cent).
32. **Telephone effects**: 4 (3 per cent; 4.8 per cent of cases since 1901, when the first telephone exchange in Scotland was opened).
33. **Voices imitating the living**: 4 (3 per cent).
34. **'Possession'/trance**: 4 (3 per cent).
35. **Noxious substances** (blood, maggots): 3 (2.2 per cent).
36. **Ouija board**: 3 (2.2 per cent).
37. **Thrown items warm to the touch**: 2 (1.5 per cent).

ABOUT THIS BOOK

The cases are numbered chronologically, starting with No.1 in 1635, and ending with No.134 in 2012. Each chapter has its own map, and cases can also be found by place name in the index. To assist with locating a particular case geographically, current local authority names have been used, e.g. South or North Lanarkshire rather than just Lanarkshire. For the vast Highland Region, however, I have also added the district, such as Lochaber or Caithness. Most cases are structured around the same format: the period (how long the disturbances lasted, where known); a description of the phenomena; an evaluation of the sources; a discussion of the context for the case, which is often crucial to its understanding; and the interpretation of the participants at the time, sometimes with my own (doubtless biased) comments. Where minor or repetitive cases have strained the boundaries of available space, I have retained them within the case numbering system, but reduced their content to the bare bones.

Chapter One

The Seventeenth Century

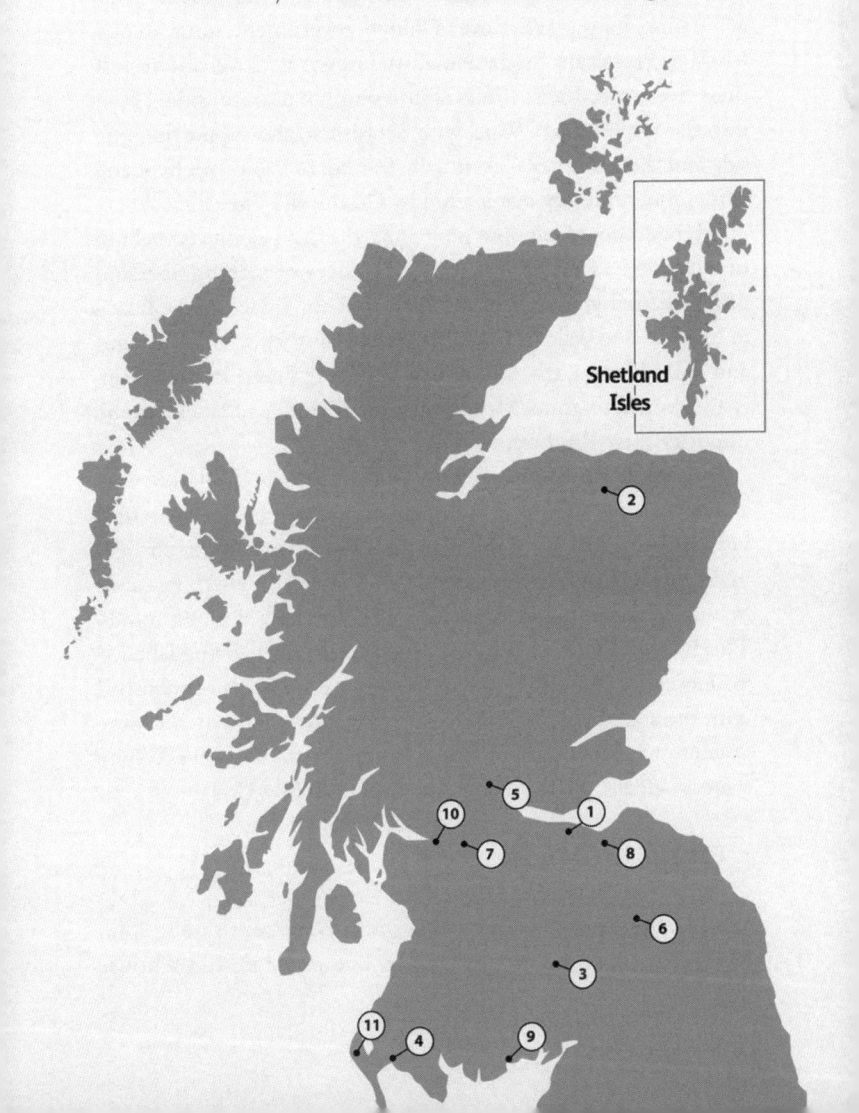

Poltergeist over Scotland

> Here's a knocking indeed!... Knock! knock! knock!... Who's there, i' the name o' Beelzebub?... Who's there, i' the Devil's name? Knock! knock! knock!-- Never at quiet?
>
> William Shakespeare, *Macbeth*

The seventeenth century was a tumultuous period in Scotland, with wars and rebellions often fracturing along religious lines. In a generation-long conflict over Church government, some 30,000 hardline Protestant fundamentalists, known as Covenanters, lost their lives to Royalist forces. This complex dispute spilled over into the English Civil Wars, with Scottish armies supporting one side and then another – eventually leading to Protestant Scotland being under military occupation by Cromwell's Puritans.

After decades of religious ping pong, the first Jacobite Rebellion of 1689-90 had the unintended side-effect of making Scotland officially Presbyterian – even today, while the Established Church in England and Wales is Anglican (Episcopal, that is, led by bishops and archbishops), the Church of Scotland, being Presbyterian, is a bishop-free zone. Meanwhile, the fortunes of the Catholic minority waxed and waned.

Executions for witchcraft reached their peak in the 1660s, with a steady decline thereafter (although punctuated by the occasional burst of ferocity). Part of this reduction was attributable to changes in the intellectual world. A new way of thinking – something called 'natural philosophy' or 'science' – was attracting the best minds. This too led to a backlash, with such freethinkers being labelled 'Saduccees' or 'Atheists' – and, as we shall see, books were published with the stated purpose of proving that spirits and witches were a) genuine and b) part of God's design for the universe. Where there are devils, the argument ran, there must be a God.

1. EDINBURGH: 1635?

We owe the earliest record of a Scottish poltergeist case to John Maitland, 1st Duke of Lauderdale. The polt infested a house occupied by an unnamed elderly Presbyterian minister and his son, less than 4 miles from Edinburgh – which would place it very much within the suburbs of the present city.

Period
Several weeks (?).

Phenomena
'Their house was extraordinarily troubled with noises,' writes Maitland:

> ... which they and their family, and many neighbours (who for divers weeks used to go watch with them) did ordinarily hear. It troubled them most on the Saturday night, and the night before their weekly lecture day. Sometimes they would hear all the locks in the house, on doors and chests, to fly open; yea, their clothes, which were at night locked up into trunks and chests, they found in the morning all hanging about the walls. Once they found their best linen taken out, the table covered with it, napkins as if they had been used, yea, and liquor in their cups as if company had been there at meat. The rumbling was extraordinary; the good old man commonly called his family to prayer when it was most troublesome, and immediately it was converted into gentle knocking, like the modest knock of a finger; but as soon as prayer was done, they should hear excessive knocking, as if a beam had been heaved by strength of many men against the floor.

Maitland adds another intriguing detail:

> Never was there voice or apparition; but one thing was remarkable (you must know that it is ordinary in Scotland to have a half cannon-bullet in the chimney-corner, on which they break their great coals), a merry maid in the house, being accustomed to the rumblings, and so her fear gone, told her fellow maid-servant that if the Devil troubled them that night, she would brain him, so she took the half cannon-bullet [cannon-ball] into bed; the noise did not fail to awake her, nor did she fail in her design, but took up the great

bullet, and with a threatening, threw it, as she thought, on the floor, but the bullet was never more seen; the minister turned her away for meddling and talking to it.

If we look at a contemporary work, such as *Diary of the Marches of the Royal Army during the Great Civil War*, written by Richard Symonds in 1644, we see that a typical cannon-ball of the period tipped the scales at 9lb (4.1kg).

Sources

Maitland did not witness the events himself, but heard of them some years later from the minister's son (himself a clergyman); the episodes were also described to him by several other witnesses, including the Duke's own steward, whose father and servants lived close to the infested house, and saw the events with their own eyes. The Duke vouched for the character of all these witnesses.

Context

Maitland was a central figure in the complex weft of seventeenth-century Scottish politics, in which religious affiliations, self-interest and brute force created alliances built on quicksand.

Starting as a supporter of the ultra-Presbyterian Covenanters, he switched to the party of King Charles. During the Civil Wars he was captured by Parliamentarian forces at the Battle of Worcester (1651) and held prisoner in Windsor Castle for nine years. From his confinement the Scottish Royalist aristocrat wrote a number of letters to Richard Baxter (1615-1691), an influential English Puritan minister (Baxter's replies have not survived). The letter describing the Edinburgh poltergeist was dated 12 March 1659, and includes a hint of an even earlier poltergeist episode: 'I could tell you an ancienter story before my time, in the house of one Burnet, in the north of Scotland, where strange things were seen, which I can get sufficiently attested.' Unfortunately no further details were forthcoming.

Baxter reproduced Maitland's letter in *The Certainty of the World of Spirits Fully Evinced by the Unquestionable Histories of Apparitions, Operations, Witchcrafts, Voices, etc., written for the conviction of Sadducees and Infidels*. Published in 1691, the book was ideologically designed to combat the growing intellectual scepticism of the age.

Maitland stated that the events occurred 'since I was a married man'. The Duke married Lady Anne Home in 1632, so we can guess that the polt may have been active sometime around 1632–35. Maitland signed off his letter asking that it not be printed, for patriotic reasons: 'Scottish stories would make the disaffected jeer Scotland, which is the object of scorn enough already.'

Interpretation

Baxter's ideological commitment is clear from the title of *The Certainty of the World of Spirits*. He did not comment on Maitland's story of a house 'disquieted with noises', but the reader is left to assume that the agency involved was an evil spirit or demon.

2. BOTARY, ABERDEENSHIRE: 1644

Period

Twenty days.

Phenomena

Patrik Malcolme was a poor labourer with a reputation as a 'charmer', a term which meant a practitioner of folk magic. While lodging at the farm of Alexander Chrystie he asked Chrystie's servant Margaret Barbour for sex. She refused, upon which Malcolme took the girl's left shoe, told her she would not earn her wages that year and described what she had hidden in a locked cupboard. That night, stones and clods of peat rained down on the roof of the farm in Grange. The 'clodding' – a term specific to north-east Scotland – continued for twenty days and nights, and only ceased when Margaret Barbour was removed from the house.

Sources

On 28 February 1644 Patrik Malcolme was investigated by the kirk session at Botarie (Botary – now the hamlet of Cairnie, 4 miles north-west of Huntly). Kirk sessions were the Presbyterian frontline in maintaining social order, usually dealing with fornication, drinking, gambling, and minor crimes of theft and violence. Occasionally they found themselves up against magic, supernatural beliefs, and witchcraft. According to witnesses, Malcolme begged milk from the wife of John Maltman in Botarie; when he was rebuffed, he cursed the cow, and it died shortly afterwards. He took away the 'goodness' or substance of Alexander Gray's cornfield and transferred it onto a neighbour's crop, and then told Gray he would bring the goodness back in exchange for the gift of a shirt. Both of these were standard accusations of low-level witchcraft of the time, and established Malcolme's reputation (the Strathbogie Presbytery had also investigated another charmer, Issobell Malcolme, who was almost certainly a relative of Patrik). As for the clodding, it was witnessed by Alexander Chrystie and his neighbour Walter Brabner. Margaret Barbour did not appear at the investigation. The Presbytery deferred the case for a month, and thereafter it vanishes from the records. The original text can be found in *Extracts from the Presbytery Book of Strathbogie 1631-1654*, published by John Stuart in 1843.

Context

Charming – folk magic below the serious level of witchcraft – preoccupied many a rural minister or church elder at the time. In 1637 the representatives of the Strathbogie Presbytery asked the Synod of Moray for advice on how to deal with the plague of charmers operating in their area. Again in 1672 Strathbogie charmers were described as using 'spells and other heathenish superstitions, expressions and practices over sick persons for their recovery'.

Interpretation

This is a deeply frustrating case, in which the scant records only hint at what must have been going on. Did the Presbytery think that Malcolme initiated the clodding through sorcery? Or did Alexander Chrystie eject Margaret Barbour because he deemed she was either responsible for or the focus of the events? And why did Malcolme regard Margaret's left shoe as a ritual object in his quest for sexual power over her?

3. MOFFAT, DUMFRIES & GALLOWAY: 1650

Period
Days? Years? Decades?

Phenomena
Poldean Holm, 4 miles from Moffat, was plagued by 'noises and apparitions, drums and trumpets'. In August 1650 Charles II and his English troops lodged at the house, and some of the soldiers were 'soundly beaten by that irresistible inhabitant'. By 1659 it was manifesting as a disembodied naked arm, and discussing politics with the officers. The house had supposedly been haunted for fifty or sixty years.

Sources
The source is Lauderdale's letter to Richard Baxter, 12 March 1659, although here the details are scanty. The Duke said he heard the tale from the house's owner, a Mr [Ambrose] Johnstone, when the latter was in England in 1651, while the information about the arm and speechifying was supplied to him by a Puritan minister, James Sharp. Agnes Marchbank, in *Upper Annandale: Its History and Traditions* (1901), quoting the scholarly Revd William Bennet of Moffat (d.1899), supports the tradition of the ghost arguing with Royalist officers and taking a political stance opposite to that of the laird.

Context
The Civil Wars generated supernatural tales a-plenty, often with an eye to propaganda.

Interpretation

A minor poltergeist outbreak, or a more conventional haunting? In 1909, in a history of the Johnstone clan, C.L. Johnstone sceptically suggested the spirit was a device invented to prevent hungry soldiers from eating the inhabitants of Poldean out of house and home.

4. GLENLUCE, DUMFRIES & GALLOWAY: 1654-56

If Moffat was an information famine, this is a glut; the 'Devil of Glenluce' is one of the best-attested Scottish polts, with a wealth of details.

Period

November 1654 to September 1656 (twenty-two months, with gaps).

Phenomena

The locus of the astonishing set of phenomena was the home of Gilbert Campbell, a weaver who lived in the rural Galloway village of Glenluce, some 9 miles east of Stranraer. Weavers worked long hours on large home looms. In the household were Gilbert's wife, Grizel, several children of various ages, and a servant named Margaret. The episodes had three principal phases, with several months of peace between each.

Phase One: November 1654–April 1655

As with many poltergeist outbreaks, it started with sounds – in this case, shrill whistling both outside and inside the house, 'such as children use to make with their small slender grass whistles.' Sometime in early November 1654, Gilbert's daughter Janet was at the well, with the whistling all around, when both she and another woman heard a voice that resembled Janet's say threateningly, 'I'll cast thee, Janet, into the well.'

Around mid-November the polt graduated to throwing great quantities of stones through the doors and windows and down the chimney, although, despite the force with which they were

The Seventeenth Century

thrown, they did not injure anyone. At this point the parish minister, the Revd John Scott, along with neighbours and friends, became aware of the disturbances, which now included the slashing and cutting of the family's hats, clothes, and shoes, even while they were wearing them, and the severing of the threads on Gilbert's weaving loom. At night, blankets were pulled off beds. The contents of chests and trunks were strewn around the house. Work items and tools were displaced into tiny holes and clefts. Gilbert was forced to move his remaining equipment to a neighbour's house, and temporarily lost his livelihood.

Some neighbours suggested the troubles were centred on one member of Gilbert's family, and so he sent all his children away to various houses for five days – and the disturbances ceased. They returned one by one – and when one son, Thomas, arrived, the phenomena kicked off again, this time with fires breaking out on two separate days. The weaver, now convinced Thomas was the focus, lodged the boy with the Revd Scott. But even with the lad out of the picture, the phenomena just kept getting worse, with peats hitting the house, turf being pulled off the roof and walls, clothes being slashed or stolen, and attacks with pins that left bloody prick-marks on skin. When Thomas returned he heard a forbidding voice ordering him not to enter the dwelling – and when he did so, he suffered so badly that the Revd Scott was forced to re-accommodate him.

One day, three months into the outbreak, the entire family heard a voice speak to them, and spent many hours in casual conversation with it. The next day, Tuesday, 13 February 1655, the Revd Scott, fearing fraternisation with Satan, turned up with a task force: his wife, accompanied by a gentlewoman of the name of Mrs Douglas, and a troupe of gentlemen of good standing – James Bailie of Carphin, Alexander Bailie of Dunragged, and Mr Robert Hay. As they entered the voice addressed them in Latin and then in Lowland Scots. It was the start of a truly extraordinary day, in which the group became convinced they were speaking with the Son of Satan.

Poltergeist over Scotland

Throughout the day, the voice was silent whenever the group prayed, but at other times it was garrulous. It revealed the names of 'the witches of Glenluce'. When Gilbert Campbell said that one of the women named had died, the voice replied: 'It is true she is dead long ago, but her spirit is living with us in the world.' The voice threatened to set the roof on fire if Thomas Campbell did not leave. It asked for a shovel to make its own grave. It claimed to have a written commission from Christ to vex the family. It argued Scripture with the minister, trading back and forth endless quotations from the Gospels. It stated it lived in the 'bottomless pit of hell', and that Satan was its father. It accused Robert Hay of being a witch and mocked Alexander Bailie for his broad-rimmed hat. It called for the candles to be extinguished, so it could appear in the darkness as a fireball. It cried for oatcakes out of hunger, asked Janet Campbell to hand over her belt so it could bind its bones together, and threatened to dash out the brains of a younger daughter (to show how familiar the family were with the voice, the young girl just shrugged this off and went back to her chores).

When, late into the night, the party prepared to leave, it threatened to burn the house down or strike the children. The voice appeared to come from the ground beneath a bed, or from the children lying on the beds, or from outside. When it roared for the candles to be put out, the noise was so great the visitors thought the voice was shouting into their ears.

Perhaps most peculiar of all, at some point during the day the voice created an apparition of Satan's own forearm:

> Presently there appeared a naked hand, and an arm from the elbow down, beating upon the floor till the house did shake again, and also he uttered a most fearful and loud cry, saying, 'Come up, my father; come up. I will send my father among you; see, there he is behind your backs.' Then the minister said, 'I saw indeed a hand and an arm, when the stroke was given and heard.' The Devil said to him, 'Saw you that? It was not my hand, it was my father's; my hand is more black in the loof [palm].'

The Seventeenth Century

Despite a later visit by five ministers – in which their continuous prayers remained uninterrupted by Lucifer Jnr – the Campbell household continued to suffer the visitations until April 1655. At which point, after six months of torment, the disturbances just stopped.

Phase Two: July 1655-April 1656
Four months of peace was shattered in July 1655, with a renewed series of assaults, including the destruction or spoiling of food, so that the family were close to starving. In October Gilbert Campbell approached the Synod, the regional body of Presbyteries, for help. Acting with glacial speed, the Synod committee met at Glenluce in February 1656, implored God in his mercy to assist the afflicted family, and declared a day of fasting and humiliation throughout south-west Scotland. Such fast days were common at the time, part of Presbyterian attempts to attract the attention of the Almighty. The Synod's slow reaction may have been caused by the death of the Revd Scott in December 1655, aged forty-six. Back in February 1655, the voice had predicted (correctly, as it turned out) that it would have a longer life than the minister. Phenomena slowly declined, and by April 1656 had vanished altogether.

Phase Three: August 1656-September 1656
A second four-month gap came to an end in August 1656, with cooked food being displaced from the table into holes, under beds, within the bedclothes, and out of the house. Making breakfast one morning, Grizel had the plate snatched from her. She called out, 'Let me have my plate again,' and the item flew at her, but without causing any harm. Throughout August, noises and disturbances raged through the house every night. In September events built up to a climax of sorts: the noises got worse, stones cascaded on the house, the family were assaulted in their beds by wooden staves, and the voice roared out that it was going to burn the house down. On 21 or 22 September, one of the beds caught fire, the blaze being quickly extinguished. And then, that was that.

⚔ Poltergeist over Scotland ⚔

After almost two years, the terrifying phenomena simply ceased, and the principal narrative breaks off:

> Thus I have written a short and true account of all the material passages which occurred. To write every particular, especially of lesser moment, would fill a large volume. The goodman lived several years after this in the same house; and it seems, by some conjuration or other, the Devil suffered himself to be put away, and gave the weaver a peaceable habitation. This weaver has been a very old man, that endured so long these marvellous disturbances.

In January 1661 Robert Baillie, Principal of the University of Glasgow, wrote one of his habitual long letters to his friend William Sprang, mentioning the Glenluce case, which he said was notorious throughout Galloway (although he called Mr Campbell John, not Gilbert). Baillie noted that nothing had been heard of the disturbing spirit for at least a twelve-month.

Sources

The primary source is George Sinclair, Professor of Philosophy at the University of Glasgow, who says he received some details from one of the clergymen present at the five-minister prayer session, but that the bulk of the narrative was supplied by one of Gilbert Campbell's sons, who was a philosophy student at Glasgow ('philosophy' at this point meant natural philosophy, i.e. science). Sinclair himself taught at Glasgow between 1655 and 1667. This son is not named in the piece, but he does feature in the text. On 13 February 1655, the famous day when the Revd Scott and others argued with the Devil's offspring, the voice stated: 'If the goodman's son's prayers at the College of Glasgow did not prevail with God, my father and I had wrought a mischief here ere now.' In other words, Gilbert's college boy, through his prayers, had kept Satan & Son at bay.

The story first appeared in print in 1672, rather bizarrely inserted into Sinclair's engineering treatise *The Hydrostaticks, or, the Weight, Force, and Pressure of Fluid Bodies... together with a Short History of Coal*. He reprinted it – as 'The Devil of Glenluce, enlarged with several remarkable additions from an eye and ear witness, a person of undoubted authority' – in his compendium of the supernatural, *Satan's Invisible World Discovered* (1685). This was another book designed to shore up the popular belief in the supernatural, as can be seen from its subtitle: *A choice Collection of Modern Relations, proving evidently against the Saducees and Atheists of this present Age, that there are Devils, Spirits, Witches, and Apparitions, from Authentic Records, Attestations of Famous Witnesses and undoubted Verity.* The Glenluce narrative also appeared in the second edition (1689) of Joseph Glanvil's hugely influential book *Saducismus triumphatus: or, Full and plain evidence concerning witches and apparitions*, which gave the initial boost of publicity to famous English poltergeist cases such as the Drummer of Tedworth. The editor of the second edition, Henry More, wrote of the Glenluce case: 'I have heard the Truth of the Story averr'd with all assurance myself by some of that Country.' Robert Baillie's comment in 1661 shows that the episode was well known long before Sinclair published his account.

Context

Sinclair opens with a reference to Alexander Agnew, 'a bold and sturdy beggar, who afterwards was hanged at Dumfries for blasphemy... [he] had threatened hurt to the family, because he had not gotten such an alms as he required.' In the next sentence, the whistling begins, as the herald of the full poltergeist outbreak. The unstated implication is that Agnew, by some form of sorcery or cursing, had conjured up the evil spirit in revenge for being rebuffed. Volume five of David Masson's monumental *Life of John Milton* (1877) tells us more about Alexander Agnew. He was commonly known as 'Jock of Broad Scotland', and was an itinerant beggar infamous for his religious views. The English Civil Wars had unleashed a hurricane of sects, cults and revolutionary beliefs across the land, with the result that many people at the lower end of the social scale were openly espousing their opposition to orthodox religious tenets. As both England and Scotland were both effectively theocracies, the authorities did not look kindly on these challenges to established Christian norms. Big-mouthed Agnew was arrested for blasphemy. He was charged with refusing to attend church, denying the reality of the Trinity, Heaven, Hell and the efficacy of prayer, claiming he owed nothing to God and that God provided nothing for him, mocking all religious beliefs, and indeed regarding the entire Christian worldview as a charade. 'He declared that he knew not whether God or the Devil had the greater power; but he thought the Devil had the greatest; and "When I die," said he, "let God and the Devil strive for my soul, and let him that is strongest take it".' On Wednesday, 21 May 1656, for expressing these views, Jock of Broad Scotland was hanged from a gibbet.

In his letter of 1661, Robert Baillie states that the Campbells obtained some temporary relief in the period after Agnew was executed. In reality, the phenomena had stopped in April 1656, at least a month before the hanging, and then started up again in August of that year.

Interpretation

The association between Agnew's threat and the onset of the poltergeist may seem like coincidence to the modern reader, but to Sinclair or his informant it was clearly meaningful. Given the beggar's forthright views, was he thought to be an agent of the Foul Fiend? Throughout the infestation, the ministers and other gentlefolk were convinced the poltergeist was demonic, even Satanic in nature. Some of the Campbell family, in contrast, seemed to treat the voice as if it were an annoying lodger that wanted to constantly draw attention to itself.

Sinclair's account tells us very little about the family situation, the age and number of children, or any tensions within the household. Deliberate fraud may have been employed by one or more of the children, but given that the Campbells ended up almost starving, this idea can't be taken too far, and the sheer range and scale of phenomena would require a family-wide conspiracy to carry out. Thomas Campbell may have been the human focus of the poltergeist, but phenomena continued in his absence; possibly his sister Janet was the agent – we cannot tell. Fraud? RSPK? The actions of a discarnate intelligence? Sadly, it is now impossible to come to any form of conclusion about the Glenluce Devil.

5. STIRLING: 1659

If this is a poltergeist case, it is one that centres exclusively on spontaneous fires. As such it bears comparison with the 1982 case of Carole Compton (No.100).

Period
January 1659 (two or three weeks?).

Phenomena
Fires broke out wherever Margaret Gourlay went. Around the second week of January her bed caught fire on two consecutive days. After a third blaze in her house, three separate fires broke out in the home of her neighbour Andrew Wright. Two days later the bed of the male servants in the byre went alight. Another two days brought what appears to be the climax, with five fires starting up simultaneously in different parts of the barnyard, while Margaret, who was winding wool at the time, ignored a fire flickering under her very feet.

Sources
Margaret Gourlay was examined by local magistrates on 25 February 1659, and, along with five other women and one man, tried for witchcraft by the Circuit Court in Stirling on 22 and 23 March. The accusations against the six overlapped, and were mostly concerned with ritual healing, and magical harm to humans and animals – Margaret alone was associated with fiery outbreaks. The proceedings are recorded in the Circuit Court Books listed as JC10/1 and the Process Notes JC26/26, both held in the National

Records of Scotland. There is a good summary of the events in Professor Maxwell-Stuart's *The Great Scottish Witch-Hunt* (2007).

In addition to the fires, Margaret was implicated in various uncanny events, such as the appearance of a sinister black man and a mysterious flight of crows. A day or two before the fires started, a bizarre clap of thunder was heard at her window, there were bangs at her door, and stones were thrown at her wall (these episodes of course hint at poltergeist activity, although they could just as easily have a mundane human explanation). Margaret's principal accuser was Janet Millar, apparently a neighbour, associate or even a servant, and one of Margaret's co-accused. In the end two of the accused were found guilty and executed, while four, including Margaret and Janet, were acquitted and set free.

Context

If Margaret really was a pyrokinetic poltergeist agent, her powers could, within the context of the times, have only been regarded as sorcery. Spontaneous outbreaks of fire are extremely rare within the corpus of Scottish witchcraft cases.

Interpretation

The simplest interpretation is that Margaret Gourlay was an arsonist – and, indeed, on one occasion she was witnessed planting a burning peat on the property of her neighbour John Wright, who had refused to lend her a broom. On the other hand, she was charged with witchcraft, not the much more common crime of fire-raising. There again, we know nothing of the relationship between Margaret and Janet Millar, so we cannot tell how reliable the latter's testimony was. This may have been a case of a pyro-polt; equally, it may not have been.

6. GALASHIELS, SCOTTISH BORDERS: BETWEEN 1668 & 1672

Period

Several days or weeks.

The Seventeenth Century

Phenomena

Over one long evening, loud knockings came from the bed, chair and floor on which young Margaret Wilson rested or prayed. A scratching sound issued from the bed, and a noise like that of a rasping-iron or metal file came from her chest. Asleep, her body levitated from the bed, so that 'many strong men were not able to keep it down.' An invisible force gripped her by the feet and pulled her up and down. Once awake, she related how the Devil spoke to her and offered gifts, and that one time in the recent past Satan had appeared in a man's likeness and told her not to go to church that day.

After an unspecified period, the child, who was twelve or thirteen years old, moved to a friend's house in Edinburgh, then became a servant in Leith, before marrying and living out the rest of her life in Magdalen-Pans, an industrial salt-pan community east of Edinburgh. Once leaving Galashiels, Margaret Wilson was never again disturbed by anything sinister.

Sources

The episode appears in *Satan's Invisible World Discovered* (1685). George Sinclair states that his account is true, given to him by an eyewitness. The phenomena had been active for some time previous, but Sinclair writes regretfully, 'What passed other nights I cannot relate, since I want information. ... If all the particulars of this business were truly collected, they would amount to a far longer Relation than I have set down.'

Context

This was a period when the concept of a Devil who was actively recruiting witches in Scotland was at its height. The girl, having woken from her demon-haunted sleep, was unable to say the words of prayer, so she was made to sign a religious tract (*The Christian's Great Interest* by the Puritan intellectual William Guthrie) as a way of forging a personal covenant between herself and God. Sinclair writes: 'When she had done this the Devil persuaded her with many Arguments to break it. This was the Method the Devil observed ordinarily every Night, during her long trouble.' Sinclair did not know when the events happened, but the principal witness was the Revd Thomas Wilkie, the minister at Galashiels between 1665 and 1672, and Guthrie's tract was published in 1668, so our timeframe is between 1668 and 1672.

Interpretation

The witnesses knew Satan was in the house. We moderns may see a classic human poltergeist focus, a troubled young girl. Or possibly a hoax. But there is a curious coda. After the troubling events, the Revd Wilkie took the girl's uncle for a midnight stroll around the garden, to talk things over in private. The clergyman 'exhorted him to reflect upon his ways, and consider if he had done any thing that had provoked the Lord against him, and particularly he charged him with one thing, whereof there was a loud report [i.e. gossip]'. The uncle 'solemnly protested, and that with dreadful imprecations, he was innocent of that particular, which was said of him, and absolutely denied it.' The 'it' the two men were arguing about goes resolutely unmentioned, which, in the repressive religious atmosphere of the era, probably meant it was to do with sex. Did the uncle have incestuous designs on his pubescent niece? Was the poltergeist a shammed or even authentically psychokinetic cry for help? We will never know.

7. KEPPOCH, GLASGOW: 1670

'There was a Devil that troubled a house in Keppoch, within a mile of Glasgow, for the matter of eight days time, (but disappeared again) in casting peats, and dropping stones from the roof, yet not hurting any.'

This is the entire entry, to be found in *Memorialls, or the memorable things that fell out within this island of Britain from 1638–1684*, by the Revd Robert Law (published in 1819).

8. ORMISTON, EAST LOTHIAN: 1680

Period
Eight or nine weeks, perhaps from November 1680 through to January 1681.

Phenomena
Three or four nights after she died, Isabel Heriot was seen at midnight walking from the chapel to her former place of employment, the manse at Ormiston. She was dressed in her white coffin-shroud, and her face was extremely black, as it had been in the final days of her illness. She spoke to another servant, Isabel Murray, and was seen to gather stones in her lap.

A few nights later, stones rained down on the manse, hitting the roof, hall-door and windows, but without causing damage. The stones were found on the ground the following morning. At other times, Isabel Murray was struck hard by a stone, while a groom, working in the garden, was the target of several stones – although only one hit him, and that but gently. In the stables the same groom was gripped by an invisible force on his heel, and in the mornings the horses were found sweaty and nervous, as if they had been frightened in the night. Meanwhile a large rock was cast at the minister, hitting the back door just as he closed it, and leaving a dent. Clods of peat were thrown and a horse-comb, missing for several years, was flung hard at the servant-men's bed in the byre. A burning coal turned up under a bed. And, most absurdly, a nightcap was removed from a sleeping family member and hidden in the chimney, where it was found full of cinders and ashes. Phenomena were intermittent, not appearing every night. The events were much gossiped about in the local area, with some people amused that the minister could not cast out a devil in his own home.

Sources
This is another episode from *Satan's Invisible World Discovered* (1685). Sinclair's informant was not only one of the eyewitnesses

but his own brother, the Revd John Sinclair, minister of Ormiston. The brothers Sinclair were dubious about Isabel Murray's testimony: she was the only one who saw the ghost, while the stone-throwing and other events had multiple witnesses.

Context
The period was a difficult one for many ministers riding the ideological U-turns of the political establishment. Four years after the poltergeist, John Sinclair was forcibly removed from his ministry. He died in 1687, aged about sixty-nine.

Interpretation
According to Isabel Murray, the spirit of Isabel Heriot told her of many meetings with the Devil, who had charged her with destroying the minister of Ormiston, or his friend the schoolmaster. She had been forced to return from the dead, she said, because she had stolen money from the minister. Elsewhere we learn that the woman had also been stroppy, rude and unchristian, and eventually the minister turned her out. After service elsewhere, she returned secretly to Ormiston, where she died. Isabel Murray did not have a high opinion of her fellow-servant, and as far as she was concerned, the evil spirit in the house was Heriot's cantankerous ghost.

The Revd Sinclair, however, could not countenance the idea of souls being given day-release from either Heaven or Hell. If Murray had indeed seen a phantom (of which the minister was not entirely convinced), then it could only be a zombie or a demon in disguise: 'Either her real Body informed and acted by the Devil (for her soul could not be brought back) or only the Devil taking upon him her shape and form, acting and imitating her to the life, which is more probable.'

Another interpretation is added by G. David Keyworth, writing in the journal *Folklore* in 2006. Isabel Heriot's deeply blackened face links her to the draugr, an animated corpse, a revenant, and one of the folkloric ancestors of the vampire. As a result of Viking colonisation since the Dark Ages, Scandinavian draugr-lore had become loosely incorporated into Scottish supernatural belief.

We are told nothing about the make-up of the household, but of the minister's four children, at least three had already left home; it's possible his youngest, Sarah, was still in the house. We have nothing to go on in trying to pin down either a fraudster or a psychokinetic agent within the Sinclair manse. As with so many historical cases, the Ormiston polt remains a mystery.

9. RERRICK, DUMFRIES & GALLOWAY: 1695

This is probably the best-attested early case. The location was a farm steading called Ringcroft of Stocking, just outside the coastal village of Rerrick (now Auchencairn), on the A711 between Dalbeattie and Kirkcudbright. The primary account is presented in the form of a chronological diary, based on notes taken at the time. For each episode, we are given the names of those who witnessed it, including farmers, ministers and the landowner whose tenants were plagued by the poltergeist. The entire document is then affirmed as true by fourteen upstanding members of the community, each of them an eyewitness to some part of the proceedings.

Period
February 1695-1 May 1695 (around nine-ten weeks).

Phenomena
February, 1695: Andrew Mackie, a mason, noticed that each night the tethers holding his cattle in the byre were loosened or broken. One morning, having penned the beasts up in the yard overnight, he found that one young cow had been secured to the back of the house with a rope of hair pulled so tight that the animal's hooves only just touched the ground. This would have been a feat normally requiring three men (and a great deal of noise). On another night, a large pile of peats was emptied onto the floor and set alight, the smoke waking the family, who extinguished the fire.

March:

7th-11th: Many stones were thrown in and around the house, most frequently at night. 'It was observed, that the stones which hit any person had not half their natural weight; and the throwing was more frequent on the Sabbath than at other times; and especially in time of prayer, above all other times, it was busiest, then throwing most at the person praying.'

10th: The Mackie children saw a figure beside the fire; it turned out to be a stool and blanket set up in the shape of a person.

11th: The metal crook for the cooking-pot and the pot-clips vanished for four days, eventually being discovered in a loft that had already been searched several times.

13th: The Revd Alexander Telfair arrived for the first time. He held a prayer session, and nothing happened. As he was about to leave he saw two small stones fall onto the croft; and when he went back inside, he was pelted with stones as he prayed, although he was not hurt.

18th-21st: More motile stones, these ones stinging as they hit. One night Telfair was beaten with a large stick, and the portable wooden side of the bed was thrown off. Raps rang out from chests and boards. Telfair felt a pressure on his arm, caused by a white childlike hand that faded into nothingness at the elbow. This was one of the few apparitions during the infestation; the others – a red-faced youth with yellow hair, and a teenage lad wearing grey clothes and a bonnet – are the only events that have no named witnesses. Perhaps Telfair was uncertain about their veracity.

22nd: Curious neighbours were now turning up, and were duly attacked with stones and staves both inside and outside the building. Several men were painfully gripped by unseen hands and pulled through the house. Andrew Mackie was scratched as if by fingernails, pulled by his hair and suffered a wound on his forehead. That night the children were deprived of their bedclothes and beaten loudly. The heavy bar for the door was found in different parts of the house. A wooden staff rattled on the chests and bedsides.

23 March–3 April: Stone-throwing, rattling noises and banging with sticks, augmented by shrill whistling. During this period the polt found its voice, crying 'Wisht' (hush) every time someone prayed.

April:
4th: Things having got worse, Andrew Mackie and his landlord, Charles Macklelane of Colline, approached a meeting of ministers taking place at Buttle, several miles away. That night the Revds Andrew Ewart and John Murdo held a prayer meeting at the house, only to suffer beatings, head wounds from large stones weighing up to 7lbs (3.1kg), and veritable downpours of smaller stones. Mr Ewart's wig was knocked off as he prayed, and a burning peat was cast into the praying group.

5th: Straw stacked in the farmyard was set alight. A throng of visiting neighbours was pelted with stones.

6th: Events entered another new phase. The previous night Mrs Mackie had noticed that a large floorstone outside the door was newly loose. Early in the morning she lifted it, to find what seemed to be a witchcraft or curse package: 'seven small bones, with blood, and some flesh, all closed in a piece of old saddled paper; the blood was fresh and bright.' Thoroughly frightened, she ran the quarter of a mile to the home of the nearest authority figure, her landlord Charles Macklelane. In the time it took him to come, airborne stones and fireballs shot through the house, a staff smashed through the wall above the children's bed, and a thrown stone burned through a set of bedclothes; ninety minutes later, the stone was still too hot to hold. The crescendo of noise and assaults only ceased when Macklelane, having fortified himself with prayer, lifted the bones. That night the Revd Telfair prayed in the house, and was hit by several large stones which did not hurt him.

7th: Two fires broke out, to be quickly quenched by the neighbours, who were by now practically camped in the house. A metal ploughing tool and a trough-stone weighing some 40lb (19kg) were tossed at the local blacksmith without injuring him, but a small stone bloodied the man's forehead. At twilight John Mackie, the eldest son of the family, was approaching the house when: 'there was an extraordinary light fell about him, and went before him to the house with a swift motion.' Beams from hovering UFOs aside, that night had its usual quota of bangings and displaced items.

8th: Another sinister item turned up, this time a letter found outside the house, apparently both written and sealed in blood. On the back was the message: '3 years thou shall have to repent a nett [note] it well.' Inside was written: 'Wo [woe] be to thee Scotland. Repent and tak warning for the doors of haven ar all Redy bart against thee, I am sent for a warning to thee to flee to God yet troublt shall this man be for twenty days repent repent repent Scotland or else thou shall.' At midday, by order of the civil magistrate, all current and former tenants of the Mackie farm assembled in Charles Macklelane's home. There, in front of the Revd Telfair, each was required to touch the package of bones. It was believed at the time that a murdered corpse would react to its murderer; but the bones remained inert, and so the suspicion that a secret murder had taken place at the farm was abandoned.

10th: A delegation of six ministers including Telfair turned up to do battle with the spirit, which responded in kind. Whichever minister was leading the prayers always got the worst of it. Showers of stones weighing as much as 28lb (12.7kg) crashed through a hole punched through the roof; the house shook as if in an earthquake; the door and mid-wall of the adjoining barn were torn down; and the ministers, along with a neighbour, were pushed and pulled mercilessly.

11th-13th: Every visitor to the house was beaten. Three young men were praying inside when they were smacked about the head by a dead polecat, which had earlier been dumped by a hunter at the side of the house.

14th: Straw in the yard was set alight, stones were thrown, a sieve levitated and energetically resisted attempts to keep it still; when it came apart, the mesh of the sieve was thrown at a neighbour, while a spade was fired at Andrew Mackie.

The Seventeenth Century

15th: The Mackie boys were badly hurt by stones as they approached the house. Inside, a drover named William Anderson bled profusely from a stone cast at his head. As the men prayed the spirit whistled, groaned and cried, 'Whisht.'

16th: More whistling, groaning, 'hushing', shoving, grabbing, shaking, and throwing stones during times of prayer. New words were added to its vocabulary: 'Bo, bo,' and 'Kick, cuck'. By now the Mackies were clearly at their wits' end. They left the house for two nights, while five neighbours took up residence. None of the visitors were assaulted, but the cattle on the farm were either pushed over, or had their tethers loosened.

18th: The family returned. That night, sheep in a nearby byre were found tied together in pairs by ropes fashioned out of straw taken from the stable.

19th: Straw in the barn caught fire, and while extinguishing it, Andrew Mackie had staves thrust at him through the wall.

20th: Amidst the whistling and 'whishting', it learned more words. When stones hit someone, they heard, 'Take you that till you get more' (in which case further stones were forthcoming) or simply, 'Take you that,' and no more stones appeared for a while.

21st-23rd: People were assaulted with stones, staves, and peat-mud, especially when at prayer.

24th: This was a 'day of humiliation', in which everyone in the parish was supposed to fast and pray, as a way of asking God to intercede for the Mackies. Little good it did: the poltergeist was especially active the entire day, 'in a most fearful manner without intermission, throwing stones with such cruelty and force, that all in the house feared lest they should be killed.' More lithobolia occurred the following day, but with less force.

26th: Phenomena escalated as the end-game approached. After knocking on a chest several times, as if to call everyone to attention, the voice was now up for a thoroughgoing conversation. It insulted everyone in the house, calling them witches and rakes, saying it would drag them all to Hell. It told Andrew Mackie, 'Thou shalt be troubled till Tuesday,' (the 26th was Friday).

Poltergeist over Scotland

Andrew asked, 'Who gave thee a commission?' to which the voice answered, 'God gave me a commission; and I am sent to warn the land to repent; for a judgement is to come, if the land do not quickly repent.' If Scotland did not repent, it said it would go to its father, and get a commission to return with a hundred worse than itself, and would trouble every family in the land. When a man named James Telfair spoke out of turn, the voice said to him: 'You are basely bred, meddling in other men's discourse, wherein you are not concerned.' There now ensued a debate between the voice and Andrew Mackie:

> Voice: 'Praise me, and I will whistle to you; worship me, and I will trouble you no more.'
>
> Andrew: 'The Lord, who delivered the three children out of the fiery furnace, deliver me and mine this night from the temptations of Satan.'
>
> Voice: 'You might as well have said, Shadrach, Meshach, and Abednego.' [These were the names of the three Jews miraculously saved from the furnace.]
>
> Andrew: 'The Lord stop Satan's fury, and hinder him of his designs.'
>
> Voice: 'I will do it, or you shall guide well. Remove your goods, for I will burn the house.'

27th: Seven fires broke out in the house.

28th: Endless fires: 'as it was quenched in one part, instantly it was fired in another.' In the evening, an entire stone-built gable of the house was pulled down. A huge piece of a tree was suspended above the children in their bed, and the voice said: 'If I had a commission I would brain them.'

29th: Andrew Mackie extinguished all household fires for a quarter mile around, but yet more parts of the house caught alight. In the barn, the voice spoke out of the wall, telling Andrew: 'Be not troubled, you shall have no more trouble, except some casting of stones upon the Tuesday to fulfil the promise.' The Revd Telfair arrived around 11 p.m., and witnessed another fiery outbreak and two small stones dropping at the fireside.

30th: This was the Tuesday promised as the cessation of the events. Several neighbours were praying in the barn when Charles Macklelane observed: 'A black thing in the corner of the barn, and it did increase, as if it would fill the whole house. He could not discern it to have any form, but as if it had been a black cloud.' Mud and chaff was thrown into the faces of the prayer group, and several men were gripped hard about the waist and arms.

1 May: The sheep-house burned to the ground, but the animals were saved in time. And with this final flourish, the Rerrick poltergeist abruptly ceased.

Sources

The Revd Telfair's pamphlet, entitled *A True Relation of an Apparition, Expressions, and Actings, of a Spirit, which infested the House of Andrew Mackie, in Ring-Croft of Stocking, in the Paroch of Rerrick, in the Stewarty of Kirkcudbright, in Scotland* was completed in December 1695, less than eight months after the events. It was published in Edinburgh and went through two editions, with a third printed in London. The full account appears in several later books, such as the 1818 edition of the *Memorialls* of the Revd Robert Law, edited by Charles Kirkpatrick Sharpe.

The pamphlet ends with the names of those who swore what they had experienced was true. These included five ministers: Andrew Ewart of Kells, James Monteith of Borg, John Murdo of Corsmichael, Samuel Spalding of Partan and William Falconer of Keltoun. Also listed were the landlord, Charles Macklelane of Colline, and eight neighbours: William Lennox of Millhouse, Andrew and John Tait in Torr, John Cairns in Hardhills, blacksmith William Mackminn, John Corsby, Thomas Mackminn, and Andrew Paline. Other parts of the text are attested by John Telfair in Achinleck. Further witnesses are also named in the body of the account: Samuel Thomson, a chapman; William Anderson, a drover; James Paterson, his son-in-law; and John Keige, miller in Auchincairn.

Given that it is unlikely that six Presbyterian ministers, a land-owner, and several farmers and tradesmen of good reputation would

all put their names to a false document, I think we can assume that
at least some of the phenomena described were genuine.

Context
The Glorious Revolution of 1689 had finally secured the
Established Church in Scotland as Presbyterian in nature. After
decades in which first one Protestant ideology held sway, and
then another, the nature of official religious worship for Scots
was now fixed. This had huge consequences for individual clergy.
In 1687, Alexander Telfair was an Episcopalian chaplain; after the
Revolution, having – like so many others – changed his spots, he
was a Presbyterian minister. At Rerrick, Telfair would have been
conscious that he had to toe the line of orthodoxy.

The farm buildings were twenty-eight years old, and had been
home to several tenants in that time. Andrew Mackie had a number
of children, the youngest of which was nine or ten. We are told that
the father was a respectable, well-liked and pious man.

Interpretation
Telfair makes it clear that the 'spirit' he encountered was demonic
in nature. His pamphlet starts with three quotes:

> 'Put on the whole armour of God, that ye may be able to stand against
> the wiles of the Devil.' (Ephesians 6:11)
>
> 'For we wrestle not against flesh and blood, but against principalities,
> and powers.' (Ephesians 6:12)
>
> 'Resist the Devil, and he will flee from you.' (James 4:7)

In his introduction, Telfair tells us that he hopes the pamphlet will be
proof against the sceptical spirit of the age, which regards descriptions of good and evil spirits as merely the ramblings of disordered
minds. He also wants it to act as a warning in praise of orthodox
piety: '[I seek] to induce all persons, particularly masters of families,
to private and family prayer, lest the neglect of it provoke the Lord,
not only to pour out his wrath upon them otherwise, but to let

The Seventeenth Century

Satan loose to haunt their persons and families with audible voices, apparitions, and hurt to their persons and goods.'

Telfair also wished to dispose of three rumours that were clearly doing the rounds in Galloway and providing 'reasons' for the visitation by the spirit. The first was that Mackie had dedicated his eldest child to the Devil, on account of him having undertaken the dread oath known as the Mason's Word. The second was that the Mackies had wrongly kept for themselves some clothes left behind in the house by a woman suspected of witchcraft. And the third claimed that the previous tenant of the farm, a man named Macknaught, had suffered ill-fortune because a cursed tooth had been planted beneath the threshold (the same place where Mrs Mackie found the bag of bones and flesh; hiding items at the threshold was a standard practice of malign folk magic). Having investigated, the minister declared the first two rumours to be nonsense. It was true that the tenant before the Mackies, a Thomas Telfair, had found something like a tooth beneath the entrance to the house, and burned it; but the reverend could not say whether this had any bearing on the Mackies' infestation.

So witchcraft was clearly thought to be a possible catalyst for the events, even if this was not a firm conviction. As for the Satanic interpretation, in some respects the voice was similar in tone to that in Glenluce, but unlike that case, at no point did the Rerrick 'spirit' claim to be a demon. Misperception could have played a role, and the apparitions, in particular, could have been imagined and invented. We can easily imagine that an opportunistic neighbour with a grudge took advantage of the situation to plant the bag of bones and the letter written in blood. Was there some kind of neighbourhood vendetta in the background? Did someone else covet the tenancy of the farm and hope to drive the Mackies out? Telfair gives no hint about such matters. If, however, we accept most of the witnesses' testimony as accurate, then we have one of the most astonishing and violent poltergeist outbreaks recorded anywhere in the world.

Over ten months in 1696-97, a poltergeist brought misery to a Catholic household in Naples, dispensing almost exactly the same kind of phenomena as unleashed in Protestant Galloway. 'It is almost as though the same demon,' wrote Alan Gauld and Tony Cornell in their classic study, *Poltergeists*, 'having completed his mission in Rerrick, and improved his skills in the process, then undertook a fresh assignment in Italy.'

10. BARGARRAN, EAST RENFREWSHIRE: 1696-97

Uniquely in the context of Scottish poltergeists, this episode led to people being executed for witchcraft. Was it, indeed, a poltergeist at all?

Period
22 August 1696-28 March 1697 (seven months).

Phenomena
The setting was Bargarran, a modest three-storey laird's house in a semi-rural area in what is now the urbanscape of Johnstone. Following an encounter with Katherine Campbell, a thieving servant who pronounced a curse on her, and Agnes Naismith, an elderly and poor widow with an uncanny aspect, eleven-year-old Christian Shaw, the laird's daughter, began to suffer 'fits'. Over the next seven months she exhibited a battalion of symptoms, including:

- Trance, rigidity of the body, manic episodes, and great strength.
- Extreme distortions of the throat, face, eyes, stomach and limbs.
- Appearing to be dumb, blind, insensible or even dead.
- Coughing up hair, straw, feathers, animal bones, stones, bent pins, hot candle wax, glowing coals, and excrement.
- Complaining of being stabbed, cut and otherwise assaulted by an invisible 'crew' of assailants.

Most of the listed symptoms occurred dozens of times over the months. At first Christian was treated by doctors, who could do nothing, so the diagnosis turned to one of witchcraft. The girl

The Seventeenth Century

said she was visited by the Devil and starting naming her unseen tormentors, which included Campbell and Naismith and a host of other local people and casual visitors to the house. Her accusations acted as a catalyst, which eventually led to a full-scale witch-hunt with over twenty people accused. By now Christian's testimony was less important than the various accusations the suspected witches were throwing at each other, combined with the confessions of some who were suspiciously eager to tell everything they knew about magical murder parties and carnal relations with that nice Mr Lucifer. Eventually one accused man committed suicide in jail, and another seven men and women were found guilty and hanged at Paisley on 10 June 1697 – the last mass execution for witchcraft in Scotland.

From our point of view, however, the interest lies in some supernormal phenomena ascribed to Christian:

11 January 1697: 'She was suddenly carried away from her parents and others that were about her, with a sudden flight, and in the first of these (to their great amazement) through the chamber and hall, down a long winding stair toward the tower-gate, with such a swift and unaccountable motion, that it was not in the power of any to prevent her, her feet not touching the ground, so far as any of the beholders could discern.'

12 January: 'She was suddenly carried away... through the chamber and hall, and sixteen large steps of a winding stair, up toward the top of the house ... but was carried down ... toward the gate again, where accordingly she was found, and was carried up as formerly, all the parts of her body distended and stiff as one dead.'

Sometime in January: 'She was again suddenly carried from them in the former manner down a stair, which goes off from a corner of the chamber to a cellar just below it ... Mr King having caught hold of her, kept her in his arms till a lighted candle was brought; and endeavouring to bring her up stairs, did declare that he found something forcibly drawing her downwards....

Sometimes she cried out of violent pain, by reason of furious blows and strokes she had received from the hands of her tormentors, the noise of which strokes bystanders distinctly heard, though they perceived not the hands that gave them.'

20 February: A large pile of peats burned to ashes overnight, even though no fire had been nearby.

27 February: A fireplace was found completely swept clean of ashes and cinders overnight, yet no servant or member of the family had been near it.

9 March: Christian was floated up from the tower gate to an upper floor, although on this occasion there was no direct eyewitness.

14 March: 'She being in church in the forenoon, her glove falling from her, the same was again put into her hand by some invisible agent, to the amazement of beholders.'

28 March: Christian suddenly recovered completely, and was never troubled again. In adult life she went on to found a successful textile business in Paisley.

Sources

The primary document is a pamphlet entitled *A True Narrative of the Sufferings and Relief of a Young Girle; Strangely molested by Evil spirits and their instruments in the West: With a preface and postscript containing Reflections on what is most Material or Curious either in the history or trial of the Seven Witches who were Condemn'd to be Execute in the country*. All the quotations above come from this work. Published less than a year after the executions, it was reprinted, with additional material, in two anonymous works of 1809 and 1877, each entitled *A History of the Witches of Renfrewshire*. The second version includes relevant extracts from the proceedings of the Presbytery of Paisley, 1696-97. The records of the investigation and witch-trials are in the National Records of Scotland (Privy Council PC1/51 and Circuit Court Books JC10/4).

A True Narrative is anonymous, but it was almost certainly the work of three men: John McGilchrist, a Glasgow solicitor and Christian's uncle; James Brisbane, minister of Kilmacolm; and

Andrew Turner, minister at Erskine. The latter two had been charged by the Presbytery to write a record and history of the case, while McGilchrist was known to have kept a journal of the events. It is not clear who wrote what, or which man was the overall editor.

In 2006 a third version of *A History of the Witches of Renfrewshire* came out. Entitled *The Kirk, Satan and Salem*, its editor, Hugh McLachlan, suggested *A True Narrative* was deeply compromised. It is not only yet another tract explicitly designed to bolster the belief in supernaturalism (and hence God); its style and language also owe a great deal to one of the primary documents of the better-known Salem witchtrials in New England. *A Brief and True Narrative of some Remarkable Passages Relating to Sundry Persons Afflicted by Witchcraft, at Salem Village*, transcribed from his notes at the trials by the Revd Deodat Lawson in 1692, may have provided the template for the way the Scottish text is written. McLachlan also suggests some of the Bargarran events may have been 'spiced up' to pile on the supernatural detail and convince the sceptical.

We know from the Presbytery, Privy Council and court records that Christian Shaw did suffer terribly over the given period, and we know the authorities took the record of those sufferings sufficiently seriously to initiate a witchcraft investigation. What we do not know is to what degree the record was rewritten or 'improved' before its publication as a propaganda tract.

A True Narrative trumpets its authenticity by listing the names of dozens of important people who witnessed at least some of the events. But if it is untrustworthy as a document, does this mean we also have to seriously doubt the veracity of the Revd Telfair's account of the Rerrick case (No.9)?

Context
The Shaws were long-established landowners: comfortable, but not wealthy. Christian was the oldest of their six children, and had been taught to read and write. The family had six servants and a

herdsman. One of the bizarre elements of the case is that once Christian started exhibiting extreme symptoms, she was turned into a public spectacle. The Shaws kept open house for curious gentlefolk who wanted to observe the demoniac in action, and the girl's bedroom often had a dozen people in it. Sadly, however, none of these visitors seems to have kept an independent account of the proceedings. Under the tutelage of Revd Blackwell (minister of Paisley from 1694-1700), interest was rekindled in seeking out witches in the parishes of Kilmacolm, Erskine, and Inchinnan. This may have had an influence on the zealotry of the Bargarran investigation.

Interpretation

A True Narrative explicitly tells us Christian was possessed by the Devil and his crew of invisible witches. James Sharpe, in his 1996 book *Instruments of Darkness: Witchcraft in England 1550-1750*, points out that the seventeenth century was a golden age for cases of children possessed by demons. At least twelve other examples are known in England, and many are so similar to each other that Satan seemed to be working in very stereotyped ways. Perhaps reports of one case influenced others. We cannot tell whether this happened with the Bargarran case, but it had all the elements of what became the standard pattern of the era.

Later generations dubbed the girl 'The Bargarran Imposter', demonising her as a manipulative attention-seeker. Messrs Mitchell and Dickie revealed in their 1839 book *The Philosophy of Witchcraft* that they had discovered an angled hole in the wall beside Christian Shaw's bedhead; they took the view that an accomplice was passing the various 'vomited-up' items from the adjacent room. And it is easy to see the hand of deliberate fraud or misperception in the various phenomena, such as the alleged levitations, telekinesis and the episode with the cleaned fireplace. The atmosphere in the Shaw household must have been so fraught with expectation that the slightest odd thing would have taken on a sinister aspect.

The Seventeenth Century

An article in the *Scottish Medical Journal* in 1996 (and reprinted in *The Kirk, Satan and Salem*) gave a retrospective diagnosis on Christian Shaw as possibly suffering from one or more of: dissociative disorder/conversion disorder; trance and possession disorder; pica of infancy and childhood; localisation-related (focal) (partial) idiopathic epilepsy; and acute and transient psychotic disorder. Many of these temporary conditions cease after childhood or adolescence, which fits with Christian's history of living a normal adult life.

The question is, did the eleven-year-old girl's distress escalate into poltergeist phenomena? The 'fits', distorted body parts and disgorging of unpleasant materials all fall within the recognised spectrum of extreme mental states, and we need not concern ourselves with those here. As for the supernormal aspects, the interpretation is: 'maybe'. If the account is reliable and accurate, then we do have a polt; but as *A True Narrative* may be full of lies, we cannot be sure.

11. GALDENOCH, DUMFRIES & GALLOWAY: 1680(?)-1697(?)

Ruined Galdenoch Castle, a small L-plan tower house built sometime in the mid-sixteenth century, lies on the B738 7 miles north-west of Stranraer. The castle can be viewed externally from the Meikle Galdenoch carpark.

Period
At least seventeen years, if the reports can be trusted.

Phenomena
A son of the Agnew family, having fought in a battle on the losing (Covenanter) side, sought refuge with a farmer of Royalist inclinations, probably in Ayrshire. In the morning, when his host attempted to prevent him leaving, the soldier shot the man dead. The day the Agnew lad returned home to Galdenoch, the tower became infested with poltergeist phenomena. We are not told

the initial nature of the events, only that they included noises and 'pranks'.

Some time later the ownership of the tower changed hands. One wintry night the family were sitting round the fire playing the game of 'priest-cat', in which a burning stick was passed from hand to hand while the players chanted:

> About wi' that! About wi' that!
> Keep alive the priest-cat!

Whoever held the stick when the flame died was required to pay a forfeit. At the moment the spark was extinguished, a glowing peat vanished from the fire, 'leaving as clear a vacuum in the fire as when a brick is displaced from a solid archway.' A few minutes later the farm-steading was in flames, and the identical peat from the fire was seen burning in the thatch. On another occasion the tenant's elderly mother was snatched from her spinning wheel and dumped in the stream. When the family went looking for her, a voice was heard: 'I've washed grannie in the burn, and laid her on the dyke to dry!'

Several of the neighbouring clergymen failed spectacularly to lay the spirit, finding their hymns drowned out and the cunning and manipulative voice able to win any argument. Threads were cut on the spinning wheel; peat clots fell into the porridge; dung was found in the cooking-pot. After many years of trouble, peace was finally restored by the Revd Archibald Marshall, minister of Kirkmaiden. Gifted with a loud and powerful voice, the minister went head-to-head with the spirit in a singing contest, each trying to bellow louder than the other. After many hours his accompanying choir were too exhausted to continue, but the Revd Marshall carried on, and eventually in the early hours of the morning the spirit cried out, 'Boar awa', Marshall, I can roar nae mair!' And after that it vanished for ever.

According to tradition, the tenant was too fearful to remain in the haunted tower, and after he moved out, Galdenoch sank into ruin. In 1916 C.H. Dick, in *Highways and Byways in Galloway and Carrick*, stated that the tower had for many years been in use as a cowshed, as the structure was considered to be 'too haunted for human occupation.'

Sources
The story first appears in print only in 1893, when Andrew Agnew published *The Hereditary Sheriffs of Galloway*. Agnew made it clear the tale had been well known in the area for nearly 200 years, but almost certainly exaggeration and invention had crept in during its many retellings. With the sole exception of the Revd Marshall, we are not given the names of any of the participants or witnesses, any dates, or even the name of the battle at the start of the narrative. There were Covenanter defeats at Rullion Green, south of Edinburgh (1688); Bothwell Brig, South Lanarkshire (1679); and Ayrs (Airds) Moss, East Ayrshire (1680). If we take the gentlest interpretation both geographically and chronologically, then the Agnew soldier probably fled from Airds Moss. The Revd Marshall was ordained in 1697. So if the core details of the tale are correct, Galdenoch was troubled for at least seventeen years (1680 to 1697), if not longer.

Context
South-west Scotland was the Covenanting heartland, and tales from the period have percolated into local folklore. The Agnews did indeed quit Galdenoch because they were financially broken by the end of the seventeenth century, partly through fines levied for supporting the Covenanters, and partly because their salt-pans business venture failed.

Interpretation
For Andrew Agnew this is a straightforward haunting by a vengeful ghost. According to Andrew Donaldson's *Guide to Kirkmaiden* (1908), however, the Revd Marshall was a zealot when it came to extirpating witchcraft; in revenge the local witches magically

prevented him from speaking in his own pulpit, so in 1700 he had to be transferred to neighbouring Kirkholm parish, where he regained his famously stentorian voice. It is possible that Marshall regarded the spirit as an emissary from Hell, but we have no records supporting this. In fact, we have no records at all regarding what really happened. It may be that the 'ghost murdered by a Covenanter' is a piece of folk narrative grafted on to a standalone poltergeist outbreak, as an invention designed to 'explain' the infestation. To add to the complexity, Alan Temperley's *Tales of Galloway* (1979) states that during the late eighteenth century the tower was used by pirates, who may have invented the story to keep nosy parkers away…

Chapter Two

The Eighteenth Century

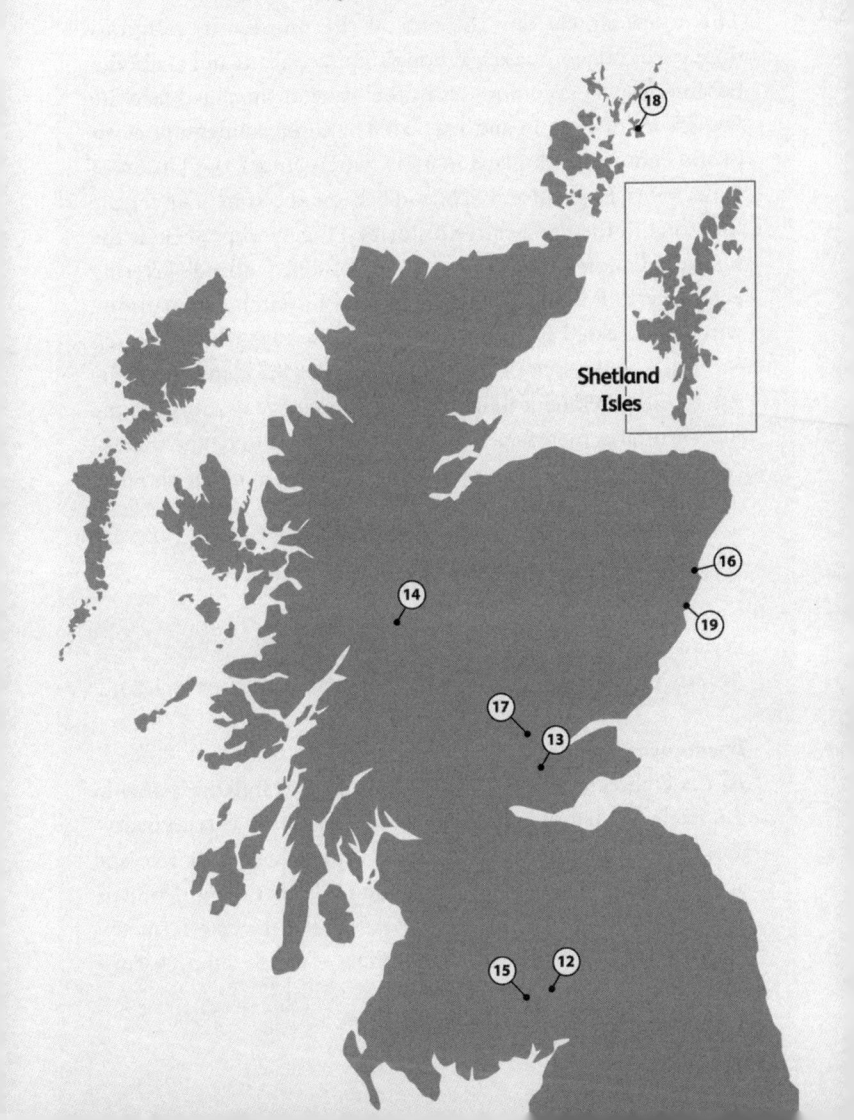

'I don't care to deny poltergeists, because I suspect that later, when we're more enlightened, or when we widen the range of our credulities, or take on more of that increase of ignorance that is called knowledge, poltergeists may become assimilable. Then they'll be as reasonable as trees.'

Charles Fort, *The Book of the Damned*, 1919

The 1700s slowly saw the ebb of the murderous religious disputes of previous years, although Episcopalians and Catholics became suspect communities in the wake of the failed Jacobite Rebellions of 1715-16 and 1745-46. The most momentous event of the century took place in 1707, when, under the Union of Parliaments, England and Scotland became the same state for the first time in their respective histories. Hugely unpopular at the time, the Union actually secured and boosted Scotland's faltering economy. Following a massive decline in witch prosecutions, witchcraft ceased to be a capital crime in 1735 (the last witch execution took place in 1727). Intellectually, the century saw the rise of Enlightenment thinking, with a tendency to disparage the supernatural as mere superstition. Devils ceased to be the source-code of poltergeists, which were now regarded as either ghosts of the dead, or entirely fraudulent.

12. MELLANTAE, DUMFRIES & GALLOWAY: 1707

Period
At least a month (late August to 23 September 1707, or longer).

Phenomena
As the eighteen-year-old Miss Johnstone was milking a cow in the stable of Mellantae Farm in broad daylight, an extraordinary-looking man appeared, stole the milk, slapped her on the face, and acted in such a strange and threatening way that the girl fainted, and took a long time to recover. After that day the farm was plagued day and night with flying stones – which did no harm –

and the disappearance of clothes, which were found a day or two later thrown over bushes and dykes. Beehives were overturned, the sound of thundering hammer- or axe-blows came from a bed, and at night the kitchen resounded with the pewter vessels being cast onto the floor, even though by the morning all the items appeared undisturbed. Miss Johnstone was especially targeted, with bedclothes removed, her foot pulled by an invisible force, and her body so frequently assaulted that she became ill. A servant who said to others working with him in a field, 'Lord be thanked, the ghost has not troubled us this last night!' was instantly struck hard with a stone.

Sources
The account appears in Robert Wodrow's *Analecta, Or, Materials for a History of Remarkable Providences; Mostly Relating to Scottish Ministers and Christians*, written in journal form between 1705 and 1732, and finally published in 1842-43. Wodrow was the minister at Eastwood, Glasgow, and also wrote a monumental history of the Covenanter times. The *Analecta* ('scraps' or 'crumbs') is full of ecclesiastical gossip and reports of supernatural events.

Wodrow learned of the episode from his friend James Cowan, who had been staying in Annandale with the Revd James Short, minister of Drysdale. They got the details in September 1707 – while the events were still ongoing – from their old acquaintance the Revd James Murray, minister of the neighbouring parish of St Mungo's. Murray himself got the tale from the distressed Mr Johnstone, the farmer at Mellantae. Cowan and Short picked up further intelligence from a chap called 'young Dornock', who witnessed the tumbling of the beehives, and other incidents. Cowan received more details from another (unnamed) witness, one of a group of gentlemen who had been staying at the farm overnight. So the material is third-hand, with few named witnesses, but it was gathered as the events were unfolding. When James Cowan left the area on 23 September, the disturbances were still going on.

Context
Mellantae Farm (also known as Mellintae and Millintae) was south-east of Lockerbie. The Johnstones appear to have been quite prosperous farmers. We know nothing abut the family situation.

Interpretation
Farmer Johnstone clearly linked the phenomena to the advent of the strange man. His daughter described him thus: 'he was almost all naked, except that he had a white night-cape on his head, a white sheet about his shoulders, and white socks on his legs.' He was tall, red-haired and had very large feet, and 'made a great many odd faces, gaping and staring upon her, and grasping at her with his hand.' He could conceivably have been an itinerant beggar, or perhaps someone with a disordered mind who had escaped from confinement.

Satan is never mentioned, and there are no religious elements; the actions are throughout simply ascribed to a 'ghost'. It seems plausible that the eighteen year old was so alarmed by her experience that she spontaneously developed poltergeist powers. But there may be a geological explanation: Mr Dornock, while setting the beehives upright again, 'thought he felt a shaking and trembling of the earth beneath him.' But even if tremors were present, it is surely a stretch too far to suggest that earthquakes throw directed stones or displace clothing. Is it possible, in a bizarre coincidence, that the beehives were tumbled by a minor tremor at the same time as the poltergeist outbreak?

13. KINROSS, PERTH & KINROSS: 1718

Period
Several days or weeks in the first half of 1718.

Phenomena
The disturbances at the household of the Revd Robert McGill started with silver spoons and knives being found sticking upright in the floor of the barn. Next to them was a large dish

'all nipped to pieces'. Thereafter all food, including boiled eggs, was found polluted by pins. Any bread made on the premises was uneatable. Even when Isabel, the minister's wife, performed every stage of the cooking herself, as soon as the meal was presented on the table it was found to contain pins. One pin in particular was noted – a large specimen with which the minister fastened his gown.

Other phenomena followed: drying sheets cut to pieces; clothes destroyed while in a locked chest; and a woman's hood, gown tail, and underwear cut while she was wearing them. A dresser toppled, smashing the stored vessels. A stone thrown down the chimney 'wambled a space in the floor, and then took a flight out at the window'. The minister's Bible was cast on the fire, but did not burn, while a similarly thrown plate and two silver spoons melted immediately in the flames. The events lasted 'a considerable time' and were witnessed not only by the family but also by others who spent the night watching and praying.

Sources
The account is the entire contents of a pamphlet published by a Mr Sinclair in June 1718, called *Endorism, or a strange relation of dreams or spirits that troubled the minister's house of Kinross*. It was republished in James Maidment's 1834 miscellany of historical documents, *Analecta Scotica*, and Charles Kirkpatrick Sharpe's *Historical Account of the Belief in Witchcraft in Scotland* (1884). The author clearly knew the McGill family, but no eyewitnesses are directly quoted, and no specific dates are given.

Context
Robert McGill had been the minister at Kinross since 1699; he was about forty-six at the time of the disturbances. He had one son, Alexander, but we do not know his age. 'Endorism' refers to the Witch of Endor, the only named witch in the Bible. The manse was demolished in 1769 and replaced by a larger building.

Interpretation

The pamphlet nails its colours to the mast at the very start: 'Many deny that there are any such as witches… to be sure there are both spirits and angels good and bad, and, according to Scripture, there may be witches.' As with many earlier tracts, here the phenomena are enlisted in the campaign to shore up belief in the supernatural. In a slightly confused argument, the writer laments that these days so many accused witches are being set at liberty because they are 'dreamers' – presumably this means their confessions are dismissed as imagination or ravings, as part of the sceptical thinking of the era. Elsewhere in the pamphlet 'dreamers' are conflated with 'evil spirits', and it seems the writer believes that witches can use their mental powers to send invisible spirits into houses – which is a version of the psychokinetic idea of the origin of poltergeists.

And as to why the minister should be targeted: 'the godly are the only objects of the Devil's fury, for such as the Devil is sure of, he does not heed them.' The pamphlet also decries the wicked and irreligious nature of the times: 'Is it not very sad, that such a good and godly family should be so molested, that employ their time no other way but by praying, reading, and serious meditation, while others who are wicked livers all their lifetime, and in a manner avowedly serve that wicked one, are never troubled.' The pamphlet is one of the last hurrahs of the Satanic school of poltergeist interpretation.

There is a minor hint at fraud hidden within the text: 'A certain girl, eating some meat [food], turned so very sick, that being necessitate to vomit, cast up five pins.' As far as I can tell, the McGills had no daughter, so was this 'certain girl' a servant, and was her vomiting of the pins another version of the fraud that was suspected in the Bargarran case (No.10)?

14. MONESSIE, LOCHABER, HIGHLAND REGION: 1750s?

Period
Weeks? Months? Years?

The Eighteenth Century

Phenomena

Donald Bán lived at Mounessie or Monessie, close to the spectacular waterfalls on the A86 some 6 miles east of Spean Bridge. After being wounded fighting on the losing Jacobite side at the Battle of Culloden in 1746, he spent some time in a government prison. When he returned home he found himself haunted by a Bócan, a Gaelic word meaning goblin or spirit. He was thus known as Domhnall Bán a' Bhocain, Donald Bán of the Bócan.

Donald was a huntsman, and it was said he first encountered the Bócan in the wild Lochaber hills of his homeland. It was an invisible, speaking spirit, and soon moved in with him. Stones and peat clods flew onto and through the house. Noises erupted from Donald's bedhead. Food, especially butter, was polluted. A visitor, Angus mac Alister Ban, was seized by his two big toes. Eventually Donald and his family decided to move to another house. They took everything with them except a harrow; but they had just gone a little way when they saw the implement following them. 'Stop, stop,' cried Donald, 'if the harrow is coming after us we may as well go back again.' The Bócan had a particular animus against Donald's wife, a MacGregor woman, and often insulted her in speech.

The Bócan ordered Donald to come with him and leave behind all metal items, such as his dirk. The duo tramped for 3 miles through the darkness until they reached a spot beside a burn. Here the spirit showed Donald a cache of valuable plough-irons it had hidden when alive. While Donald was digging them out he was terrified by the Bócan's glowing eyes. Once the pair had returned to Donald's home, the Bócan departed and troubled the man no more.

Donald composed a hymn about the affair, part of which runs:

> Always at the time when I go to bed
> The stones and the clods will arise –
> How could a saint get sleep there?
> I am without peace or rest,
> Without repose or sleep till the morning.

Poltergeist over Scotland

Sources
The story first found its way into print in 1877, when a Gaelic version written by D.C. Macpherson appeared in Volume 6 of *The Gael* magazine. In 1890 the Revd A. Maclean Sinclair contributed a different version to *The Glenbard Collection of Gaelic Poetry*. The first English translation, and my source, was an article written in 1896 by W.A. Craigie for the journal *Folklore*. The Revd Sinclair stated that he had heard the tale from an old Lochaber tailor who happened to be the grandson of the man whose toes had been tweaked by the Bócan.

Context
For the first time in this book, we find a poltergeist within the context of Gaelic culture. A Bócan can be many different things in Highland folktales, the English term 'goblin' being only one translation; its use simply signifies 'something supernatural' rather than a specific entity.

Interpretation
This is a spectacularly weird story. What is the significance of the harrow they deliberately left behind, and which then followed them? And the insistence on not taking metal weapons on a journey is folklorically reminiscent of the fairies' dislike of iron, even though the plough coulters – which feature widely in Highland traditional narratives as objects of value – were of course themselves metal. It is almost as if there are meanings to the story which were once blindingly obvious to its listeners, but which are now utterly obscure.

With more than a century during which the story flourished as a purely oral narrative, there was obviously plenty of opportunity for the tale to gain arms and legs. It was rumoured that the Bócan was the restless ghost of a man Donald had wronged in life, although the hunter always denied this. Donald was no stranger to the supernatural, having had precognitive dreams, and met fairies and a strange being riding a deer. So is the story of the

Bócan to be interpreted as another one of these liminal events? The sense I have is that, despite its elaboration and aggrandisement over the decades, the story contains core elements which are probably memories of genuine poltergeist incidents.

15. DUMFRIES: 1782

> [One] place was inhabited by a highly respectable gentleman, a magistrate of Dumfries, whose family were perpetually annoyed by knockings and drummings in all parts of the house, as though some powerful hand had been exercising a heavy mallet on the partitions and floors. Although these noises were so loud as to be distinctly heard by the labourers in the neighbouring fields, no clue to their origin was ever discovered. Tenant after tenant occupied the house, but the invisible rapper continued among the fixtures.

The house was for many years known as 'Knock-a-big's Close', after the stone mortar used to hull barley. This is the entire story, as found in an 1863 book on Spiritualism, Henry Spicer's *Sights and Sounds*. Spicer does not give his source.

16. ABERDEEN: 1783

> The sound [made by this poltergeist] resembled that of a sledge-hammer striking upon an anvil, but as if both hammer and anvil were muffled;—dull, dismal, and heavy,—So heavy indeed, that it made the poker and tongs rattle in the fireplace. Soon after the first blow came a second,—and another, and another,—then one not so loud,—then several in quick succession;—by and by, the shuffling of feet, or the dancing;—and so on, more or less, till day-break.

Sceptical twenty-year-old student George Colman lived for a summer in this haunted house near what is now Links Road, and after investigation concluded the noises were genuine. The account is in Colman's autobiography of 1830, *Random Records*.

17. PERTH: 1790s? / 1800s?

An 'incessant racket' proceeded day and night from an old empty tenement in Bridgend, the suburb on the east side of the Tay. Crowds gathered, and more than one minister attempted to lay the spirit, to no avail. The sparse details are in *Traditions of Perth*, published in 1836 by George Penny.

18. STRONSAY, ORKNEY: 1791

From April to August hammering noises were heard from a boat under construction by carpenter John Spence, and, when the boat was delivered, the noises infected his home. (*The Statistical Account of Scotland 1791-1799*, County of Orkney.)

19. DUNNOTTAR, ABERDEENSHIRE: 1793?

A clodding was found to be fraudulent, practiced by 'a young country girl' (Sir Walter Scott, *Letters on Demonology and Witchcraft*, 1830).

Chapter Three

The Nineteenth Century

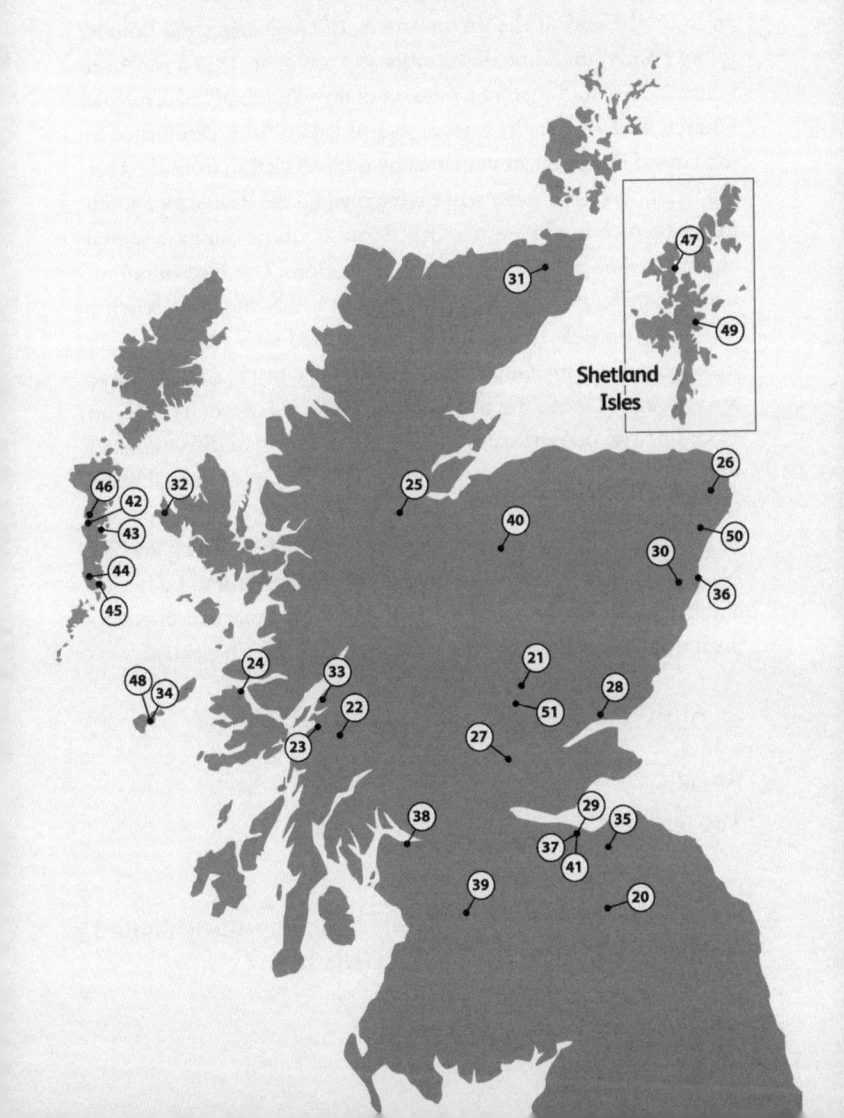

> There are powers mysterious, miraculous, and diabolic frequently let loose mid the ordinary affairs of human life. It is this 'something' which ... glamours us in the recital of the weird and eerie stories so plentiful in the bye-gone life of Scotland.
>
> William Walker, *A Longside Legend*, 1913

At the start of the nineteenth century, most Scots still lived in country areas; by the end of the Victorian era, the majority were housed (often poorly) in industrialised cities and towns. In 1843 a row over who exactly could appoint a minister of the Church of Scotland (the Church itself, or wealthy patrons such as landowners) culminated in the Great Disruption, in which many ministers left to form the Free Church of Scotland. Later schisms fragmented the Protestant faithful further, which is why even a small Scottish village can have several church buildings for different denominations. The blossoming of science and scepticism saw the decline in beliefs in fairies, witches and demons, while British intellectuals started taking an interest in the supernatural: the Ghost Club was founded in 1862, the Folklore Society in 1878, and the Society for Psychical Research (SPR) in 1882. The rise of Spiritualism brought the notion of direct contact with the dead into the homes of thousands of people – probably the single greatest change in the paranormal landscape of the century. In 1888 Margaret Fox confessed that the very first raps – in Hydesville, New York, 1848 – had been fraudulently manufactured by herself and her sisters; by this point the momentum of Spiritualism was so great that it carried on as if the confession had never happened.

20. ABBOTSFORD, SCOTTISH BORDERS: 1818

Period

Two nights, 28 and 29 April 1818.

Phenomena

On 30 April Sir Walter Scott wrote from his partially finished mansion at Abbotsford to his friend David Terry:

> The exposed state of my house has led to a mysterious disturbance. The night before last we were awakened by a violent noise, like drawing heavy boards along the new part of the house. I fancied something had fallen, and thought no more about it; this was about two in the morning. Last night, at the same witching hour, the very same noise occurred.

With an antique sword in hand, Scott investigated, but found no cause for the sounds. On 16 May he wrote again to Terry: 'The noise resembled half a dozen men hard at work putting up boards and furniture, and nothing can be more certain than that there was nobody on the premises at the time.'

The noises took place on Tuesday and Wednesday night. George Bullock, Scott's agent for the building work, died suddenly on the Wednesday, between 9 p.m. and 10 p.m. The author connected Bullock's demise in London with the noises *chez* Scott. As Scott retold the story over the years, the original five-hour gap between the two events shortened and shortened until his friend's death exactly matched the time of the noises.

Sources
The correspondence is in John Gibson Lockhart's *Memoirs of the life of Sir Walter Scott* (1838). The full evolution of the ghost story over the years is elucidated in Coleman Parsons' 1964 study, *Witchcraft and Demonology in Scott's Fiction*.

Context
Scott was the premier novelist of his age, with an on-going interest in folklore and the supernatural. In 1826 he wrote *Woodstock*, a fictional version of the 1649 poltergeist episode at Woodstock, Oxfordshire.

Interpretation
Were the noises caused by careless builders? Possibly. Possibly not. If nothing else, this is an object lesson in the way the description of an uncanny event can become 'improved' over the years.

21. BONSKEID, PERTH & KINROSS: 1820

Period
Several weeks in the summer of 1820.

Phenomena
Here we have two different versions of the same event, both located on the River Tummel a few miles north-west of Pitlochry, but each set in slightly different locations. In version one, the theft of some gravestones from the Cladh Chille burial ground, to help build a new farmhouse at Mains of Bonskeid, resulted in both locations becoming haunted. 'While the farm-servants were at supper, stones came rattling down the chimney; and when the inmates went to bed, low moaning sounds were heard which would not let them sleep.' A pig trough moved across the ground and up over a roof in view of the Revd John Stewart, the minister of Blair Atholl.

In version two, the events took place at Bonskeid House, which is a few hundred yards north of the graveyard and a mile south-east of Mains of Bonskeid. 'Turnips and peats, thrown by unseen hands, flew about the house, lights were blown out, furniture was mysteriously moved, bedclothes were pulled off.' Sometimes the turnips seemed to come through the walls. On two occasions a spinning wheel made its way down the stairs and dismantled itself.

Sources
Version one is in *Memoir of Mrs Stewart Sandeman of Bonskeid and Springland*, first published in 1883. Written by her daughter Margaret Frazer Barbour, the book describes how, at the age of seventeen, Margaret Stewart spent the summer of 1820 at her parents' home, Bonskeid House. Both she and her father, Dr Alexander Stewart, found the tenants and servants on the estate in the grip of ghost fever. The mystery was solved when the Revd Alexander Irvine of Little Dunkeld parish discovered that a young couple who wished to marry and live in Mains of Bonskeid were trying to scare the old people out of the house. Once the scheme

was exposed, the disturbances stopped. The stones which had descended the chimney were, however, still regarded with fear, so the minister had them taken away and built into the wall being erected around his manse in Birnam.

Version two can be found in *Witchcraft and Second Sight in the Highlands and Islands of Scotland*, published posthumously in 1902 (now more easily explored in *The Gaelic Otherworld*, a re-issue which also includes the same author's *Superstitions of the Highlands and Islands*, all expertly edited by Ronald Black). Its author, J.G. Campbell, was one of the greatest Scottish folklorists of all time. He collected his stories between 1850 and 1874, relying entirely on his informants' memories, without any recourse to letters or books. His account names no witnesses, is vague on dates, and claims that the anonymous owner of the house (i.e. Dr Stewart) had married a woman from Badenoch, the area on the River Spey around Kingussie and Boat of Garten. In fact Dr Stewart had in 1790 married Jane Bissett of Dunkeld. According to Campbell's version, the disturbances were caused by the Badenoch servants the wife brought with her, probably by trickery, and once they were expelled the troubles ceased.

Context

The Stewarts had owned the lands around Bonskeid for centuries, although their fortunes had ebbed and flowed. Bonskeid House was built some time after 1796, and occupied by the Stewarts in 1811. Margaret Stewart went on to marry Glas Sandeman of Perth and, as Mrs Stewart Sandeman, became a well-known local figure. The house was aggrandised in Scottish Baronial style in the 1860s.

Interpretation

The local people believed the noises were the restless dead, aggrieved at the desecration of their gravestones. Margaret Frazer Barbour is clear that the disturbances were fraudulent. Campbell is equally suspicious: 'The tricks are such as it is perfectly possible for human agency to perform... These cantrips are exaggerated by fear and rumour, till at last the Devil is believed to be unusually busy in the locality. Once this belief becomes popular, the delusion is easily carried on.'

22. INVERAWE HOUSE, ARGYLL & BUTE

This tale, and the three that follow, are undated scraps and also taken from Campbell's *Witchcraft and Second Sight*. All are concerned with a glaistig, a 'tutelary being' usually regarded as a former human woman who had acquired a fairy nature. She was attached to a house, farm or location, not a person or family. Like a brownie, she usually helped tidy things up, and was particularly adept at cattle husbandry. Tales of glaistigs and their cousins, the gruagachs, are widespread in Gaelic folklore.

A glaistig known as Maighdeann Inbhir Atha ('the Maiden of Inverawe') would overturn water stoups overnight and move chairs. She was supposed to be a former mistress of the house who was unfaithful, and so buried alive. In this sense she is more a restless ghost than a fairy.

23. DUNSTAFFNAGE CASTLE, ARGYLL & BUTE

A visitor had his bedclothes twice pulled off by the invisible Sianag or Elle-maid, who also stomped loudly around the room and adjoining passages.

24. ERRAY, MULL

The glaistig regularly overturned and disturbed everything in the barn, and was heard trampling at night.

25. STRATHGLASS, INVERNESS-SHIRE, HIGHLAND

A giggling glaistig delighted in regularly pulling the bedclothes off a shepherd's bed, and making coats and cheese temporarily vanish before returning both. The man tried to keep her away by placing the New Testament above the door, but to no effect. One evening a party of young men came over to hear the noises. After a disappointing evening, they were about to leave when the pot floated off the fire onto the floor, and they were badly attacked with clods. This event may possibly have been in around 1834.

26. LONGSIDE, ABERDEENSHIRE: 1822

Period
Six months of 1822.

Phenomena
Every night James Wylie, tenant of a croft at Braehead of Auchtydonald, Longside, was plagued by poltergeist attacks, so much so that many local people visited the house to witness the disturbances for themselves. One night five men and an old woman went to watch. Around midnight, unearthly sounds started to make themselves heard. The old woman took hold of Wylie's blankets to see if the spirit had the power to pull them from her, when:

> ...out came one of the pails of water and after cutting some capers emptied its contents around her, while at the same time all the blankets in the bed were lifted, as if by their own accord, and tumbled out of the bed upon the floor with great force, and everything in the house moved as if there had been an earthquake.

The male witness described how chairs, tables and crockery danced about; two of his friends were struck down by a peat and a bowl respectively, while he himself was hit in the cheek by a potato-chopper. 'Everything was in motion and flying in all directions through the house, and the poor man was walloping up and down in his bed and screaming fearfully.'

The five men searched the place and failed to find any lurking prankster, at which point some of them fled in fear. Those who remained enjoyed an hour of peace, but then the chaos started up again, lasting until dawn. Other visitors, including doctors and Bible-sporting ministers, suffered similar assaults. All this is in the Grant account (see below).

On 9 November 1822 Wylie's cousin, Mr Allardyce, arrived, having travelled some distance and fully resolved to solve the mystery. He ordered everyone out of the house, except Wylie and two young servants (male and female). Allardyce sat up all night with 'a steady lad' to keep watch. Between 11 p.m. and midnight he heard two smart knocks, and so lit a candle and proceeded to explore the entire building, knocking at every wooden surface – but he could not reproduce the exact sound of the original taps. The following night he heard a knock – and fired his pistol at the source of the sound. By 4 a.m. Allardyce and his fellow-watcher had fired at noises twice outside, and five times inside the house, all with no effect. The knocks did not sound like strokes with a hammer upon iron, stone, or timber; rather, they resembled the crack of a wind- or pen-gun, a popular boys' pop-gun toy made from a quill.

Another witness told Anderson (see below) that the noises were akin to 'a smart crack on a table with a cane', and that Wylie had complained of being attacked and nearly smothered in his bed, while a stick was once snatched out of his hand by an invisible force. Wylie also claimed to have seen a tall, white-clad figure rise out of the hearthstone. All of this preyed on the man's nerves.

Wylie quit the croft before 28 November, and went to live with his father. Despite being a young man, his health deteriorated (allegedly due to the disturbances), and he died soon thereafter. The easternmost croft was henceforth known as Boodie Brae, 'boodie' being a local dialect word meaning 'devil' or 'evil spirit'. The house was later let to tradesmen; no further phenomena were reported.

Sources

On 28 November 1822 John Allardyce of Cairnbulg wrote to a friend in Peterhead, describing his son's adventure at Longside: 'He has no fear. I was rather afraid he should lodge a bullet in someone's guts.' James Wylie was the son of John Allardyce's wife's brother, hence the family interest. The letter was included in full in '"Boodie Brae": A Longside Legend', by bibliophile publisher William Walker, who inserted it in the *Aberdeen Buchan Association Magazine* in November 1913, and then reprinted it as a booklet of the same title in an edition of twelve copies. Walker's booklet also included the full account of the episode written by David Grant in a pamphlet (probably from 1862) entitled *A descriptive account of the Formantine and Buchan Railway*, the original of which I have not been able to trace. Grant had clearly spoken to several witnesses, possibly while researching *A Hand Book to the Great North of Scotland Railway and Branches*. A shorter and more sceptical piece, with contributions from another unnamed witness, appeared in William Anderson's *Guide to the Formantine and Buchan Railway* (1862), which (inaccurately) redates the events to 1824, and the story was then retold in J.M. McPherson's *Primitive Beliefs in the North-East of Scotland* (1929), in which the name was changed to Broodie Brae, and the date to 1825.

Context

The 13-mile section of railway between Maud and Peterhead, passing Longside, was opened on 3 July 1862.

Interpretation

According to Grant, the neighbours were convinced that someone had raised the disturbance by means of the Black Arts, i.e. diabolism or witchcraft. Anderson thought the noises were the drying-out of the green wood used to repair the house, while the rest was down to imagination and nerves.

27. AUCHTERARDER, PERTH & KINROSS: 1830s

'Money rumbled in the drawers, and leaped from places, where it was not under lock and key, to the floor. Tables shook – the plate rack, or its contents, danced and rattled with startling fury – the house bells would ring for many minutes on end.'

After a visit by a religious gentleman to this 'respectable mansion', the disturbances ceased. The scanty report is in the *Perthshire Courier*, 29 October 1840.

28. LOCHEE, DUNDEE: 1831

An elderly couple in the Lochee district were disturbed nightly between midnight and 3 a.m. by repeated loud batterings. Fourteen neighbours stationed within and without the house failed to locate any cause, and a request to the Lochee Kirk Session for an exorcism was turned down. The item appeared in the *Dundee Advertiser* for 29 September 1831. There was no follow-up story.

29. TRINITY, EDINBURGH: 1835

Period
Several weeks or months in 1835.

Phenomena
In May or June 1835 Captain Molesworth rented a house in fashionable Trinity. Within two months of moving in, the officer complained of strange noises to his landlord, Mr Webster, who lived next door. He even accused the property owner of being behind the disturbances for nefarious purposes. Mr Webster responded robustly, stating that it was not likely that he would damage the reputation of his own property, nor alienate a paying tenant.

The knockings, scratchings, rustlings and footsteps continued, day and night. Sometimes a tune could be discerned within the knocks, as well as a rudimentary intelligence capable of communication: when asked out loud, 'How many people are there in this room?' the knocks would respond with the correct number. Beds were heaved into the air, and the walls trembled with the bangs. Sheriff's officers, masons, justices of the peace and military officers were called in. Hoping to trap a malicious prankster, a number of them formed a cordon around the house, but no intruder was discovered. Mr Webster accused Captain Molesworth's bed-bound thirteen-year-old daughter, Jane, of being behind the noises, and perhaps the sick girl's father also entertained that possibility, as on one occasion she was tied up in a bag to prevent any sleight of hand. The disturbances, however, continued unabated.

Eventually, Captain Molesworth must have been driven into a frenzy of anxiety and frustration. When he quit the house in 1835, Mr Webster brought a suit against him, partly for tarnishing the reputation of the house, making it difficult to rent out again – but also because the captain had torn up the floorboards, made holes in the walls, and even shot at the wainscot. The suit was heard on 7 August 1837 – Captain Molesworth was ordered to pay for the repairs.

Sources

The case was first written up in *The Night-Side of Nature* by Catherine Crowe (1848). Crowe's informant was a solicitor engaged by Mr Webster to pursue the case, and so had spent 'many hours in examining the numerous witnesses, several of whom were officers of the army, and gentlemen of undoubted honour and capacity for observation.' Crowe gave the lawyer's name as 'M.L.'. Robert Dale Owen, writing in *Footfalls on the Boundary of Another World* in 1860, identified him as Maurice Lothian, who later went on to become Procurator Fiscal for Edinburgh. The outcome is tersely recorded in the Advising Books for Edinburgh Sheriff Court, held in the National Records for Scotland (item SC39/3/32). Unfortunately the related processes, or case papers (which would hopefully include some of the witness statements), appear to be missing or misplaced.

Context

Trinity was situated north-east of the New Town, between Ferry Road, Leith Port and Lower Granton Road.

Interpretation

For the neighbourhood, the polt was obviously the warning ghost of Jane's recently deceased sister Matilda, and Jane did indeed pass away shortly after the family quit the house. Mr Webster contended that Jane was behind the noises – and perhaps she was, if we take the view that a sickly, unhappy adolescent girl, as so often seems to be the case, can project her frustration outward by some form of psychokinesis.

30. BALDARROCH, ABERDEENSHIRE: 1838

> Afore the fire folk couldna' sit for fear,
> For peats and clods cam' bunging ben the flear;
> The Parson cam' and sained the house wi' prayer,
> But still the clods were thuddin' here and there.
> The spoons an' dishes, knives an' forks,
> They frisked aboot as light as corks,
> And cups and ladles joined the dancing,
> An' thro' the house they a' gaed prancing.
> They say the De'il's come to Baldarroch,
> Or some unearthly Devilish warroch [warlock]
>
> William Walker, *The De'il at Baldarroch* (1839)

Period

Several weeks from 5 December 1838.

Phenomena

The farmyard of Baldarroch, 2 miles east of Banchory, became a hurricane of flying stones, clods and sticks. After five days the chaos moved indoors, with the farmhouse enlivened by flying articles: cutlery, shoes, plates, mustard-pots, mortars, rolling-pins, and warming irons. 'The lid of a mustard-pot was put into a cupboard by the servant-girl in the presence of scores of people, and in a few minutes afterwards came bouncing down the chimney... There was also a tremendous knocking at the doors and on the roof, and pieces of stick and pebble-stones rattled against the windows and broke them.'

This at least was the description in Charles Mackay's *Memoirs of Extraordinary Popular Delusions and the Madness of Crowds*, published in 1852.

Another account comes from a Banchory schoolteacher (and later a minister), Charles Ogg, who, under the pseudonym of 'An Old Residenter', wrote *Banchory-Ternan 60 years ago* in 1870. Domestic utensils were disarranged or hidden in unlikely places, agricultural implements allegedly moved without hands, horses were unharnessed, and stones, peats and potatoes were thrown day and night. Ogg was one of a pair of investigators who suspected fraud; he was unimpressed by the testimony of two of the farm residents, mason James Thomson and ground officer William Downie, both of whom swore they had seen stones, cooking implements and shoes doing acrobatics, including flying out of walls. A young servant girl seemed to be enjoying herself too much. 'Concealing my suspicions,' wrote Ogg, 'I said I had come far to see something strange, and hoped I would not be disappointed. She said it did not work well when there were so many people in the house...'

Shortly after, the girl was taken by the parish constable to the adjacent Crathes Castle, to be questioned by the local laird, Sir Thomas Burnett. While she was absent the movable items within the farmhouse remained within the laws of known physics, only to regain their vivacity when she returned. The following day a second investigation by the parish minister and the laird's brother caught the girl red-handed, squirting wet potatoes through her fingers so they scattered on the floor. Through the agency of Sir Thomas, the Procurator Fiscal in the county town of Stonehaven became involved, and the following report appeared in the Aberdeen Constitutional on 8 February 1839:

Two young women, Ann Leighton, aged 32, sister of the farmer at Baldarroch, and Catherine Mackie, aged 16, his servant, have each been ordered to find caution to the amount of 200 merks Scots, that they will appear any time within six months to answer to any libel that may be brought against them for the crime of wickedly, maliciously, and wantonly throwing about peats, stones, spoons, knives, or other missiles or articles, and with striking therewith, or with part thereof, his Majesties' lieges; and removing in a secret or concealed manner articles of furniture or other articles from the place in which they were usually kept, and causing them unexpectedly to appear in other places, and then asserting and giving out to the lieges that such occurrences had been seen to take place when no person was present by whom they were occasioned; and all this they are charged to have done to the great annoyance, molestation, and disturbance of others, and with an intent to produce an impression and belief that the same was the result of some supernatural or invisible agency or influence, and with the intent of creating fear, terror and alarm to the lieges; as also assault; as also malicious mischief, or the wilful destruction of the property of others.

Sources

The newspaper report was included in William Walker's *Boodie Brae* booklet (see No.26). Mackay's 1852 account, which is the best known, cites not a single name, eyewitness or source, but his version is so detailed that he must have got it from somewhere – Mackay worked variously for *The Morning Chronicle*, the *Glasgow Argus*, and the *Illustrated London News*. Only a few months after the events, two local works were published on the subject – William Walker's *The De'il at Baldarroch*, quoted above, and *The Dance of Baldarroch*, an anonymous work attributed to Andrew Edwar, a bookseller from Stonehaven. Later, James Skinner, a Banchory musician, composed a strathspey reel entitled 'The Deil o' Baldarroch', and Johnny Milne o' Leevit's Glen, a smuggler turned itinerant poet, hawked his contribution, 'The Deil o' Baldarroch, or the Banchory "Ghaist"', around the farms, the work finally finding a publisher in 1871:

The Nineteenth Century

> The bere-beater, of great wecht and size,
> Aff like a bird into the air did rise;
> It flew ower the houses like a lark.
> And down on the fouk's taes fell wi' a yark.

Context

While popular opinion in the district went into overdrive, inventing ever more outlandish rumours (pirouetting hayricks, enchanted horses, Satan himself dancing on the roof), both the secular and religious investigators were convinced from the very start that the events were fraudulent. How times had changed.

The North East has distinctive, localised folk traditions, and 'The Baldarroch De'il' sucked in several examples, as if the tale were some kind of folkloric black hole. According to J.M. McPherson's *Primitive Beliefs in the North-East of Scotland* (1929) the clodding originated because a woman had learned the Horseman's Word, the secret knowledge passed on by the quasi-Masonic all-male fraternity of Aberdeenshire horseworkers. Ogg, meanwhile, claimed the farmer consulted Adam Donald, the 'Wizard of Bethelnie', a locally famous healer and cunning-man – yet, as Ogg clearly knew (because he mentioned it elsewhere in his book), the 'Wizard' actually died several decades before the events of 1838.

Interpretation

There had apparently been a family dispute about inheritance at Baldarroch, and Ann Leighton was unhappy about the outcome. Were all the disturbances hoaxes by herself and Catherine Mackie, or did a genuine poltergeist outbreak inspire them to help things along a bit? Your guess, my guess: they're as good as each other.

31. CAITHNESS, HIGHLAND REGION: 1840s?

'Stones were flung, which never hit people, but fell at their feet, in rooms perfectly closed on all sides.' The excruciatingly terse report of an event 'not long ago' is in Crowe's *The Night-Side of Nature* (1848).

32. GLENDALE, SKYE, HIGHLAND: 1840s

Every time they got into bed, a newly married crofting couple were assailed with flying objects and alarming noises. When the church elders arrived to drive the spirit out by prayer, they were pelted with peat clods. A group of Glendale lads spent the night on watch, and caught the tenant's two grown-up daughters making the noises. It seemed the girls disapproved of their recently widowed father's new marriage, and had hoped the clodding would be interpreted as the vengeful spirit of their mother. Source: Norman Matheson, in Volume 18 of the *Transactions of the Gaelic Society of Inverness*, 1891-92.

33. PORT APPIN, ARGYLL & BUTE: c.1844?

The inhabitants of a pair of houses all heard bottles rattling in an upstairs cupboard. After several nights of this, a death unexpectedly took place in one of the dwellings, and the bottles were subsequently used at the funeral for refreshments. Around the time of the man's death, a girl entered a room and said 'every article in the room' met her at the door. This is another fragment from Campbell's *Witchcraft and Second Sight* (see No.34 below).

34. KILMOLUAG, TIREE, ARGYLL & BUTE: c.1854

Period
Possibly several weeks, around 1854.

Phenomena
'The annoyance began,' said the report, 'by the trickling of dirty water (mixed with sand) from the roof. Then burning peats were found among the bedclothes, and pebbles in bowls of milk, where no peats or pebbles ought to be; linen was lifted mysteriously from the washing and found in another room; articles of furniture were moved without being touched by visible hands; and stones flew about the house.'

The Nineteenth Century

The disturbances were exclusively nocturnal, and became shy when large groups assembled at the house. Firing guns into the air – a long-established way of dispersing evil spirits – had no effect. The family moved to another house, but the cantrips followed them. Eventually peace was restored – according to local rumour, only because some missing or stolen money was restored to its rightful owner.

Sources
The account comes from *Witchcraft and Second Sight in the Highlands and Islands of Scotland* (1902). The author, folklorist John Gregorson Campbell (1836-91), was minister of the island of Tiree from 1861, and his unnamed informants would all have been local people. The location was the scattered township of Kilmoluag (these days usually spelt Kilmoluaig). Through the kindness of two Tiree residents – Dr John Holliday, chair of the An Iodhlann heritage centre, and Lachie Campbell of Crossapol – the 'haunted house' can be identified as the long-ruined Kilmoluaig croft of Taigh Ailein Oig, next to Loch Bhasapoll. In a personal communication (April 2012), Lachie Campbell, who was born in 1933, remembered being told about the place by the old folk when he was a boy. Milk pails went tumbling and 'sticks with caps on' flew about. He was told that the minister – which would have been the Revd Neil MacLean, Campbell's predecessor – stayed all night with the Bible in his hand to try and combat the spirit, but Lachie could not recall whether this was effective. Dr Holliday, using the genealogical history of the owners of buildings, dated Taigh Ailein Oig to approximately the mid-nineteenth century, which dovetails with the approximate date of 1854 which Ronald Black (Campbell's editor on *The Gaelic Otherworld* re-issue) ascribes to the Kilmoluag polt.

Context
Supernormal movements were not all that unusual at Kilmoluag – Campbell mentions glasses rattling of their own accord, which, as with the Port Appin case above, indicated they would soon be used for refreshments at a funeral in the village.

Interpretation
Campbell unequivocally stated the phenomena were fraudulent and darkly hinted at some kind of dispute behind it all (probably money-related). Of course, he was not present on the island at the time and most (but not all) of the islanders subscribed to the preternatural explanation.

35. PEASTON, EAST LOTHIAN: 1853

Period
Several days or weeks in August 1853.

Phenomena
A number of children walking to school one morning were accosted by 'a rough, strange-looking man' who stole their food. One eight-year-old girl refused to give up her dinner, so the sinister assailant drew a circle round her on the road, and walked away. That night Peaston, the farm where the girl lived, erupted with knocks and raps. The sounds, which were most active during the hours of darkness, seemed to issue from the walls and furniture, and if anyone banged on a wall, they instantly received a reply in kind. Curious visitors, numbering in their hundreds, flocked to hear the noises, which always accompanied the eight year old, who was described as having 'wild and peculiar' eyes. A Mr List, police superintendant, was called in, declared that the raps were fraudulent, had the girl taken elsewhere – and the noises promptly stopped.

Sources
The accounts come from two books on Spiritualism by Henry Spicer: *Sights and Sounds* and its sequel, *Facts and Fantasies* (both 1853).

Context
The 1850s was the first flush of the worldwide interest in Spiritualism, and the Peaston raps seem to have mimicked those (fraudulently) produced by the Fox sisters in America in 1848.

The Nineteenth Century

Interpretation

It is possible that, with 'rapping mediums' the talk of the day, a farmer's daughter 14 miles south-east of Edinburgh was inspired to create her own sensation. The policeman clearly believed the child was the knowing instigator of the noises, and that either she, or her sister-accomplice, was surreptitiously striking the boarding of the box-bed in which she slept. A doctor gave his opinion that the girl could crack some of her bones at will.

The story of the threatening thief stands apart from these mechanistic theories. The act of drawing a circle around the belligerent child is an act of folk magic or cursing. Here, after some years' absence, we see the return of witchcraft as a hinted explanation for the disturbances. Note, however, that as with the cases of Bargarran (No.10) and Mellantae (No.12), the phenomena commenced soon after the young female at the heart of the events suffered a great fright. I wonder if, in each case, the fright was the catalyst that altered the subject's neurology and 'set free' the psychokinetic poltergeist. Or perhaps it was just a hoax – we will never know.

36. FOUNTAINHALL HOUSE, ABERDEEN: *c.*1860

Period

Several days or weeks.

Phenomena

In 1860 a clergyman and his family rented Fountainhall House, a sizeable detached dwelling in the West End of the city, only to find the otherwise attractive location decidedly haunted. Heavy footsteps were heard on the stairs and knocks, both gentle and violent, resounded on the doors. 'At midnight, on several occasions, there was a constant, uninterrupted sound in one room, as if a large sledgehammer (having been wrapped in a blanket folded several times), was steadily and regularly struck against the wall, at the head of the bed in the room, by some particularly powerful arms.' These tremendous hammerings lasted for up to three hours.

One night a great crash was heard, 'as if all the shutters of the windows of the house had been suddenly and simultaneously burst open with the greatest violence.' Like Walter Scott before him, the vicar timorously investigated with a sword in his hand; but nothing had been disturbed. Ten minutes after he returned to bed, an explosive crash shook the house for a second time. On other occasions, eddies in the air suggested an invisible presence passing along the corridors. Most sensationally, it was claimed that a servant girl had followed the footsteps to an attic room and encountered something that made her swoon. She later had to be confined to a lunatic asylum.

Sources

The account appears in *Glimpses of the Supernatural* (1875) by the Revd Frederick George Lee, vicar of Lambeth in London. It is presented as the experience of an unnamed English clergyman, attested by his equally anonymous wife ('I can testify of my own personal knowledge that it is neither understated nor exaggerated but is in all its details strictly true and accurate – June, 1874.'). Further, Lee writes: 'These are facts. As to the general accuracy of the foregoing, the Editor is enabled, on the testimony of several, to pledge his word thereto.' In one of my earlier books (*Haunted Aberdeen*, 2010) I followed these clues and suggested that the clergyman concerned was the Revd Robert Skinner, vicar from 1856-69 at St Andrew's Episcopal church in Aberdeen. Embarrassingly, I got this completely wrong, missing the obvious – for the occupant of Fountainhall House from 1860 to 1864 was none other than the Revd Frederick Lee.

Lee reluctantly came north to Aberdeen to take up the post of vicar at St John's Episcopal church, after the previous incumbent left under difficult circumstances. Lee arrived in November 1859 for his induction, returned south for a few months, and then installed both himself and his family in Aberdeen from spring 1860. The following year an ongoing row with part of his congregation led to him depart with half his flock, to form a new church, eventually opening St Mary's Episcopal church on Carden Place in 1864. That same year he resigned and headed back to London. These details can be found in *The Churches of Aberdeen: Historical and Descriptive* (Alexander Gammie, 1909) and Lee's own *A Statement of Facts with regard to his resignation of the incumbency of St John's, Aberdeen* (1861).

Context
Fountainhall House was built in 1753 or so. Lee's seemingly endless dispute centred on how far he wanted to move his Episcopal (Anglican) form of worship towards what many thought was uncomfortably close to the Roman church. In later life he fully converted to Catholicism.

Interpretation
Lee's wife had come across the rumour that the haunting was connected to a murder: 'Many years previously,' Lee wrote, 'the cast-off mistress of a Scotch nobleman, having been handed over to a physician and university professor for marriage, and the latter having received from the nobleman in consideration of the marriage the gift of the house and lands in question, subsequently murdered the woman, for whom he had conceived a special dislike, and buried her body on the premises.'

This allegedly murderous academic can only have been Dr Patrick Copland, Professor of Mathematics and Natural Philosophy at Aberdeen's Marischal College for forty-seven years. Copland purchased the house in around 1803, and died in it in 1822. But the rest of the rumour was nonsense: Copland did not receive the house gratis, had not married an aristocrat's former mistress, and his wife, Elizabeth Ogilvie, outlived him by many years. The origin of the calumny against Copland is a mystery, but it effectively acted as a smokescreen for the strange noises, which apparently received no further investigation once the unfounded 'explanation' had been broadcast. We know nothing about the nature of the Lee household. Did a servant really lose her mind?

What was her name? How long did the noises continue? When did they end? We are not told.

It is impossible to tell whether the bitterness of the religious dispute had anything to do with the events at Fountainhall; but if Lee was under stress, could he himself have been the unconscious poltergeist?

37. HUNTERS' TRYST, EDINBURGH: 1860s?

Period

Several years(?), possibly in the 1860s or earlier.

Phenomena

The Hunters' Tryst, once a roadside inn, was:

> ...not so long ago haunted by the Devil in person. Satan led the inhabitants a pitiful existence. He shook the four corners of the building with lamentable outcries, beat at the doors and windows, over-threw crockery in the dead hours of the morning, and danced unholy dances on the roof. Every kind of spiritual disinfectant was put in requisition; chosen ministers were summoned out of Edinburgh and prayed by the hour; pious neighbours sat up all night making a noise of psalmody; but Satan minded them no more than the wind about the hill-tops; and it was only after years of persecution, that he left the Hunters' Tryst in peace.

Sources

The quote is from *Edinburgh: Picturesque Notes* (1878), a series of essays on his home city by Robert Louis Stevenson. I have been unable to find any other supporting documents for the events, such as newspaper accounts.

Context

The Hunters' Tryst on Oxgangs Road, on the southern edge of Edinburgh, was a popular eighteenth-century howff. By the time Stevenson was writing, the inn had been converted into a farmhouse. From 1867 the Stevenson family spent summers at Swanston Cottage, in the hills south of Oxgangs. In 1870 RLS, then nineteen years old, found himself alone at the cottage, so he socialized with the young gentlemen farmers of the area, including Charles Macara of Swanston House and George Scott at Oxgangs Farm. The latter was just a short distance from Hunters' Tryst. My guess (for there is no evidence either way) is that it was during this summer of 1870 that Stevenson picked up the story of the Devil's antics at the inn. The infestation must therefore be from the 1860s at the latest, although of course it could be very much earlier. Stevenson later included the inn by name in his unfinished novel *St Ives: Being the Adventures of a French Prisoner in England* (published in 1897).

Interpretation
It is impossible to come to any kind of conclusion, but this certainly has all the hallmarks of a classic poltergeist incident.

38. PORT GLASGOW, INVERCLYDE: 1864

Period
About two weeks in April 1864.

Phenomena
Knocks having been regularly heard in Hugh McCardle's apartment in Scott's Lane, large numbers of curious onlookers started turning up, crowding the stair and lobby of the tenement and the lane outside. In this rather intense situation, an investigation was undertaken by a prominent local man, Andrew Glendinning, and a police sergeant and constable, with several other witnesses present.

As the sounds had been reported to be most active between 7 p.m. and 10 p.m., the investigators waited for a while; then, about 9 p.m., a kind of scratching was heard. This was followed by hammerblows on the floor beneath the bed. Glendinning and the sergeant examined the spot with a candle, but could find no obvious source. Someone present asked various questions out loud, and received three knocks for 'yes', and one knock for 'no'. Glendinning thought some of the knocks were imitating the tune 'There is nae luck about the house', so he whistled it, and the knocks banged away in time. Glendinning then whistled other popular Scottish airs, such as 'Let us gang to Kelvin grove, bonnie lassie, oh' and 'Scots wha hae wi' Wallace bled'. In each case the knocks joined in on the second line, keeping exact tempo. As 10 p.m. struck on the town clock, each stroke was supplemented by a knock in the wall, above the bed.

The investigators were nothing if not thorough. They tore up part of the flooring with a pickaxe, which caused the sounds to shift location for a while, but then the knocks hammered loudly on the very edge of the hole. The beds were taken apart, and the walls and ceiling, along with the staircase and cellars, were all examined, to no avail. They tried knocking on various surfaces throughout the building, but could not reproduce the nature of the mysterious sounds.

While the investigators were present, only noises occurred. But at other times different phenomena had been observed, as recorded by Mr McCardle:

> There were various articles scattered about from their places, as if thrown by some person, although no one was near where they were thrown from; such as small pieces of coal, broken crockery, and potatoes. We also saw, at times, at the back of the bed, the appearance of a hand moving up and down, and we sometimes tried to catch it, but could not, for (however quickly we reached out our hands) it as quickly vanished, and we only felt cold air. And sometimes, when the hours were striking on the town clock, low knocks were made on the inner partition between the bed and the press.

Sources

The case is in the *Report on Spiritualism of the Committee of the London Dialectical Society*, published in 1871. Glendinning had written to the committee on 30 August 1869. His evidence included: his own description of the events, written up on 15 October 1866 from notes taken in April 1862; sworn attestations of the truth of the events from Sergeant James McDonald and another witness, grocer James Fegan; a statement from Fegan that Hugh McCardle was 'an honest, sober, industrious, straightforward, truthful man'; and a sworn statement from Mr McCardle and family that, 'We did not do any of these things, nor cause, nor allow them to be done, and that we have no idea whatever how to account for them, as they were all quite mysterious to us.'

Context
The London Dialectical Society was an association dedicated to intellectual inquiry. The burgeoning popularity of Spiritualism prompted an examination of the movement, with a committee being appointed to take evidence between 1869 and 1870. The society declined to publish the final report because it seemed to favour the reality of Spiritualist phenomena, but the committee independently printed the findings in 1871.

Andrew Glendinning was thirty-six at the time of the disturbances. He later moved to London and went on to become well known within Spiritualist circles, being mentioned in an episode from 1870 in W.T. Stead's 1891 work *Real Ghost Stories*, and editing *The Veil Lifted: Modern Developments of Spirit Photography* (1897). The Port Glasgow polt was probably his first 'case'.

Interpretation
Glendinning may have had his own Spiritualist agenda when he wrote to the committee, but with what appears to be good witness testimony and a solid attempt to eliminate fraud, this could well be an accurate record of an authentic poltergeist outbreak.

39. MUIRKIRK, EAST AYRSHIRE: 1867

Period
One night in November 1867, and possibly some years previously.

Poltergeist over Scotland

Phenomena

Midhouse-of-Kames, a former farmhouse on Springhill Road, was the home of an incomer, a railwayman. The locals told him that the place was haunted, but the rent was cheap and for more than three years nothing untoward occurred. Then one night in 1867 his three sons, asleep in the attic, were disturbed by a moaning, as if from someone in great pain. Seconds later, 'bedclothes, boys, bed, and bed rungs were tossed on to the centre of the floor. And there they were – a mix-up of yelling boys and a sound as if two individuals were wrestling round the attic in a death struggle.' The father rushed in and the disturbance ceased, leaving only the sobbing of two of the boys, the third having fainted. As his wife, candle in hand, comforted the children, the man searched the closets and the chimney-place and examined the window, but could find no sign of an intruder. He promptly took the boys downstairs for the night, secured the attic door, and kept it locked until the family found another house in the village.

Sources

The account is in a 1929 book, *Cairntable Rhymes* by Thomas Floyd (1858-1933), a local poet who spent fifty years working for the Glasgow and South Western Railway and its successors. He writes: 'I can vouch for the truth of the attic incident, as the railwayman was my father, and I was one of the boys.'

Context

Muirkirk is a moorland village on the A70 between Cumnock and Douglas. Midhouse-of-Kames was demolished during Floyd's lifetime.

Interpretation

For the local people, Midhouse-of-Kames definitely had a ghost. An old shepherd named Tweedie had once heard loud footsteps in the attic while he was staying in the farmhouse, and the sounds had caused his dog to leap through the closed window, injuring itself on the glass. A Mrs Gibson said her sister had witnessed the apparition of a white lady at the house, the experience of which led to a nervous breakdown and eventually death. Most interestingly, from a poltergeist point of view, a milliner named Miss Macfarlane, who hung the hats she made on the snags of an old tree stump she kept in the attic, one night saw the stump crash to the floor for no reason, destroying her hats. In the morning the stump was standing as it always had been, and the hats were undamaged. Floyd, of course, could not verify any of these tales, and his child's-eye account of the one-off outburst is difficult to evaluate.

40. BOAT OF GARTEN, STRATHSPEY, HIGHLAND: 1870s?

Period
Unknown. Possibly the 1870s?

Phenomena
In some ways this is one of the most bizarre tales in this book, largely due to the curious religious passions that preceded the poltergeist.

In 1865 an unusual stone was erected in Boat of Garten. Its purpose was to commemorate a local miracle, in which the boiling waters of the River Spey had parted, like the Red Sea before Moses, this time to allow a funeral party to cross. The name of the saintly woman in the coffin changed depending on whoever was telling the story and the miracle had supposedly taken place in the thirteenth, or the fourteenth, or fifteenth, or sixteenth, or seventeenth century…

This miracle had caught the attention of William Grant, a small farmer from Slochd (Slock), a few miles north-west. Grant was one of a group known as The Men, a grassroots movement of ultra-conservative Presbyterians. Depending on your point of view, you could regard them as pious and serious-minded – or religious fanatics. Grant was described as a mystic who retired into the windswept Highland wilderness to commune with – again depending on your perspective – either God, or his own vivid imagination. A short while before his death, he had a vision: despite having never seen the spot, he knew exactly where the miraculous river crossing had occurred, and so he instructed his fellows that a monumental stone – also identified in the vision – should be set up at the site. On 9 March 1865 the stone was duly erected. Grant had predicted that two bushes of yellow broom would grow up on each side of the stone, and when the vegetation covered it, it would herald a dire time for Scotland. Just to make certain of the prophecy, Grant's followers managed to fix the stone exactly between a pair of broom bushes.

'The Miracle Stone of Spey' brought forth choleric local passions, and the Free Church minister the Revd John Logan denounced it from his pulpit. 'Pro-stone' adherents started visiting the monument rather than attend Sunday worship. The community was divided. Then on 19 February 1867 person or persons unknown smashed the stone and threw the fragments into the river. The iconoclasm only served to polarise local opinion. When Dr Arthur Mitchell visited the area in 1874, he found that just mentioning the Miracle Stone could start an argument, and received dark hints that one of the perpetrators of the destruction had shortly afterwards suffered a fatal accident, this being in the nature of divine punishment for his 'sacrilege'. Mitchell was also told some people ventured into the river to break off pieces for relics or charms, and that the entire subject was widely regarded with superstitious awe.

The story goes that, some unnumbered years later, the largest part of the stone was taken out of the waters for use as a doorstep at nearby Knock of Drumuillie Farm. At this point the poltergeist made its entrance. Straw and turnips descended the chimney, stones flew through closed windows without causing damage, furniture was displaced between floors, hailstones the size of cricket-balls fell in mid-summer, and phantom lights furtled about. A minister suggested the slow burning of a rowan tree outside the house; rowan was the classic apotropaic against evil, but here it had no effect. According to the story, the inhabitants of the farm died off one by one, and when the last resident passed away – an old woman with a reputation as a wart-charmer – the first action of the next tenant was to uproot the doorstep and return it to the river. After this there were no further disturbances, although the river-washed stone continued to attract uncanny rumours. It is still there, just north of Garten Bridge.

Sources
The history of the Miracle Stone was conveyed by Arthur Mitchell to the Society of Antiquaries of Scotland in 1874 and reprinted in his book *The Past in the Present: What is Civilization?* (1881). The nature of the dispute is outlined in Donald MacLean's *Duthil, Past and Present* (1910), although he states the stone was smashed a mere week or two after its erection. The description of the poltergeist can be found in Peter Underwood's *Gazetteer of Scottish Ghosts* (1975), but with no sources given.

Context
Readers who are not steeped in the alternative world-view that is Scottish religious nitpicking could be forgiven for assuming that a time-slip had taken Boat of Garten back to the seventeenth century. Well, at least this time no one was burned or run through with bladed weapons.

Interpretation
It seems there was strong support locally for the idea that the poltergeist was acting out because it was unhappy about the relocation of the Miracle Stone, of which it was presumably the guardian. So does this mean that the polt was the Wrath of God? Or perhaps an evil spirit imprisoned in the river by the stone? Obviously other scenarios can be constructed, such as the presence of the stone being merely coincidental to the poltergeist's visitation, but where's the fun in that? A cursed stone makes for a much better story.

41. BLACKET PLACE, EDINBURGH: 1871-78

In 1871 the MacMurdo family took up residence in a large detached villa in Blacket Place, an upmarket garden suburb in

Newington. Over the next seven years a classic haunting transpired, with numerous people witnessing a range of apparitions. Sounds, as if of doors opening and shutting, or a big heavy table and chairs shifting, came from the dining-room flat when it was unoccupied. An explosion-like noise frequently shook the whole house around 6 a.m.; people were called by name from empty rooms. One evening the unlocked bathroom door refused to open, only to then swing wide of its own accord. A woman was pushed down the staircase with great violence. Rustlings, as if of dried leaves or silk dresses, were heard on the staircase, and several witnesses felt invisible hands on theirs on the banisters. Four sisters – Misses P., K., E., and Z. MacMurdo – all wrote out their respective experiences for the SPR's *Journal* in July 1886. The youngest, Z., was around ten years old when she saw her first apparition. All the sisters commented on the extreme dampness of the gloomy house, and that several rooms had an unpleasant atmosphere. Not wishing to admit a belief in ghosts, they put the experiences down to a combination of the damp, neuralgia, and indigestion.

42. IOCHDAR, SOUTH UIST, WESTERN ISLES: 1880s?

This case, and the four that follow it, were all recorded by Father Allan McDonald, the Catholic priest of Eriskay, between 1887 and 1893. The events described are very difficult to date, and could be from the 1880s, or from much earlier decades.

Mr MacEachen of Iochdar, at the north end of South Uist, died before he could live in the new house he had built, although his corpse lay in it prior to the funeral. Afterwards, the building was said to be haunted. Mrs Ronald MacDonald of Dalibrog spent a night in it, and heard a cacophony of noises – as if of doors banging, footsteps tramping up and down, and hammerblows on the floor. Archibald MacDonald (Beag), a one-time tenant, was said to have quit the house because of the noises.

43. LOCH CARNAN, SOUTH UIST, WESTERN ISLES: 1880s?

Showers of stones frequently fell on the house of invalid Uisdean Mac Thormoid, near Loch Carnan in Iochdar. One day two women saw writing form in the ashes of the fire but they could not read it (was this because they were illiterate or because it was in a language unknown to them?). At this point a minister arrived, and the writing vanished.

44. KILPHEDIR, SOUTH UIST, WESTERN ISLES: 1885?

The house occupied by joiner Alexander Steele and his wife, and an old man named John Steele, was frequently troubled by strange noises. This was in Kilphedir (Cille Pheadair), a township west of Lochboisdale, and the noises may have been still current in about 1885, when the Steeles emigrated to Canada.

45. BÀGH HÀRTABHAGH, SOUTH UIST, WESTERN ISLES: 1880s?

Archibald MacDiarmid, who died no later than 1885, was a fisherman from Eriskay. One evening he took his boat to Bàgh Hàrtabhagh, on the east coast of South Uist, for a pre-arranged meeting with Malcolm MacDonald of South Lochboisdale. Finding no one there, he lit a fire in a sheiling to keep warm. He was then hit by a stick thrown through the smoke-hole in the ceiling. When he swore at Malcolm, whom he thought was hiding outside, a second stick struck him. After a search he realised he was entirely alone, and promptly departed in his boat.

46. LIANICLET, BENBECULA, WESTERN ISLES: C19TH?

Aonghas MacNeill dug a potato pit at a spot supposed to be an old grave. Soon after, sticks and peats were thrown inside his house, and anyone sitting round the fire had their feet beaten by a shinty (a stick or club). No matter where this shinty was hidden, it always returned to beat the inhabitants. One day Aonghas threw the stick far out to sea, but that night it was up to its usual tricks in the house. A Protestant man decided to lay the spirit, but, according to the story, barely escaped with his life. Some time later a small hand started to appear through the bedside boards. After a year a voice was heard to say, 'I will not come any more,' and the disturbances ceased. By the time Father McDonald collected the story, the house in question was in ruins.

Sources (Cases 42-46)
Father McDonald arrived on Eriskay in 1884, and starting collecting folklore in his notebooks in 1887. He died in 1905, much-loved. The accounts are reprinted entire in John L. Campbell and Trevor H. Hall's book *Strange Things* (1968).

Context (Cases 42-46)
Eriskay and South Uist are overwhelmingly Catholic, while Benbecula is equally divided between Catholics and Protestants. North Uist, Harris and Lewis are Protestant (sometimes fearsomely so). Anecdotal Gaelic storytelling can sometimes drift through decades unanchored by notions such as conventional dates, and 'recent' can mean 'within my great-grandfather's time'.

Interpretation (Cases 42-46)
Some of these intriguing fragments are connected folklorically to the restless dead, while others lack any context to help us understand what was going on.

47. OLLABERRY, SHETLAND: 1880s?

Period
Several weeks, probably in the early 1880s.

Phenomena
This case started, rather unusually, with vicious assaults on children. Schoolmaster James Manson and his wife Andrea Cluness

The Nineteenth Century

had a large family; one day several of them rushed in, bleeding from wounds on their faces and hands – and, in one case, from scratches inside the mouth. Before any investigation could be carried out, utensils were thrown across the kitchen and crockery was smashed. Phenomena escalated over the following days to include the slashing of clothing, bedding, quilts and pillows. One day a braid hem was delicately removed from a dress without otherwise damaging the garment. Animal-like cries and other unearthly noises resonated through the house, and some of the children claimed to have seen a sinister black man.

Also victimised was the servant-girl, who was often violently pushed from one side of the kitchen to another. On one occasion the local 'strong-man' sat on a chair, clasped the girl firmly in his arms, and swore nothing short of the Devil himself would be able to loosen his grip. Scarcely were the words spoken when the servant was pulled out of his hands and sent staggering to the opposite wall.

Sleepless nights followed disturbed days, and eventually James Manson was forced to close the school for two or three weeks. As family worship was also constantly being interrupted by noises from above the kitchen, the Mansons decided to approach the parish minister. This was probably the Revd James Rose Sutherland, who had been in the post since 1848. He gathered the family in the kitchen for prayer, but the noises above them reached such a crescendo that Mrs Manson begged the minister to cease and desist. The reverend gentleman left, saying he could do no more, as the forces of darkness were too powerful for him.

The disturbances came to an end when a packman who had travelled on the Scottish mainland visited the house and, on learning of the trouble, told the family they were victims of the Black Ert (witchcraft). It appeared that Mrs Manson had recently quarrelled with her next-door neighbour, Mrs Nicolson – the obvious culprit. The packman had a remedy – the witch had to be attacked with fire and steel, so that blood was drawn 'above the breath' (on the forehead). This was an age-old antidote for witchcraft. Later that day, Mrs Manson encountered Mrs Nicolson – so she rushed inside, picked up a burning peat with the firetongs and struck the old woman on the head, setting fire to her mutch (cap) and drawing blood. (In an alternative version, it was the minister who suggested the solution: the Mansons were to invite the neighbour in, give her hospitality, and as she was leaving, throw fire over her.) Whoever came up with the idea, and whatever actually happened, all versions agree that the disturbances immediately ceased.

Sources
The episode is described in two documents held by Shetland Archives. The most detailed is an undated and anonymous handwritten manuscript entitled *The Black Ert*, while further corroboratory detail is in the transcript of an oral history tape recording made with Joan Williamson of Ollaberry in 1982. From the conversation between Mrs Williamson and the interviewer Robert L. Johnson, it is clear the story was well-known locally, but there are slight variations between the two versions and the question obviously arises: how much has the story changed over the years? Based on the similarity of language, the first manuscript account must be the source for the only time the story made it to the press, when the *Shetland Times* published an article entitled 'A Trowie Story' on 23 January 1959. The newspaper version renamed Ollaberry as 'Grunneberg' and the family as 'Smith'. The anonymous manuscript uses the originals, and also names Mrs Nicolson as the 'witch'.

Context
Ollaberry is a small coastal community in Northmavine, some 36 miles north of Lerwick. James Manson was from Sullom Voe, Andrea Cluness from Yell. Mr Manson taught at the school next door to his home from 1877 to 1888. Joan Williamson stated that the family continued to live at Ollaberry for several years after the poltergeist, so that may date it to the early 1880s. The story has become known as the 'Ollaberry Trowie'. Trowies or trows are the Shetland version of Scandinavian trolls, and like the Gaelic Bócan, the word is a catch-all term for goblins, ghosts, fairies and other supernaturals.

Interpretation
Malign witchcraft is explicitly indicated in both accounts. The anonymous manuscript states that the neighbour, who already had something of a bad reputation, gained her knowledge of black magic from a dread book her merchant seaman son brought back from Asia. The volume supposedly bore the legend 'Whosoever readeth this book shall not enter the kingdom of heaven'. Joan Williamson also mentioned the book, and said it had been found hidden in the byre by Mrs Nicolson's grandson, who promptly burned it. Another element is cited in all the accounts: the day-girl, who lived a short distance away, was protected from assaults once she passed through the boundary into the neighbouring district. Only when she entered the schoolhouse area did she become victimised. Significantly, the boundary between the two districts was also the limit of the croft occupied by the Nicolsons. The inference was that the witchcraft could not progress beyond this border. When author Norman Adams was researching his book *Haunted Scotland* (1998) he made enquiries locally and came to the conclusion that Mrs Nicolson had been unfairly maligned.

48. GREENHILL FARM, TIREE, ARGYLL & BUTE: 1880s?

The following three cases are largely taken from oral history recordings made by the School of Scottish Studies in the 1960s and '70s. These tape recordings – which feature ordinary people sharing stories, songs, music, poetry and information about working and living conditions – are now available on the Tobar an Dualchais ('Kist o' Riches') website, www.tobarandualchais.co.uk, which is a veritable treasure trove for researchers.

Period
Unknown. Possibly 1880s, and much later.

Phenomena
Taigh Mòr Ghrianail ('the big house at Greenhill') had a long history of phenomena. Milk pails were upset overnight, fires broke

out without causing damage or giving off heat, and the workers' beds in the barn-loft were often found disturbed. These events were linked to a female servant. An old man visiting from the neighbouring village of Sandaig exited, pursued by a peat from the fire. A slightly different version of this story states the visitor overstayed his welcome, so, as a hint, a table lamp floated through the air and a pair of boots started walking around the room.

Sources

A number of years later a farmworker heard strange noises in the room in which he slept – this was Donald Sinclair (Dòmhnall Mac na Ceàrdaich), born in West Hynish, Tiree in 1885. Most of the information above comes from his taped interviews conducted in Gaelic in 1968, 1970 and 1974; Donald thought that the main disturbances had taken place about 1888. The detail of the mobile boots is in *Townships and Echoes of Tiree* by Niall M. Brownlie (1995). According to Dr John Holiday's 'Tiree Place-Names' website, in recent years the lid of the geirneal (grain-store) has been seen to lift of its own accord.

Context

Greenhill was one of the larger farms on the island. In 1885-86 landless crofters tried to wrest land from the estate. The police and 250 marines were called in to restore order, although there was no violence. Could this dispute be somehow connected to the stories?

Interpretation

Brownlie's book notes that Lachlan MacLean, the Greenhill tacksman or tenant until his death in 1885, had a reputation for magic, and it was his boots that effectively kicked out the unwelcome guest from Sandaig. Supernatural black pigs were also seen to come out of the sea to root around on the beach below Greenhill. In an oral interview from 1974, Hector Kennedy (born on Tiree in 1897) recalled stories told to him about the

MacLeans having paranormal powers over recalcitrant horses. A later tenant was known to have the second sight. Does all this somehow suggest that the house was/is the focus of some kind of low-level phenomena? Or that the MacLeans were the focus? Or that the MacLeans' reputation inflected otherwise mundane events with a supernormal interpretation? In another interview, from 1971, Donald Sinclair mentioned the milk pails incident again, and seemed ambivalent as to whether the problem was caused through magic or just mischief.

49. NESTING, SHETLAND: 1890s?

Period
Unknown; probably 1890s.

Phenomena
When Andrew Hunter was a boy, two elderly sisters who lived in a croft nearby were plagued by disturbances. When they came in from work, the cups, saucers and other kitchen items had been moved, and at night dreadful noises prevented them from sleeping. One sister said the only solution was to read the Bible.

Sources
Andrew Hunter was born in Nesting in 1888, and interviewed in 1974.

Context
The eastern Shetland mainland is an area of indented coastline and scattered settlements.

Interpretation
Mr Hunter recalled seeing one of the elderly sisters accompanied by a host of little people wearing dark clothes (the little women also had something like a white apron in front). 'I saw them just as plain as I see you sitting there,' he told the interviewer.

Just before they appeared, the family dog refused to go further and made strange noises. Although just a small boy, Andrew knew the fairy-like beings were somehow connected to the old woman, although his mother told him he was talking nonsense and to never mention the subject again. Did this mean that the fairies were somehow connected to the poltergeist incidents? Or simply that the old woman was a focus for uncanny events?

50. ELLON(?), ABERDEENSHIRE: 1890s?

Period
Unknown.

Phenomena
When working on a farm as a lad, Willie Mathieson witnessed a man in the chaumer (farmservants' quarters) recite some words from the Bible seven times backwards. Known as 'raising the Devil', this caused a pail of coal to dance over the floor, and when another man spoke, a piece of coal flew out and struck him in the face. This apparently took place at Kirkhill of Ellon (there are two locations where this could be), but Mr Mathieson later told the same tale about a different man in a different farm. Perhaps at the same place, although probably at a farm elsewhere in Aberdeenshire or Banffshire, a woman raised the Devil and caused the master's boots to dance on the roof. Willie was feeding the horse when the minister arrived, and he saw the clergyman pelted with clods, thus barring access to the house.

Sources
Willie Mathieson was born in Ellon in 1879, and spent a lifetime working as a servant at various farms. He was interviewed in 1952.

Context
Once again, a distinctive Aberdeenshire agricultural folk-belief comes to the fore.

Interpretation
Did the poltergeist outbreaks, if accurately described, start up only after the folk-ritual of 'raising the Devil', or was the occult act later tacked on as the 'reason' for the disturbances? Note that the 'Devil' in this case is better interpreted as meaning 'evil spirit' rather than His Satanic Majesty in all his infernal glory.

51. BALLECHIN HOUSE, PERTH & KINROSS: 1896-97

Period
Various periods between 1878 (possibly) and May 1897.

Phenomena
This is such a complex case it needs to be considered in several phases.

Phase One: 1878-92
Sometime between 1878 and 1880 a Miss Yates quit her job as the governess at Ballechin House because of the 'queer noises'. From 14 to 21 July 1892 Jesuit priest Father Patrick Hayden was rendered sleepless by loud explosion-like noises, taps, and what sounded like a heavy weight falling against the outside of his bedroom door. On the ninth night, 22 July, he heard nothing, and slept peacefully.

Phase Two: 1896
In 1896 Ballechin was taken as a summer holiday home by the family of Joseph R. Heaven of Gloucestershire. The butler and two maidservants arrived on 15 July, followed by most of the family on different days. By the time Mr Heaven turned up at the start of August, the entire household was alive with tales of ghosts and nocturnal noises. Rustlings, bangs, footsteps, knocks and other noises were reported by the servants, the family, and guests. Courageous young men, one armed with a revolver, stayed up all night in an attempt to locate the source of the sounds.

The butler, Harold Sanders, was shocked out of his scepticism – he initially thought the culprit was the hot-water system – by unnerving bangs on his door. He later wrote: 'Sometimes the whole house would be aroused. One night I remember five gentlemen meeting at the top of the stairs in their night-suits, some with sticks or pokers, one had a revolver, vowing vengeance on the disturbers of their sleep.' The butler's own vigils included a powerful sensation of presence or sharp cold just before the noises began. In the second week of September, Sanders experienced more intense poltergeistic effects:

> My bedclothes were lifted up and let fall again – first at the foot of my bed, but gradually coming towards my head. I held the clothes around my neck with my hands, but they were gently lifted in spite of my efforts to hold them. I then reached around me with my hand, but could feel nothing. This was immediately followed by my being fanned as though some bird was flying around my head, and I could distinctly hear and feel something breathing on me. I then tried to reach some matches that were on a chair by my bedside, but my hand was held back as if by some invisible power. Then the thing seemed to retire to the foot of my bed. Then I suddenly found the foot of my bed lifted up and carried around towards the window for about three or four feet, then replaced to its former position.

At the end of September the Heaven family quit Ballechin, two months earlier than their planned departure date.

Phase Three: 1897
From 3 February to 13 May 1897 Ballechin became the locus of a large-scale 'ghost-hunt'. Leased by members of the Society for Psychical Research (SPR), and filled with numerous other well-heeled temporary guests, the house was to function as a great laboratory. It was hoped that with so many eyes and ears present over an extended period, good-quality evidence would be obtained regarding the reality (or otherwise) of the phenomena. A journal was kept, listing who experienced what, when, and where.

The noises included: explosive or percussive bangs; monotonous reading aloud; voices in conversation; footsteps; knocks; animal movements; groans; blows on tables, doors and walls; detonations, as if a cannon had been fired some distance away; clangs, like 'tuning a kettle-drum'; and heavy objects falling (without physical evidence of same). These reports came from almost thirty people over three months.

On 23 March a medium named Miss Fyfe found her bed shaking and bucking violently, as if she were riding a rollercoaster. The following night Lizzie, the kitchenmaid, saw 'a cloud which changed rapidly in colour, shape, and size, and alarmed her greatly' and then felt her blankets being pulled off the bed. On 25 March Miss Fyfe again felt her bed shake, only this time not as extravagantly as before. There were other accounts of nudges by 'invisible dogs', cold areas, and a sense of presence, while from mid-April more and more guests were complaining of a feeling of palpable malevolence in the house. Apparitions were reported – a nun, a grey-garbed lady, a black dog, an old woman, and others. On 6 May a Catholic bishop and two priests performed a ceremony of blessing, sprinkling the most 'active' rooms with holy water. Thereafter the phenomena declined into nothingness, and soon the tenancy came to an end. A greatly extended discussion of the chronology and events at Ballechin, including the history of the house and its former owners, can be found in the present writer's *Paranormal Perthshire* (2011).

Sources

On 8 June 1897 the investigation at Ballechin was thoroughly ridiculed in a piercing article in *The Times*, and over the next few weeks the letter columns of the top people's newspaper echoed with accusation and counter-accusation. It is within this arena that the testimonies of Joseph Heaven and Harold Sanders were made public. The scandal inflected everything that followed: the owners of Ballechin were aggrieved they had been told nothing about the 'ghost-hunt'; no official report on the investigation was published by the SPR; the society publicly distanced itself from the affair; there was a falling-out; and when the entire episode was aired again in a book published in 1899 by one of the participants, it was acidly reviewed by the SPR. That book, *The Alleged Haunting of B-------- House* by Ada Goodrich Freer and Lord Bute, remains the key primary document. Ms Freer was the 'house manager' during the tenancy, and kept the journal of events. Much has been written on her character – for example, a spectacularly detailed hatchet-job appears in *Strange Things* by Campbell and Hall (1968). It is only fair to point out that some of these accusations were refuted in an article penned by G.W. Lambert for the *Journal* of the SPR in June 1969. Whatever the verité, it cannot be denied that Ms Freer was not entirely trustworthy, and as so many of the phenomena (especially the apparitions) were reported by her alone, dubiety is the natural consequence. Nevertheless, the noises were witnessed by dozens of individuals, so we can assume the sounds had objective reality.

Context
The relatively modest mansion of Ballechin had a colourful history (owners included a dog-loving eccentric India veteran who apparently believed in the transmigration of souls, and a devout Catholic who threw the house open to nuns and priests), and this was incorporated into what could be regarded as the 'mythology' of the house. By the time of the Heaven and SPR tenancies, Ballechin was being offered as a let for those seeking long sojourns in the increasingly fashionable Scottish Highlands. In 1932 the property was sold, fell into ruin and was eventually demolished in 1963.

Interpretation
On 10 June 1897 Joseph Heaven wrote to *The Times*, vehemently denying that his family had had anything to do with fraudulent actions during the 1896 'haunting'. He was responding to an accusation in the paper's letter columns two days earlier, which pointed the finger at one or more of the Heavens' lively children: 'One of their pranks was to drop or throw a weight upon the floor, and to draw it back by means of a string.' W.A.F. Balfour-Browne, one of the more athletic of the visitors in 1897, found a

round-the-house crawlspace above the top floor, which may have enabled any number of pranksters to play the ghost.

As for the 1897 investigation, it was deeply flawed. Messages 'received' via Ouija board were allowed to influence the subsequent interpretations of the phenomena. It is clear from the journal that many of those attending were positively giddy at the thought of encountering a real-life ghost, and some of the more sceptical observers – such as John Ritchie Findlay of *The Scotsman* – found their fellow guests credulous in the extreme. Many of these views are expressed in private letters from the time and published in *Strange Things*, which makes that book an essential Ballechin source. A few of the more suggestible members of the entourage seem to have fallen prey to Ms Freer's powerful personality, so that when she said she saw a phantom, they did too. Suggestibility and expectation – 'seeing what you want to see' – very probably played a major role in turning this investigation into a debacle.

But, assuming they weren't all fraudulent or imagined, what about the noises? *Four Modern Ghosts*, by E.J. Dingwall and Trevor Hall (1958), proposed earth tremors. G.W. Lambert, writing in the *Journal* of the SPR ('Poltergeists: Some Simple Experiments and Tests', 1956, and 'Scottish Haunts and Poltergeists', 1962), finessed this idea by suggesting the noises originated from an underground stream, and that the cracks and bangs derived from subterranean ice breaking up. Several guests put the blame squarely on the hot-water pipes. Perhaps more than one of these natural audio sources was amplified by the structure of the house in a kind of resonating soundbox effect.

The damning first article in *The Times* sarcastically referred to Ballechin as 'the most haunted house in Scotland'. Was it actually a spectacularly un-haunted house? Was there anything genuinely supernormal in the events? Was there a poltergeist? Despite a three-month live-in investigation, dozens of witnesses, thousands of words in books and articles, and a controversy that continues to bubble today, we are unable to provide definitive answers to any of these questions. Like the notorious Borley Rectory, Ballechin House is the mystery that just keeps on giving.

Chapter Four

The Twentieth Century, Part I: 1900-1949

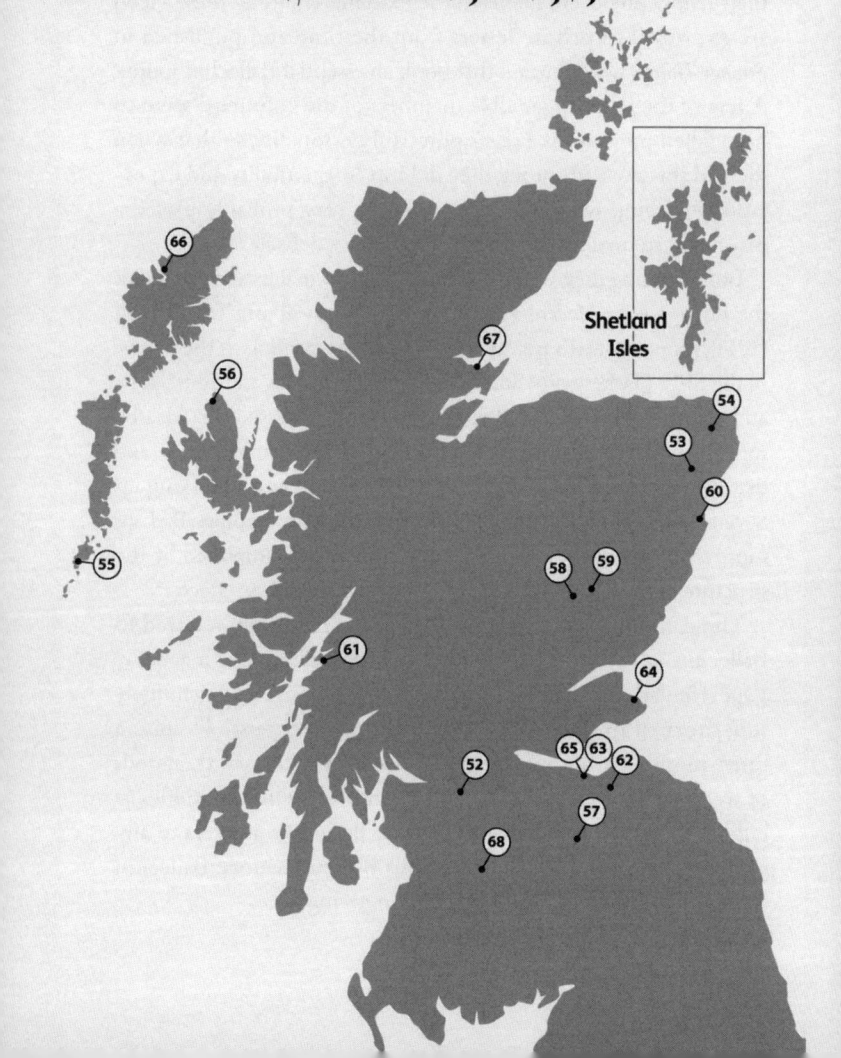

The Twentieth Century, Part 1: 1900-1949

'Poltergeists usually take place where there is a sensitive child in the family, especially when there is a young girl who is just entering puberty, but it is not definitely known whether this condition is a causative factor or is merely a coincidence.'

F. Homer Curtiss, *Personal Survival, with Physical Proofs*, 1946

The First World War and the even more apocalyptic Influenza Epidemic created millions of bereaved, all desperate to contact their deceased loved ones – making Spiritualism a major growth industry in the 1920s. In the 1930s the idea of the poltergeist as a force projected from an unhappy human focus struck a chord with psychologists and psychical investigators alike. 1945 saw the publication of the first popular book on the subject, Harry Price's *Poltergeist over England* (which included one case from Scotland). Price's book, and other media that flowed from it, made 'poltergeist' a household word for the first time.

52. GLASGOW: 1907

Period

13 August 1907-23 January 1908 (five months).

Phenomena

The location was a detached cottage somewhere in Glasgow, with two rooms on the first floor. Bedroom 1 was used by the two unmarried adult sons of the family; Bedroom 2 was occupied by the married daughter and/or the daughter-in-law, while Mr R.D. and his wife slept on the ground floor. On 13 August 1907 mysterious knockings started in Bedroom 2. These continued for several days, always around midnight, and then moved to Bedroom 1. On 30 August a small press holding bottles moved 9in from the wall in Bedroom 1 and a mahogany box atop the press fell with a great crash, waking those asleep below, while further knockings were heard. Sometime after 3 September, beds were shaken and pillows pulled in the upper bedrooms, while the knocks continued, now accompanied by footsteps ascending the stairs and entering the rooms. In early December the daughter-in-law and one son, from their beds, separately saw apparitions of a disembodied hand. On the sixteenth of the month a small washstand moved 6in-8in in Bedroom 1, as witnessed by one of the sons, and further knocks were heard.

Phenomena moved up a step on 17 December. About 10.15 a.m. the daughter-in-law, having completed some cleaning chores, returned to Bedroom 1 to find everything in disorder:

> Two basket chairs had been overturned, ashpan and front of grate removed and laid on the carpet, and clothing belonging to my sons, which had been hanging on pegs, a towel from wash-hand stand, a box from top of chest of drawers, etc., were all on floor; four pictures had also been taken from off the wall and laid, glass downwards, on the bed; all this had been done without the slightest noise, and nothing was damaged.

The young woman and her mother-in-law, the only people in the house at the time, promptly fled into the back garden, where they remained in the wintry rain until Mr R.D. came home. After this the rooms upstairs were vacated, and everyone slept downstairs. The following day, around the same time in the morning, the remaining pictures in Bedroom 1 were found on the bed, while a mirror and a small shelf of books were on the floor. Many of these events were accompanied by a 'death-bed smell'.

Three loud bangs were heard in the lobby on 21, 24 and 31 December, and 1 and 2 January. This being the festive season, several visitors were in the house at the time to witness these noises. On the morning of 13 January Bedroom 1 was again disturbed, with a chest of drawers shifted 18in, and the books, along with a dressing case and a camera, thrown on the floor. Later that afternoon the armchair in the kitchen was found relocated from its corner position to the fireside. Two days later in Bedroom 1 the chest of drawers, the bed, and an armchair were all found moved. There was more furniture relocation in the room on 18 and 20 January. The next day was the 'day of the bedding'. The mattress in Bedroom 1 was found tilted up; the daughter-in-law was 'attacked' by a mattress and bedding while downstairs; the blankets upstairs were dragged off the bed onto the floor, and bedding was pulled out of a large chest. To all this was added books and a box cast onto the floor, while the armchair moved again. On 22 January the chest of drawers and armchair shifted as before, were rearranged by Mrs R.D., and five minutes later were once again found moved. The family were frequently disturbed and frightened by these various manifestations.

Come 23 January, gentle knocks were heard downstairs. Thereafter, the poltergeist was not heard from again.

Sources

The account, dated 26 February 1908 and drawn up by the owner of the house, Mr R.D., and witnessed by the various members of his family (C.M.D., J.D., F.D. and M.R.D.), appeared in the SPR's *Journal* in April 1908. It was sent 'by a Member of the Society, who believes implicitly in the bona fides of the witnesses.' A statement from a Mr S.N.P. accompanied the report: 'I have acted as solicitor and notary public for the above Mr D. for almost twenty years past, and I certify that from what I know of him and his wife and family they would not have signed the foregoing document without believing and attesting every word of it to be true according to the best of their knowledge and belief.'

Context

Mr R.D. was described as a professional gentleman. His widowed father had lived with the family from 1875: 'He was a man of strong will, firm in his religious opinions, and took a deep interest in everything that concerned our welfare.' The daughter-in-law's husband was away in Africa. She had nursed the old man during his last illness, during which he rarely left Bedroom 1. He died in March 1907, aged ninety. After his death the room was thoroughly cleaned, to remove the smell of illness. The married daughter was present for the first few weeks of the outbreak, and then on 3 September left to join her husband in France.

Interpretation

Mr R.D. clearly believed the restless spirit of his father was haunting the house. The armchairs were being moved to the old man's favourite spots; Bedroom 1 was where he had lived out his last days; and the smell of his illness accompanied the phenomena. A modern sensibility may suspect the daughter-in-law as the focus whose frustration at her (presumably) unsatisfactory domestic arrangements energised a psychokinetic outcome. But without knowing more about the household, we are unable to do anything other than speculate.

53. ABERDEENSHIRE: 1910s?

At an unnamed farm the ploughs and carts moved by themselves and everything in the house was jumping about. A farmer known as Old Scary who had the 'power' or the 'Black Art' was brought in, at the request of the minister. Old Scary identified a female farm-servant as the perpetrator, and recognised that she had started the chaos, but could not stop it. After talking to her alone for an hour the disturbances stopped, and she promised not to use the Black Art again. This is another piece of oral history recorded by the School of Scottish Studies and available on www.tobarandualchais.co.uk. Travellers Betsy Whyte (1919-1988) and her husband Bruce Whyte (1914-2006) were taped relating versions of the tale in 1975 and 1979. Old Scary was described as living near Ellon about sixty or seventy years before 1975.

54. FETTERANGUS, ABERDEENSHIRE: 1916/17?

Fifteen-year-old Lucy Stewart had been left in charge of the other children in her extended Traveller family. They were singing hymns when suddenly the door flew open and a brick-like object was thrown in. No one was outside. Lucy Stewart (1901-1982) was recorded by the School for Scottish Studies in 1972.

The Twentieth Century, Part 1: 1900-1949

55. BERNERAY, WESTERN ISLES: 1920s/30s?

This, and the four that follow, was recorded by the School of Scottish Studies; at a guess all five are set some time between the wars.

When a religious man tried to pray in the house of a woman notorious for witchcraft, stones fell on him. Katherine Dix, a crofter born and raised in Berneray, recorded the tale in Gaelic in 1968. Her mother knew the 'ungodly' woman.

56. KILMUIR, SKYE, HIGHLAND: 1920s/30s?

A house in Kilmuir was attacked with stones and clods, because the boy who lived there had cursed the ground when he tripped. Once he swore to never do it again, the commotion ceased. The Revd Norman MacDonald (1904-1978), born and raised in Valtos, Kilmuir parish, recorded the tale in Gaelic in 1953.

57. PEEBLESSHIRE, SCOTTISH BORDERS: 1920s/30s?

One night a farmer was coming home when a stone flew out of the dyke and landed about 18in from his head. A farmworker heard footsteps on the roof of the sleeping bothy, and in the mornings the carts were found pulled out of the sheds. The man left the Peeblesshire farm because he believed he had brought the poltergeist there. Thomas Todd (born 1899) heard the story from the unnamed farmworker in Biggar, and recorded it in 1982.

58. GLEN ISLA, ANGUS: 1920s/30s?

A travelling packman took shelter in a farm-servants' bothy on a ruined farm, and was woken by an unearthly banging at the door, accompanied by weird moaning. He shifted his position to another corner, and about ten minutes later the large stone he had placed against the door flew across the room: if he had stayed where he was, it would have killed him. He fled the building, saw a white spectre on the road, and, driven by a terrible howling, ran several miles to the nearest Travellers' camp, where everyone was packing up because of the 'banshee'. The tale was recorded in 1979 by the packman's grandson, Stanley Robertson (1940-2009), a storyteller and singer who was born into a settled Traveller family in Aberdeen. Banshees were described as human beings who die without kith or kin. With no one to mourn for them, they become supernatural.

59. GLEN CLOVA, ANGUS: 1920s/30s?

Duncan Ibsen moved his Traveller family out of Glen Clova because a banshee pelted his van with rocks. This was also in Stanley Robertson's recording.

60. GORDON PLACE, ABERDEEN: 1920

Period
Several days from 7 January 1920.

Phenomena
A huge earth-shaking concussion announced the onset of the poltergeist of No. 1 Gordon Place. This was quickly followed by tappings on several separate interior walls, and then a second mighty bang. As the first police constable arrived, fourteen-year-old John Urquhart was thrown from his cot-bed by yet another explosive crash. Over the hours of darkness, eight police officers explored the entire building, including the roof and chimney, finding nothing. The noises ceased at dawn, only to return (but less loudly) the following night. Meanwhile, the municipal authorities investigated possible sources such as subsidence, structural defects, disturbance to the foundations by an adjacent telephone pole, wind-driven chunks of wood, and trapped sewer gas. A policeman was stationed permanently outside. Crowds and reporters gathered. Rumours were invented and spread like

wildfire. Alexander Urquhart, his wife and all four children were nonplussed, but they accepted the diagnosis of 'natural causes'.

A short while later it all went Spiritualist-shaped. The Bon Accord Spiritualist Association, convinced the noises were the restless dead eager to get in touch, crammed thirteen people, including a female medium and two reporters, into the tiny Urquhart dwelling. No contact was made, the medium blaming the failure on the presence of 'unbelievers'. A second séance – with only twelve attendees this time – brought the medium, via her spirit guide Paddy, in touch with Alexander Urquhart's father, speaking with the deceased man's voice. When the séance finished after an hour and a half, John Urquhart suddenly sat up in bed, claimed he could see his dead grandfather, and then became hysterical, shouting about having been pulled into a 'black hole' and returning when he saw the light in the room.

The noises were never heard from again. John Urquhart grew up with the unwelcome sobriquet 'Johnny Ghostie'. In the 1930s the cramped quarters of Gordon Place were converted into a coach-painting business, and in the late twentieth century the entire area was redeveloped, removing all trace of what was once nicknamed 'Poltergeist Alley'.

Sources
The story was in the local papers (e.g. the *Aberdeen Daily Journal*, 9 January 1920) before making it to the national press over the next few days. See also Norman Adams' *Haunted Scotland* (1998) and the present author's *Haunted Aberdeen* (2011).

Context
The Urquharts occupied the top floor of the late-Victorian two-storey building. John, their eldest son, had been an invalid since childhood.

Interpretation
For the authorities, the noises were a physical mystery that could be solved with enough engineering know-how. For the seething

crowds in the lane outside, the sounds were the calling card of a former tenant who was supposed to have committed suicide in the basement. For the newspapers, the disturbances were a goldmine. For the nation's self-appointed mystics, this was the time to pass their wisdom on to the Urquharts, who were deluged with letters. For an entrepreneur in Derby, it was an opportunity to flog 'psychic mascots' to the crowds, each amulet 'guaranteed to give immunity from the dangers of the spirit world'. For the Spiritualists, it was the chance to gain some valuable publicity, and there is a distinct sense of the proceedings being hijacked by the organisation's news-management enthusiasm. But what really was going on during and after the séance? Was John Urquhart's outburst just an attention-seeking response to the intense pressures of the séance in the cramped bedroom, or was he another poltergeist-projecting sick child? Did the noises originate with mundane forces, or a hoax?

61. LEDAIG, ARGYLL & BUTE: 1920-22

Period
January 1920-September 1922 (two years and nine months).

Phenomena
The Mackenzie family – mother, father and seven children – occupied a small cottage overlooking Ardmucknish Bay. Malcolm (thirteen) and Ian (nine) seemed to be the dual focus of rappings, the destruction of furniture and crockery, and apparently even levitation. The disturbances started in January 1920, and after several visits by interested parties, became more 'organised', with the two boys giving 'sittings' at which phenomena manifested, such as tables moving. By 27 February 1921, when the *Sunday Mail* featured the story, the 'entity' was giving answering raps to questions posed in both English and Gaelic.

The Society for Psychical Research twice brought the boys to Glasgow, but the sittings there were not particularly satisfactory. By 1922 both Malcolm and Ian were channelling the spirits of dead people. Between 18 and 28 September the boys were investigated in their home by Eric Dingwall, the SPR's Research Officer, who concluded the pair were fakers through and through.

Sources
The case was in the SPR's *Journal*, Volume 20, 1921-22.

Context
Once again, this is the era of the high-water mark of Spiritualism.

Interpretation
What may have started as a chaotic poltergeist infestation rapidly became more controlled and séance-like, probably through the influence of Spiritualist visitors. The later manifestations were clearly faked, but were the initial disturbances genuine? We will never know.

62. PENKAET CASTLE, EAST LOTHIAN: 1923-47

Footsteps, dragging noises, shrieks and groans; the unlocking of doors; the bedclothes on a seventeenth-century bed frequently found disturbed; objects and furniture occasionally moving; the possible appearance of an apported bar of soap; the disintegration of a glass globe in front of many witnesses; and sundry other uncanny events. These were the sporadic phenomena experienced in this much-converted late sixteenth-century laird's house over twenty-four years, in what sounds more like a long-term haunting than a poltergeist outbreak. A good summary of the case appears in Archie Roy's *A Sense of Something Strange* (1990).

63. EDINBURGH: 1930s/1940s?

A manse somewhere in Edinburgh was plagued with moving furniture, thrown objects, fires, and widespread destruction of ornaments and paintings. The case is briefly mentioned in Ron Halliday's *Edinburgh After Dark* (2010), citing an undated investigation by the Edinburgh Psychic College's 'Committee for the Recording of Abnormal Happenings', which was active in the 1930s and '40s. Apparently the case was so sensitive the location has not been revealed to this day.

64. PITMILLY HOUSE, FIFE: 1936?–67?

Period
From 1936 until – if later accounts are accurate – 1967. With a reign of thirty years, this is probably the longest-lasting poltergeist in this book – if we can believe the reports.

Phenomena
One evening, perhaps in 1936, the Jeffrey family sat down to dinner – and a lump of coal appeared, as if out of nowhere, in the middle of the dining-room table. This was the début of the poltergeist of Pitmilly House, and the first of many coal-related incidents that plagued the mansion in the years to come.

The pre-war years seemed to have been quiet, or at least no stories from the period have come down to us. Events escalated around the outbreak of the Second World War, and in early 1940, home on leave, twenty-five-year-old Ivan Jeffrey was gently hit on the stomach by an airborne bronze Chinese jar. Pretty much every ornament in the house seems to have taken to the air at one point or another, with frequent flyer miles being clocked up by jars, vases, pots and tumblers. One bronze item rotated through 90° in mid-flight. Paintings were endlessly found turned to the walls, or piled up after being removed from their hooks in impossibly quick timescales. Pillows, bedclothes and beds became agitated. Other objects – cosmetics, irons, billiard balls, vases and mirrors – vanished, only to turn up in unlikely places. Heavy chests of drawers, wardrobes and chairs slid across floors or moved mysteriously between floors. From his bed, Jan Rostworowski, a Polish soldier, watched as a huge wardrobe moved towards him and teetered on its edge, as if it were deliberately menacing him.

On another occasion Jan found all his belongings upended, and he witnessed an ashtray fly through the air into the fireplace. A Roman Catholic priest and an Episcopalian clergyman failed to dampen the polt's ardour.

Water-filled ewers were often dumped onto the beds, but the favourite sport involved fire. Flaming coals appeared hither and thither, scorching or burning curtains, blinds, carpets, floors, bedclothes, towels and a woman's hat (when the house was later sold, visitors found scorchmarks in the most unlikely of places). A shovel-full of coals appeared on the library sofa. Captain John Arthur Jeffrey, Ivan's father, tried to beat out a fire moving across his bedroom carpet in his bedroom — but the flame, which was cold, just dodged out of the way, leaving no marks behind. On another occasion, a clergyman's hat was whisked off his head and thrown into the fireplace. Jan Rostworowski watched as small fires appeared on the carpet in the very footsteps of Mrs Jeffrey. During the daylight hours of 7 March 1940, some seventeen separate blazes broke out, requiring a visit from the fire brigade to douse the flames and rescue an elderly servant. The episode led to the Jeffrey family making an insurance claim, which was actually paid out: various sources give the sum as being as low as £50 (around £1,500 in today's terms) or as high as £400 (the equivalent of £11,500). I have tried without success to track down the papers relating to this claim.

The fire led to visits by two investigators: James Herries, the chief reporter on *The Scotsman* and a Spiritualist and member of the Edinburgh Psychic College, who stayed overnight on 19 March 1940; and Lord Charles Hope of the Society for Psychical Research, who visited the house on 28 April 1940, having previously interviewed Mr Hole, of Gillespie and Paterson in Edinburgh, the family's lawyer. Hole was an eyewitness to some of the events mentioned above; on one occasion, he was in an armchair with an ashtray containing several used matches when he noticed that the matches had suddenly become arranged in a neat row along the arm of the chair. Herries held a séance with a medium, but this was inconclusive. Hope thought Herries was gullible, and went looking for a mundane cause, such as one or more fraudsters.

In 1941 the house's owner, Captain Jeffrey, died aged fifty-one. From 1942 the house was requisitioned by the military. Phenomena apparently did not cease. Ivan Jeffrey remembered stories of bayonets being stuck in walls, while there were reports of apparitions. The building became a hotel in June 1947, and various spooksome activities continued. A wealthy newspaper owner on a golfing holiday found his clothes emptied onto the floor, and witnessed a line of fire run down the wall of a corridor for 30 yards; the flames left no marks. Bottles of spirits emptied without the seals being broken. There were vague reports of something alarming holidaymakers in 1967. The neglected building was sold the same year and demolished to the very foundations; its location is now farmland.

Sources

Hole's unpublished notes on the case are in the SPR archive at the University of Cambridge. James Herries provided the insurance story to papers such as the *Daily Telegraph* and *Daily Mail* (both 8 April 1942) and wrote an article on the fire for *Psychic Science* (October 1942) – all discreetly, without naming Pitmilly. It seems likely that Mr Hole the solicitor was the 'professional gentleman' who provided the many details included by Harry Price in his 1945 book *Poltergeist over England* (readers will note that Fife is not exactly in England). Ivan Jeffrey gave his own account to the Radio 4 series *Scotland '67*. Most of the post-war reminiscences by friends of the family appear in Lorn Macintyre's *Pitmilly House: 'Poltergeist Manor'* (2011). The late Jan Rostworowski's anecdotes were conveyed to me by his family and appear in my 2012 book *Haunted St Andrews*. The entire story was fictionally reworked by Frank Harvey for his 1946 West End farce *The Poltergeist*, and two years later adapted as the creaky British low-budget film *Things Happen at Night*.

The Twentieth Century, Part 1: 1900-1949

Context

The Jeffreys had bought nine-bedroomed Pitmilly in 1930. The mansion stood near Kingsbarns, about 8 miles south of St Andrews. Alison Jeffrey was a domineering chatelaine who forced her daughter Mary to be educated at home. In 1940 the now seventeen-year-old Mary was being courted by Jan Rostworowski, one of the many Polish troops stationed in this part of Scotland – this was the reason why Jan was so often in the house, and why he witnessed so many events. The household also included Ivan Jeffrey's Danish wife, Vibeke; a Swiss governess who is not named; a pair of elderly female servants; and two dogs.

Interpretation

Pitmilly attracts as many interpretations as it does interpreters. Charles Hope wondered if first Captain Jeffrey and then Vibeke had, in some kind of tit-for-tat game of resentment, serially faked the phenomena, each to scare the other. Mr Hole also told Hope he suspected Captain Jeffrey of some faking. It is even possible that Hole, in his excitement, helped things along a bit. But the problem was that the scale of the reported phenomena would require either several hoaxsters, or a monumental degree of misperception and self-deception by the various witnesses. On the mechanistic front, G.W. Lambert, writing in the SPR's *Journal* in March 1964, viewed all the phenomena as caused by changes in subterranean hydraulic pressure associated with earth movements.

James Herries was convinced the events were genuinely paranormal, with a discarnate intelligence present. Leaving aside the ghost theory, there were certainly enough tensions whirling around the house to provide the energy for any putative psychokinetic poltergeist. We may look (as Lorn Macintyre does) to the frustrated, closeted and home-schooled teenager Mary Jeffrey as the focus, yet events continued long after she left the house. As for the other young woman present, Vibeke sorely missed her husband when he was away on military duty, and was accused by one of the firemen of starting a fire. Jan Rostworowski, meanwhile, thought Captain

Jeffrey was the unconscious source of the poltergeist, an expression of his rage that a foreigner was courting his daughter (Jan's relationship with Mary foundered soon after). Alison Jeffrey not only resented her husband's heavy drinking, but also thought he had psychic abilities. And of course there was a war on.

65. LEARMONTH GARDENS, EDINBURGH: 1936-37

Ancient Egypt comes to Edinburgh…

Period
November 1936-May 1937 (intermittently over seven months).

Phenomena
During a dinner party Lady Zeyla Seton entertained her guests with a story of how, on a recent trip to Egypt, she had acquired a bone from an ancient tomb. Her husband Sir Alexander Seton then unveiled the bone, displayed in a former clock-case. As their friends were leaving, a heavy piece of the roof parapet crashed to the ground about 2ft from the group. A few nights later strange noises – as if of someone wandering round – were regularly heard from the drawing room. On one occasion the table holding the bone's case was found tipped over. Footsteps echoed on the stairs. Alexander's young nephew, Alasdair Black, came to stay for a few days and saw 'a funny dressed person going upstairs'. Concerned that a burglar was trying to steal some valuable snuffboxes, Alexander decided to watch all night, having first locked the drawing room door and all the windows. Bored, he fell asleep, only to be wakened by his wife and their servant Nanny, both of whom had heard loud noises in the drawing room. When the door was unlocked, the scene was one of chaos: chairs were overturned and books scattered about. The windows were still locked and an intruder was out of the question.

At this point Alexander suspected a poltergeist was in play, and was associated with the Egyptian bone, but weeks passed with no further disturbances. Then the noises and movement of items became a regular occurrence in the drawing room, so he had the furniture – including the case containing the bone – shifted downstairs to the sitting room. About a week later the sitting room was found overturned. The baronet decided to burn the bone, but was prevented by his wife's snarling reaction. In a huff he went to his club, got a little squiffy, and when he returned home found more damage, this time including a large crack in the table on which the bone rested, as if great pressure had been exerted on one of the legs.

As a result of his unguarded remarks at the club, the press became interested, and the case now became public currency. After several more weeks of quiet, the table, glass case and bone were all found smashed. Zeyla Seton, who was deeply attached to 'her' bone, had the relic repaired. During a party on the night of Boxing Day 1836, the bone was prominently on display on a table opposite the party room. In Alexander's words: 'The entire table, bone and all, went hurtling onto the wall opposite, with a terrific thump. No-one was standing near it, nor did anyone see it happen – it just happened!' In the resulting chaos a maid and a female guest fainted. The episode was just what the press were looking for.

Over the next few months the still-unfolding story appeared in the newspapers several times, although an accurate chronology of what event actually happened when remains confused, partly because Alexander's autobiography, *The Transgressions of a Baronet*, from which the above episodes are taken, contradicts press reports of the time. Phenomena included the tipping over or breaking of flower vases, further movement of furniture, glass ornaments shattering, and alleged further sightings of the mysterious figure, which had led to maids refusing to stay in the house overnight. Fires broke out, and the family became prey to 'mysterious' ailments. Two reporters who had borrowed the bone had each supposedly suffered serious misfortunes thereafter, while the doctor who had repaired the bone after its breakage reported his servant had broken a leg running away from a robed phantom.

The alleged source of the pandemonium had by now become known as the Cursed Bone, or even the Cursed Bone of the Pharoah (or Mummy). Its origin lies in the lost world of the 1930s, when, in the wake of the Egyptomania unleashed by the discovery of the tomb of Tutankhamun in 1923, wealthy individuals could tour the largely unregulated ancient sites of Egypt and bring back the occasional ghoulish souvenir. The Setons arrived in Egypt in February 1936, exploring Luxor and the Valley of the Kings before moving north to Cairo in June. There, they learned of recent excavations that had uncovered a series of small tombs on the plateau of the Pyramids. With the assistance of their guide Abdul, and the application of certain gifts of money, the Setons gained access to one of these tombs, something which, if not actually illegal, was at least not allowed. According to his version of the events, Alexander was reluctant to go along, but Zeyla was extremely keen. 'I wish earnestly to God that we had not gone!' he wrote.

The tomb did not contain a mummy – it dated from before the period when mummification was common – but on a slab lay the remains of a skeleton: 'You could see the skull quite clearly and the leg bones but few ribs were left although the spine was almost intact,' wrote Seton. After a few minutes in the underground chamber he escaped into the sunlight for a smoke, but Zeyla went back inside. Later that day she revealed her secret – she had stolen a bone from the tomb. 'To my eyes it looked like a digestive biscuit, apart from it being slightly convex and the shape of a heart,' said Alexander. It was in fact the sacrum, the triangular-shaped bone at the base of the spine. Alexander professed to be dismayed at his wife's gleeful grave-robbing; nevertheless, the bone made its way back to Scotland in the Setons' luggage (Alexander arrived in July, Zeyla a month later). The disturbances commenced in November.

On 29 March 1937 *The Times* and many other newspapers reported that Lady Seton was going to make a special trip to Egypt to replace the bone in its tomb. This may have been a ruse, or wishful thinking, for no such trip was ever planned.

Instead, the poltergeist-plagued peer started playing to the gallery. On 9 April he addressed a packed-to-the-rafters meeting of the Edinburgh Psychic College on Heriot Row, regaling the audience with the startling events associated with the bone. 'There is one thing I am dead certain of,' he said, as quoted by *The Scotsman* the following day. 'Somehow I am trying to get this bone back. I have to believe now that this bone has got something behind it. There is something in the curse of the Pharoahs.' Even more dramatically, as he was addressing an overflow meeting, the main hall was witness to the usual weekly demonstration of clairvoyance by Mrs Boardman – only this time the well-known medium delivered a message from the spirits that unless the bone was returned within six weeks, 'blindness will come upon those who touch it.' When told of this, a visibly shaken Alexander offered the bone to a reporter, so that his newspaper could arrange for the return; despite the opportunity that this presented for an endless series of exclusive stories, the offer was politely declined.

Before the Psychic College appearance, Alexander had received about eighty letters about the subject. On 16 April *The Scotsman* reported that this had now swelled to some 1,500 letters over the past week, with many correspondents willing to return the bone in exchange for an all-expenses-paid round-trip to Egypt. One man wanted £3,000 (roughly equivalent to £110,000 today), adding the proviso that should anything happen to him, free education would be provided for his three children until they had attained the age of twenty-one. Another offer was for £5,000 upfront and £8,000 on delivery. According to Alexander, one of the letters was from Howard Carter, the discoverer of Tutankhamen's tomb, in which he claimed that: 'things quite inexplicable like this could happen, indeed had happened and will go on happening.' On the same day the *Edinburgh Evening Dispatch* noted that the previously believing baronet now emphatically stated his disbelief in the clairvoyant's message: 'I am absolutely convinced that no blindness will come to those who touch the bone and I am equally sure that neither Lady Seton nor myself shall ever go blind.'

The following day *The Scotsman* had the latest sensational revelation from the Edinburgh Psychic College: Mr N.A. Ellingsen, lecturing on 'At the Fringe of the Occult', suggested the paranormal events were the result of an immortal elemental being, created by the priests of ancient Egypt. The *Edinburgh Evening Dispatch* for the same day stated that at a séance at the Psychic College, an enigmatic female figure had materialised, wearing the cobra crown of the Pharoahs. Edinburgh, it seemed, was positively hoaching with mystical Egyptians.

On 24 April the *Evening Dispatch* reported that, following a 'blood-curdling noise' at 2 a.m., the new glass case holding the bone was found smashed, with the bone lying 8ft away, and an adjacent vase also cast into pieces. This appears to have been the penultimate hurrah; on 20 May the headline in *The Scotsman* was 'The Egyptian Bone: Destroyed in 5 a.m. Crash.' The solid glass case had been smashed to smithereens, reducing the bone itself to powder. Alexander was quoted as saying: 'I am going to put the bone and the fragments of the case in a box and give them a decent burial.' In his autobiography, however, the baronet gives a different story. He says he waited until his wife was away, then had the bone exorcized by his uncle, Father Benedict of the Fort Augustus Abbey at Loch Ness. Alexander then burned the bone until nothing was left. The disturbances were heard no more, but Alexander was convinced his family's continuing ill-health was connected to the 'curse'.

Sources

Dozens of newspaper accounts from the time fed an enduring legend that was still a staple of popular journalism many years later. *The Transgressions of a Baronet* was unpublished in book form, but the relevant extract appeared in *The Scotsman* on 21 April 2005 and can also be found on the website for the House of Seton of Scotland, www2.thesetonfamily.com.

The Twentieth Century, Part 1: 1900-1949

Context

Sir Alexander Seton (1904-1963) was the 10th Baronet of Abercorn, but his family's prestige and wealth had declined so much that the grand town house on Learmonth Gardens was probably his last major asset. He married society beauty Zeyla Daphne Sanderson (1904-1962) in 1927. By 1936 the marriage was decidedly rocky, and, possibly irrevocably driven apart by the affair of the bone, they divorced on 13 June 1939. Sir Alexander married Flavia Forbes just four days later, which suggests he had been playing away from home during the latter years of the marriage.

Interpretation

With echoes of both the so-called Curse of Tutankhamun and the 1932 horror film *The Mummy*, the case was irresistible to journalists, some of whose contributions may not be entirely reliable (especially once the story crossed the Atlantic). Stripped of the fantasy paraphernalia of Pharoahs and mummies, and the confusion over dates, the reports of the actual phenomena are consistent, and appear to have multiple witnesses. Interpretation comes down into three possibilities:

1. The sacrum did carry with it a supernatural presence, which was dispersed when the bone was burned. The tale is thus a useful teaching aid on the inadvisability of appropriating ancient bones.

2. The whole episode was fraudulent. This is the opinion of Ian Wilson, whose 1986 book *Worlds Beyond*, based on an ITV series of the same name, suggests that the disturbances were caused by Zeyla, possibly in revenge for her husband's extra-marital affair. We know the couple's marriage was strained by the time they visited Egypt, so perhaps the bone simply acted as a catalyst for further interpersonal disintegration.

3. There was a poltergeist present in the house, but it did not emanate from the bone. We could consider the highly-strung Zeyla, but many of the events took place when she was absent. My suggestion is that – under the strain of a marriage break-up

– the poltergeist was powered by the unconscious mind of the deeply stressed Sir Alexander Seton.

SEARCHING FOR THE TOMB OF THE 'CURSED' BONE

Alexander's account of the acquisition of the bone notes that the tomb was near the Great Pyramid, that he and Zeyla visited in June, and descended down a passage into a rock-cut chamber that had 'at one time been filled by the mud of the Nile'. There were no inscriptions or hieroglyphics to identify the fragmentary high-status female skeleton. Armed with these partial clues, I set out, for the first time anywhere, to identify the tomb from where the 'cursed bone' had been stolen.

The plateau at Giza known as the Central Field is a necropolis, home to many dozens of tombs belonging to state officials and minor royalty. Far removed from the ostentatious grandeur of a Pharaonic burial, these typically took the form of a mastaba, a low, flat-roofed rectangle with an entrance leading to the burial chamber, which was usually underground. Pioneering archaeologist Selim Hassan (1887-1961) discovered and excavated many mastabas in this area between 1929 and 1937, all recorded in an epic ten-volume collection. His seventh season of excavations commenced on 1 October 1935 and continued until the following May or June, when the weather became too hot to dig. In spring 1936 they uncovered one of a series of previously unrecorded and – miraculously – unplundered tombs.

The mastaba had a sloping passage leading to a burial-chamber. 'It was found to be entirely filled with mud, which must have entered with storm water following upon some violent cloud-burst,' wrote Hassan in *Excavations at Gîza 7: 1935-1936*. Inside was a limestone sarcophagus equally filled with dried mud. Sifting the debris, the team found the partial skeleton of a woman, adorned with a treasury of gold: a crown, a necklace, beads, a belt, bracelets, anklets, finger-tips, and two semi-circular clasps. The lack of inscriptions meant no identification could be made, but there was something that could date the tomb: a 'spare-head'. This was a limestone and plaster 'bust' bearing a portrait of the deceased woman. Spare-heads were typically in use in the Fourth Dynasty of the Old Kingdom. 'The situation of the Mastaba between those of two members of the royal family, and the resemblance of the features of the spare-head to those of known children of Khafra,' wrote Hassan, 'lead us to surmize that the deceased lady was also a member of this exalted family.' The Egyptologist thus identified the corpse as a probable daughter of the Pharoah Khafre (also known as Khafra and Chephren). Despite having built the Great Sphinx and the second largest pyramid at Giza, little is known of Khafre. Even the dates of his reign are disputed: he may have been Pharaoh between 2558 and 2532BC.

The mastaba bears the snappy name of 'G8250, Central Field'. Hassan also called it 'Mastaba of the Princess' or 'Mastaba of Daughter of Khephren'. Of all the tombs described in Hassan's monumental series, none of the others even come close to Seton's description. Here we have a tomb with a sloping passage in the shadow of the Pyramids, discovered in 1936, containing the skeleton of an unidentified high-status female; without inscriptions; and filled with mud. By June 1936, when the Setons bribed their way in, the gold and jewellery and the sarcophagus had been removed, leaving only the less-valuable skeleton. I therefore propose G8250 as almost certainly the tomb where Zeyla Seton performed her act of sacrum-stealing.

Do not, however, go away with the idea that the bone came from Khephre's royal daughter. Egyptology as a discipline is constantly open to revision. In 2008 Peter Jánosi of the University of Vienna published an essay whose German title translates as 'Where were Chephren's daughters buried?' In it he examined all the clues in the architecture and the grave goods and concluded that G8250 belonged not to the Fourth Dynasty, but to the end of the Fifth Dynasty, or even the Sixth Dynasty, perhaps 200 years later than Khephre. We may never know the name of whoever was buried with gold and pageantry in the rock-cut tomb 4,500 years ago. But we do know where the base of her spine ended up.

66. TOLSTA CHAOLAIS, LEWIS, WESTERN ISLES: 1938

Period
A few minutes on the morning of Sunday, 30 January 1938.

Phenomena
About 10.30 a.m. eighty-year-old Mrs Macleod was in her cottage, perched above the main family croft, when the 'caorans' – small pieces of peat used to light the fire – started to jump about. One struck her on the cheek; another plopped into her cup of tea. Then half the glass chimney of the hanging lamp smashed onto the floor. The old lady was startled, but told her granddaughter – a girl in her early teens – to take the dishes through to the adjoining scullery for safety. As soon as the connecting door was opened, however, it seemed as if the world was in motion. Two jugs containing rice and peasemeal, accompanied by food tins, utensils and the teapot, flew through the door into the main room. Dishes, egg-cups, plates, jugs, tea-cups and tumblers cracked or smashed. Almost the only crockery undamaged was the set of plates the girl was holding onto, but other items – the bread knife, the entire contents of one shelf, and a glass bottle – were also unaffected.

The noises attracted at least three other members of the family from the house close by. They arrived in time to hear the cracking and smashing but not see the actual manifestations. A toothbrush was found broken in two, a cake of Lifebuoy soap was cut into three pieces as if by a knife, and the results of the aerial bombardment – including tea leaves spattered over the wall, and multiple food and kitchen items dispersed over the bed and floor, some 10ft from the scullery – were plain for all to see. The resulting debris half filled a canvas sack.

The Twentieth Century, Part I: 1900-1949

Sources
The story was covered for the *Stornaway Gazette* by the local journalist, James Shaw Grant. There is an excellent account in Shaw's 1984 book *The Gaelic Vikings*, with background detail. A monoglot English-speaker on an island where many spoke Gaelic, Shaw visited Tolsta Chaolais the day after the events, taking with him the librarian Donald MacGregor, who happened to be a Gaelic-speaking native of the village. The eyewitnesses spoke freely, and Shaw had no doubt that they were telling the truth. *Back in the Day*, a nostalgia magazine published by the *Stornaway Gazette*, had an extensive revisit to the story in its March/April 2006 edition.

Context
Tolsta Chaolais is a crofting village on the west coast of Lewis, 18 miles from Stornoway.

Interpretation
When an elder of the Presbyterian church pompously told Mrs Macleod that it had been a judgement from Heaven (because she was house-proud, and made an 'idol' of her dishes), she retorted: 'You better be careful. You worship your cow!' Despite village rumours of dark forces, she refuted any idea of supernatural causes, and said that there had to be a natural explanation, even if she did not know what it was.

Shaw was convinced the cause was electricity. The previous few nights had been marked by extraordinarily brilliant displays of the aurora borealis, with violent thunderstorms during the day. The small house, in his opinion, was a Leyden jar. The wooden walls were non-conducting, but contained a large iron stove with an iron chimney on the roof. The electrical charge entered via the chimney, caused the caorans to jump away from the stove as the iron became charged, and once the insulating wooden door to the scullery was opened, the electrical charge entered the other room. A few months later Mrs Macleod tried to darn a sock with a ball of wool that had been one of the 'levitated' objects – but the wool crumbled in her hand, as if lightning had passed through it.

67. TAIN, ROSS & CROMARTY, HIGHLAND: 1947-48

Period

1947-48 (nine months or so).

Phenomena

Two weeks after moving into the rectory at Tain, the Revd Leonard Mordle-Barnes and his wife Mollie returned from an evening out to find the kitchen door bolted and, behind it, in great distress, their live-in help Helen Ross. Helen had had a terrifying evening – the front door had apparently burst open, and heavy footsteps had echoed through the tiled hallway and down the passage towards the kitchen. Convinced an intruder was after her, she had locked herself in, and the footsteps had patrolled outside for two or more hours. A quick check showed that the front door was locked, and the three children were asleep upstairs. A few days later Helen and Mollie both heard the front door open and footsteps proceed through the hall and up the stairs, followed by knocks, bangs and the thud of something heavy falling in the first-floor bathroom. Both women ran up but the bathroom was empty and dark. Once again, the children were asleep, and the 'opened' front door was securely locked. The sounds of steps and the door being flung open became a regular occurrence, heard by all three adults in the household. On 15 March 1948, during a children's birthday party, everyone present heard the usual sounds, and rushed out from the dining room to investigate. The hall was empty, and the 'banged open' door was as secure as ever.

Phenomena now moved up a step. Woken by an almighty noise from the kitchen, Leonard and Mollie crept downstairs armed with a long-handled clothes brush. Turning on the light, they found the saucepans and kitchen utensils scattered over the floor, and the table and chairs pushed against the far wall. All doors and windows were locked, so a human intruder was out of the question. Another evening Mollie, alone in the house, heard the usual combo of door and footsteps, now followed by crashing from the kitchen. The table and chairs had been shoved aside, and a heavy preserving pan had been thrown onto the stone hearth, but without sustaining a single dent. At this moment Helen arrived through the back door, took in the chaos, and handed in her notice. The kitchen disturbances now occurred with monotonous regularity, although nothing was ever broken. In 1948, after a nine-month reign, the events ceased as abruptly and as mysteriously as they began.

In 1952 the family relocated to Leicestershire. Some time later Mollie revisited Tain and quizzed her friend Anita Carswell. Anita told her that in 1947 three separate local women had been hired to clean the rectory before the Mordle-Barnes family arrived, and each, one after the other, had quit. Each claimed to have heard footsteps in the hall or stairway of the otherwise empty house.

Sources
Mollie Mordle-Barnes' eyewitness account, 'Merry Pranks in a Scottish Rectory', was reprinted in the anthology *True Ghost Stories of the British Isles* (2005).

Context
The Episcopalian rectory was a mid-nineteenth-century building. The three children were very young – Angela (six), Beverley (three) and Julia (a baby).

Interpretation
In many ways this is a traditional haunting, but with significant poltergeist extras. If the experiences of the three cleaners are accurately reported (the stories are of course only third-hand) then the phenomena would appear to be place-based as distinct from person-focused.

68. MUIRKIRK, EAST AYRSHIRE: 1950

In November the Revd George Robertson was quoted by the *Daily Record and Mail* saying that bedclothes in the manse had been disturbed and a child displaced, apparently by a poltergeist.

1 The now-demolished Ballechin House, Perthshire, location for the notorious SPR investigation (case No.51). (*From 'The Highland Tay' by Hugh MacMillan*)

2 Bargarran House, Renfrewshire, location for the witch-haunted case No.10 of 1696. *(Author's Collection)*

3 *The Certainty of the World of Spirits*, by Richard Baxter (1691), the book containing the first recorded poltergeist in Scotland (case No.1, 1630s). *(Author's Collection)*

4 The Mackenzie Tomb in Greyfriars Cemetery, Edinburgh (case No.115). NB This is *not* the so-called 'Black Mausoleum', which is some yards to the right in the Covenanters' Prison. *(Ségolène Dupuy)*

5 The ruined tower of Galdenoch, Galloway, home to an alleged poltergeist in the seventeenth century (case No.11). *(Leslie Barrie, under Creative Commons Licence 3.0)*

6 The Urquhart family outside their 'haunted' house at 1 Gordon Place (case No. 60). From the *Aberdeen Daily Journal* in 1920. *(The Press & Journal)*

7 Lady Zeyla Seton with the sacrum, the bone she stole from the tomb. *(Courtesy Alan Murdie)*

8 Mastaba G 8250 on the Central Field of Giza. The 'cursed bone' of case No.65 was stolen from here in June 1936. *(Courtesy Peter Jánosi)*

9 A typical 1930s popular account of the affair of the 'cursed bone'. *(Courtesy Alan Murdie)*

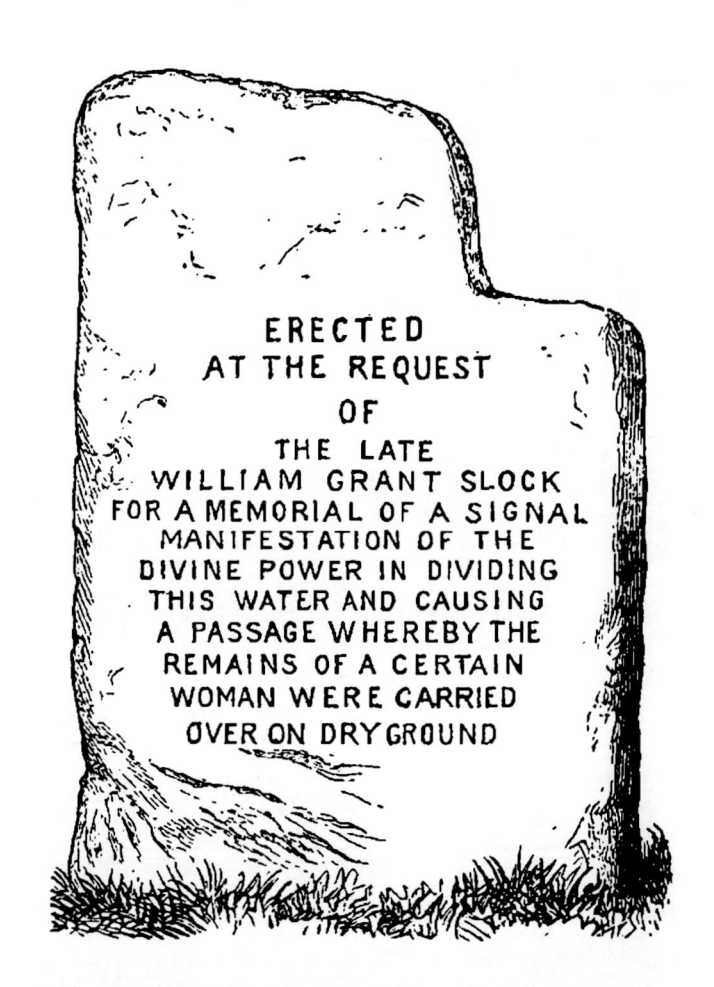

> ERECTED
> AT THE REQUEST
> OF
> THE LATE
> WILLIAM GRANT SLOCK
> FOR A MEMORIAL OF A SIGNAL
> MANIFESTATION OF THE
> DIVINE POWER IN DIVIDING
> THIS WATER AND CAUSING
> A PASSAGE WHEREBY THE
> REMAINS OF A CERTAIN
> WOMAN WERE CARRIED
> OVER ON DRY GROUND

10 The original inscription on 'The Miracle Stone of Spey' (case No.40). *(From Arthur Mitchell,* The Past In The Present, *1881)*

11 The infamous text *Saducismus Triumphatus*, which inspired lurid reports of hauntings from across the globe. *(Author's Collection)*

12 The title page of *Satan's Invisible World*. *(Author's Collection)*

13 Moorings Bar, Aberdeen, where poltergeist activity has been witnessed on many occasions. *(Geoff Holder)*

Chapter Five

The Twentieth Century, Part II: 1950-1975

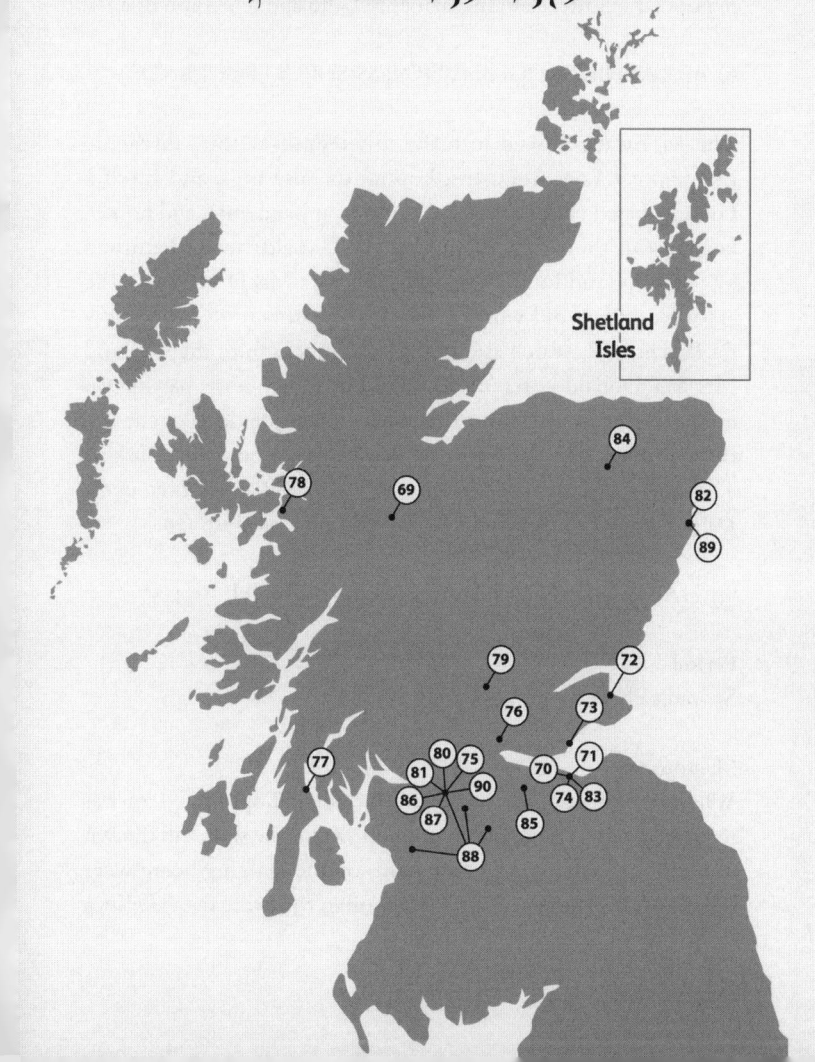

> 'The Poltergeist is rather in vogue today. The term, obscure outside the field of occult inquiries until comparatively recent days, is now accepted by the general public.'
>
> Nandor Fodor, *The Story of the Poltergeist Down the Centuries*, 1953

This is the era of the 'council-house poltergeist', as the sweeping social changes of the post-war years saw the majority of Scots come to live in public housing. It is also the era of the poltergeist in popular culture, from magazines to radio and television dramas.

69. ARDACHIE LODGE, INVERNESS-SHIRE, HIGHLAND: 1952

The McEwans moved into the nineteenth-century Ardachie Lodge, near Fort Augustus, hoping to raise pigs, and hired a London-based couple, the MacDonalds, as handyman and housekeeper. On their first night the MacDonalds were disturbed by footsteps and loud knockings, and Mrs MacDonald saw the apparition of an old woman. Two investigators from the Society for Psychical Research also heard loud knocks from the wall, and Mrs MacDonald entered some kind of trance state, passing on messages apparently from the spirit of the previous occupant. Both families quit the house, which has since been demolished. The case was dramatised in the 1977 BBC TV series *Leap in the Dark*. A good summary is in Colin Wilson's *Poltergeist!* (1981).

70. HAZELDEAN TERRACE, EDINBURGH: 1954-57

Period
Sporadically between 1954 and 1957.

Phenomena
When the kitchen was empty, the wooden chopping board was removed from its tight-fitting position within the sink, and thrown to the floor with a great crash. Items on the draining board were smashed. This happened sufficiently often to attract the *Edinburgh*

Evening Dispatch, which set up a trigger-operated camera in the hope of catching the action. At 3 a.m. the investigators heard a loud bang from the locked kitchen, like wood being smacked with a heavy object. 'We rushed into the room and found... nothing,' wrote the reporter. 'The noise had stopped as suddenly as it had started.' A fallen tumbler had been almost split in two, while a rug had been moved and bunched up. The householder, Mr Currie, said:

> One day, when I was off ill and upstairs in bed, I heard banging in the kitchen. I rushed downstairs and everything was suddenly quiet. The door to the hall and kitchen were both wide open and the rugs were thrown into a bundle. I shut the doors and tidied up the room and then went back to bed. No sooner was I beneath the covers when the noise started again.

He found the doors open once more, and the rugs heaped up. Events continued for three years, but only occasionally and with far less violence.

Sources
Ron Holiday's *Edinburgh After Dark* (2010).

Context
The terraced house lay within a post-war council-housing development.

Interpretation
Given the regular, even scheduled nature of the phenomena, there may have been something causative in the physical environment of the house. The house had a through-passage pend to the rear garden; this passed the exterior wall of the kitchen, so could there have been a human agency involved?

71. ROTHESAY PLACE, EDINBURGH: 1958-61?

Period
From 1958 to 1961?

Poltergeist over Scotland

Phenomena

This is a story with two different versions. In version one, Mrs Van Hoorne received through the post a small piece of wood from the broken staircase of Sandwood Cottage, which stands above the magnificent stretch of sand at Sandwood Bay on the far north coast of Sutherland. Why the lady should have been sent a souvenir from the most remote cottage in Scotland is unclear, as she had never visited the place. But whatever the reason, soon after the relic's arrival in 1958 knocks and footsteps were heard at night, crockery was thrown to the floor, and the smell of alcohol and tobacco-smoke pervaded the flat. On one occasion Mrs Van Hoorne glimpsed the dim outline of a bearded sailor shaking the curtains. This apparition immediately piques the paranormalist's interest, since the ghost of a sailor was reported at Sandwood Bay in 1949, 1953 and sometime before 1944. Mrs Van Hoorne, however, insisted she had no knowledge of these sightings prior to her own experience. As of 1961, the piece of wood was locked up in a cabinet in her living room.

In version two, the knockings, smells and movement/destruction of items commenced when Mrs Van Hoorne purchased some second-hand furniture which had allegedly previously belonged to a recently deceased sailor. Phenomena were concentrated on this furniture – for example, drawers on the dressing table opened and closed, and ornaments would not remain on the surfaces. A fairy-like being turned up, a 1ft-high figure dressed in a brown jacket and red trousers. A shimmering circle of light moved about the walls, apparently with a responsive intelligence. As far as can be made out, all phenomena petered out around 1961.

Sources

Version one is in *Selected Highland Folktales* (1961) by R. Macdonald Robertson, who spoke to the principal witness (and kept her anonymous). He described her as a 'citizen of high integrity and not given to exaggeration'. Version two is drawn from Dane Love's *Scottish Spectres* (2001) and Ron Halliday's *Edinburgh After Dark* (2011).

Context
The location was a flat in a rather grand nineteenth-century New Town terrace.

Interpretation
A haunting? A fairy manifestation? A poltergeist? A hoax?

72. ST ANDREWS, FIFE: 1958

Period
12-14 September 1958 (three nights).

Phenomena
A salt-cellar; a book; two scarves; and a thick leather belt. Each of these items flew from one side of the room to the other during the early hours of Friday 12 September. On one or other of the two following nights a cup and dish and an ink-bottle behaved in the like manner.

The witnesses were three young musicians, Ian Dunn, George Pitbladdo and Bob Macdonald. The room was in a small two-storey annexe adjoining Rusack's Marine Hotel on Links Crescent. In each case the items moved in darkness, and always in the same direction. After the first incidents, the musicians kept the light on for the rest of the night. The hotel under-manager commented: 'The three boys called me at 3 a.m. and they pointed out that the belt, the scarves, the salt cellar and the book had travelled from one side of the room to the other. They were certainly lying on the floor near Ian Dunn's bed.'

Sources
Dundee's *Courier* carried the story on 13 September. G.W. Lambert's article 'Scottish Haunts and Poltergeists: A Regional Study', in the 1959 *Journal* of the SPR, added the details about the ink-bottle and crockery.

Context
'Ian Dunn and his Trio' were the house band at Rusack's. On Sunday 14 September the group came to the scheduled end of their residency, and left the hotel, after which no further disturbances were reported.

Interpretation
Lambert suggested that the forces moving the objects originated with localised tremors caused by the hydraulic pressures in coastal rock formations under the action of high tides. The hotel does indeed overlook the sea. Is this a plausible explanation? Maybe. Is it the real one? Maybe not.

73. KIRKCALDY, FIFE: 1958

Period
February – September 1958 (eight months).

Phenomena
Around February 1958 the Forsyth family started to hear footsteps on the upstairs landing of their council house on Oaktree Square. Then every morning drawers were found hanging open. The noises got worse, the dog refused to go upstairs, and the family's health suffered. On 7 September the Forsyths invited Archibald McIlhatton of neighbouring Veronica Crescent to spend the night in the house. Mr McIlhatton, a self-described 'doubting Thomas', later said:

> During the night I heard six bumps like the sound of a walking stick and then there were the noises of a scuffle on the stairs as if a fight was going on between two men. I heard drawers opening after that and the sound of them being dragged along the floor. I found doors and drawers open and the cardboard I had used to jam them lying on the floor.

At 3 a.m., four of the terrified children left to spend the night at Mr McIlhatton's house, while the parents tried to find alternative accommodation for their remaining five children.

The Twentieth Century, Part II: 1950-1975

Over the next few weeks the story featured extensively in the local paper, sometimes every day. James Forsyth agitated to be rehoused, and refused to pay his rent. On 8 September an all-night vigil took place, with Kirkcaldy council housing factor John Lees and Councillor James Barron present. Neither man experienced anything untoward, but a reporter described Mrs Forsyth as 'on the verge of a breakdown'. As dawn broke, Mr Forsyth collapsed with exhaustion.

Another council tenant, Marcel Jankowsky, offered to swop, but the Forsyths refused because the hall of Jankowsky's house was too dark and scary.

On the morning of 12 September a wardrobe and wicker chair in the main bedroom were found moved several feet from their usual positions. Jeering teenagers hung around the house at night, mediums and Christian evangelists turned up, Spiritualists talked about 'earth-bound spirits', and letters arrived by the sackload. On 18 September the local MP, Tom Hubbard, spent the night in the 'haunted house' and dismissed the whole episode as 'sheer nonsense', a mix of imagination and possible fraud. 'Mr Forsyth said I would hear nothing,' he said, 'but that he could set up conditions at any time which would allow the ghost to be heard.'

The pressure mounted on the Forsyths. The education authorities told them to send their children back to school. The council went after them for the unpaid rent. Mr Forsyth, who had been off work with the stress, sank into debt. Meanwhile the noises, especially footsteps, continued. On 2 October the family finally moved into a new house. A week later the new tenants at the Oaktree Square house scoffed that the only strange noises came from a curmudgeonly cistern.

Sources

The story was in the *Courier* on no less than nine occasions – 10, 11, 13, 15, 20, 23 and 26 September, and 2 and 8 October 1958. A comprehensive run-down of the case can be found in the present author's *Haunted St Andrews* (2012).

Poltergeist over Scotland

Context

James and Ida Forsyth had nine children, aged between fifteen years and nine months, all of whom squeezed into the modest terraced house, part of a development built in 1947. The noises started a few weeks after they moved in.

Interpretation

As ever, interested parties interpreted the events along predictable lines. One visiting medium 'saw' a nine-year-old boy, who was linked with the Forsyths' son who had died in infancy nine years previously. The press suggested the house had previously been used for séances that had raised some kind of ghost, but the Spiritualist concerned, Mrs Kidd, said, 'If there is an entity in the Forsyths' home, it must have come with them. I suspect it is someone who has passed on, and the spirit, being earth-bound, wants to join them.' Another Spiritualist told Mr Forysth the incidents were caused by the unhappy spirit of a suicide.

We can suspect that with nine children under one roof, and with the four oldest children all being girls, there is ample scope for the 'troubled female adolescent/unconscious poltergeist' scenario. Equally, one or more of the siblings could have faked the noises. Or possibly it was a neighbour with a grudge, as the council found that the open pend that ran between the Forsyths' home and the neighbouring property – and which led beneath one of the bedrooms – required repairs. 'There were marks on the ceiling which may have been caused by a rake or a broomhead,' said a council spokesman, meaningfully. As for the repositioned wardrobe and chair, well, those were innocently moved by the evangelist Hope Mullin and her husband, as they openly admitted to the papers. Meanwhile, G.W. Lambert (see No.72) suggested subterranean water movements, although it is challenging to see how such geophysical events could last for eight months, and then abruptly cease once the Forsyths quitted the house.

The Forsyths' experiences led them to suffer emotionally, mentally and financially, and they were committed to the supernatural explanation, but this of course does not make it the real one. Although there may have been a poltergeist present, I suspect the solution lies in a combination of mundane noises and/or mischievous human agency, combined with runaway imagination powered by family tensions.

74. FAIRMILEHEAD, EDINBURGH: 1959

Period

Unknown.

Phenomena

> Articles being moved from one room to another (in one case a pair of eye-glasses taken from a downstairs to an upstairs room while the occupants were on the stairs – five people vouching for it)… Up to 14 or 15 people were witnesses of such incidents as ornaments, certain of them about a foot in size, being seen in a room downstairs and found half an hour later in a room upstairs. Doors in empty rooms would open and shut and there were unexplained crashing noises in other empty rooms. They were as certain of these things as they would be if giving evidence in a Court of Law.

Such was the testimony of the Revd John Wright Stevenson, in the December 1959 issue of the Church of Scotland magazine *Life and Work*, of which he was editor. The minister had been called in to help with the disturbances at a villa in Winton Terrace, Fairmilehead. It appeared to him that there was 'clear evidence of some kind of spirit presence' and he called together the household in prayer. In what seems to have been a carefully nuanced if not obscurely phrased effort to avoid any hint of the dread word 'exorcism', the Revd Stevenson wrote that the prayer:

was not for the deliverance of a house from a nuisance; it was a prayer asking simply that, where they were in uncertainty and obscurity what to pray for, their prayers might be used in ways unknown to them – for the deliverance of any spirit chained and held to this life, through the intercession of two or three 'agreed concerning something they should ask'; and in this they remembered their own sin and their own need of forgiveness and deliverance. 'Peace to this house' meant their own confession and forgiveness.

The disturbances ceased from that moment.

Sources
The *Life and Work* piece was extensively quoted in the *Glasgow Herald* on 26 December 1959. In an interview, Mr Stevenson said he had not witnessed the incidents himself, but was convinced that the members of the household were genuine in their distress. 'There was no jookery-pokery at all,' he said. No dates, names of witnesses, or other details were forthcoming.

Context
Leafy Fairmilehead is on the southern outskirts of Edinburgh. The villa in question was the home of Helen Constance Stuart (1896-1985), the feudal Baroness of Kilbride.

Interpretation
There is so much more we would like to know about this case.

75. MANSFIELD STREET, GLASGOW: 1959?-61

Period
Two years – allegedly – ending in August 1961.

Phenomena
After two years of unexplained noises, bone-chilling cold and 'a constant creepiness', events came to a head during the early

hours of Saturday, 5 August 1961, when lumps of coal were seen rising into the air and dropping back into a bucket. The witness, thirty-one-year-old Lachlan Hanlon, rushed into the bedroom to waken his wife Mary – at which point Mrs Thomas Kearney, who was also staying in the tiny flat, woke up and saw, 'a figure like a very tall man with bushy hair leaning over the children's bed.' The family left their Partick flat that same day and camped out at Lachlan's mother's tenement home in Priesthill, 6 miles away. When they were interviewed the following day, the reporter described them as shaken, anxious and lacking sleep. 'I will never step inside that house again,' said Mr Hanlon.

Meanwhile, back in Partick, the whole of Mansfield Street was standing around and gossiping about the ghost, and unwelcome midnight sightseers had to be moved on by the police. On Monday 7 August Lachlan's parents spent the night in the flat dozing in armchairs, and complained of the cold despite the fire (note that this was early August). They heard a few sounds: 'But of course,' said George Hanlon, 'the subway runs near here and perhaps that explains the knocking.' Lachlan hinted that the disturbances had followed the family to Priesthill, but refused to be drawn further by the reporters. And that, at least as far as the press were concerned, is where the story ended.

Sources

The *Evening Times*, 7 and 8 August 1961.

Context

The Hanlons lived in a typical working-class Partick residence, a kitchen-and-one room flat in a tenement. We know they had children, who were probably young given that Mary was only twenty-eight.

Interpretation

With so frustratingly little to go on, this could be anything from a genuine poltergeist to another case of a family falling prey to a runaway supernatural narrative.

76. SAUCHIE, CLACKMANNANSHIRE: 1960-61

'In my opinion the Sauchie case must be regarded as establishing beyond all reasonable doubt the objective reality of some poltergeist phenomena.'

A.R.G. Owen, *Can We Explain The Poltergeist?*, 1964

Period

22 November 1960–February 1961 (three months).

Phenomena

Here we have one of the best-attested poltergeist cases on record, which, thanks to scientific advances, continues to supply physical evidence for the reality of the phenomena. The focus or epicentre was eleven-year-old Virginia Campbell, recently arrived in Scotland from Moville, a rural area in County Donegal, in the far west of Northern Ireland. Her parents were almost sixty; James Campbell had remained in Ireland to sell the family farm, while his wife Annie got a job that required her to stay in Dollar. This was 6 miles from Sauchie, where Virginia, uprooted from her isolated country life, had to stay in the small council house occupied by her relatives, Thomas and Isabella Campbell, and share a bed with her younger cousin Margaret.

Events commenced on 22 November, just after Virginia and Margaret had gone to bed, with a 'thunking' sound like a bouncing rubber ball. This followed the two frightened girls when they came downstairs to tell the adults. Back in bed, loud knockings erupted from the headboard, and the bangs followed when the pair moved to another room. They only ceased when Virginia fell asleep. The following day, a Wednesday, Virginia was kept home from school. Around teatime, with Virginia in an armchair in the living room, Thomas and Isabella saw the sideboard move 5in from the wall and then shift back again. That night, the knocks were so loud they attracted the neighbours. Around midnight, clearly at his wits' end, Thomas Campbell brought in the Revd T.W. Lund, who established that the knocks were coming from inside the headboard, accompanied by vibrations in the wood. He also witnessed a large linen chest rock towards the bed with jerky movements, then return to its place. Margaret had long since fled the scene; when it was suggested that she get back into bed with Virginia, the knockings erupted with renewed vigour, as if in protest. Thursday 24 November was distinguished by further knockings, a sewing machine starting up, and china vases and an apple moving in front of witnesses.

On Friday 25 November Virginia returned to Sauchie Primary School. As witnessed by her teacher Margaret Stewart, the lid of Virginia's desk rose of its own accord three times, despite the girl's best efforts to keep it shut. A short while later the temporarily empty desk behind Virginia levitated about 3in above the floor. On the Saturday the Revd Lund and the local GP, Dr W.H. Nesbit, popped round, and both saw Virginia's pillow ripple and then rotate, while more raps rang out. On Sunday Virginia went into a kind of trance, calling out for her beloved dog Toby, who was back in Ireland.

At school again on Monday 28 November, a blackboard pointer vibrated to the point that it fell off a table – and then Miss Stewart could feel the table itself was vibrating. Virginia was standing close by, but not touching any of the items. The following day Virginia went to stay in a different house, where she was visited by Dr William Logan, Dr Nesbit's practice partner, and his wife Dr S. Logan. After witnessing the knockings, both were convinced they were genuine. That night Virginia went into another trance.

Thursday 1 December saw Drs Nesbit and Logan setting up a cine-camera and sound-recording equipment in Virginia's bedroom. Between 9 and 10.30 p.m. several knocks were recorded, and furniture movements were filmed (unfortunately, this 8mm film has been lost). The lid of the linen box lifted up, causing Virginia to scream. At 11 p.m. the Revd Lund, Revd Murdo Ewan Mcdonald from St George's West in Edinburgh, and two other clergymen, arrived to conduct a service of intercession and prayers. The noises continued throughout the proceedings, and almost seemed to punctuate the prayers – 'The Lord is my Shepherd,' bang! bang! bang! 'I shall not want,' bang! bang! bang! After the service, more sounds were taped between 11.30 p.m. and 12.15 a.m.

Probably during December, schoolbooks and jotters regularly floated away from wherever Virginia was sitting in the classroom. Other phenomena through December and January included a bowl filled with bulbs sliding across a school desk, the levitation of an apple and shaving brush in the house, and some knockings and footsteps — but generally the fear and tension of the last week of November had ebbed away. Virginia even became so comfortable with her poltergeist that she gave it a nickname — 'Wee Hughie'. The previously withdrawn eleven year old made a new friend at school; and, far more importantly, she was reunited with Toby. After a long decline, the phenomena had ceased by March 1961.

Sources

Early in 1961 Dr A.R.G. Owen of Cambridge University interviewed all the key participants. He considered the witness testimony of the clergyman, schoolteacher and the three physicians to be robust and accurate, and backed up by a wealth of other data. In his subsequent meticulous study *Can We Explain The Poltergeist?* (1964) Owen considered that the Sauchie case embodied solid evidence for an authentic poltergeist outbreak.

In 1994 and 2000 respectively, the case was revisited by two local investigators, Malcolm Robinson and his colleague in Scottish Paranormal Investigations, Brian Allan. Virginia's former primary school teacher, plus Dr William Logan and an anonymous Campbell family member were all interviewed, and confirmed testimony given in the 1960s, with a few added extras. These interviews can be found, in almost identical detail, in Allan's *Revenants* and Robinson's *Paranormal Case Files of Great Britain* (both 2010).

The story made it to the local *Alloa Journal* on 2 December 1961. A member of the Alloa Spiritualist Church stated that the dead were trying to communicate through Virginia, but that is what Spiritualists tend to say as a matter of course. As the phenomena declined, the press interest escalated, and soon Virginia's classmates and family were experiencing siege by media. On 13 December the BBC Scottish Home Service radio series *Scope* aired some of the recorded noises.

Dr Barrie Colvin recovered these recordings from the BBC, along with recordings of raps from nine other poltergeist cases: Andover (1974); Enfield (1977); Euston Square (2000); Thun and Schleswig (Switzerland, 1967 and 1968); Pursruck (Germany, 1971); La Machine (France, 1973); and Ipiranga and Santa Rosa (Brazil, 1971 and 1988). The raps were subjected to acoustic analysis, and compared to 'normal' raps produced by knuckles or tools hitting a variety of surfaces. In every case the poltergeist raps had a different acoustic signature to the normal raps. In normal raps the sound starts with the maximum volume as the object strikes the surface, and then decays over the next few milliseconds. The poltergeist raps, however, start at a relatively low level before escalating to the maximum volume. Colvin published his results in the SPR's *Journal* in 2010, and came to the conclusion that the distinctive acoustic waveform of the poltergeist raps meant that they were not created by a force (such as a blow from an invisible hand) striking the surface. In contrast, poltergeist raps are generated within the structure of the wood or wall where they are heard.

Context

Virginia was described by her teacher as shy, with a pronounced rustic Irish accent. She was also mature and level-headed, and on the cusp of puberty – there is a hint from Miss Stewart that the phenomena were active for a week every twenty-eight days, which may suggest a link with the young girl's hormonal changes. Virginia missed her father and Toby, and was unhappy that she could not stay with her mother. She was in a new school, and sharing a bed for the first time.

Interpretation

Owen stated categorically that the poltergeist was an exteriorization of Virginia's unhappiness; as her emotional life improved, the disturbances declined, and vanished altogether when Toby came back on the scene. Can we explain the poltergeist? In this case, yes (up to a point). We can certainly identify the source, even if we do not comprehend the mechanism.

77. 'COASTAL TOWN', ARGYLL: 1963

Period
26 June–31 August 1963 (two months).

Phenomena
It was 10.40 p.m. on 26 June 1963, in a council house in a seaside town in Argyll. Very gently, knocking started inside the wall that divided the bedrooms of Mrs D. and two of her children. The noises were described as clicks or the gnashing of teeth. Shortly afterwards the noises proceeded to much louder thuds and knocks coming from within the interior walls at twenty-minute intervals. Over the next few days several neighbours were invited inside to witness the sounds, and two policemen searched the flat thoroughly, but failed to reproduce the volume of the noises from anything available. The knocks were only heard at night. Curtains were found mysteriously opened, and a pair of shoes was discovered turned upside down. The family moved to a hotel to gain some relief, but the noises followed them, these being heard by the proprietor. After seven weeks the sounds stopped abruptly on 13 August. Then, after thirteen days' peace, they resumed on the 26th of the month. Mrs D. sought medical help for sleeplessness and anxiety, and as part of the process, her twelve-year-old daughter Rosalind (a pseudonym) was also interviewed.

After this session at the clinic the poltergeist phenomena ceased completely, to be replaced by mediumistic events. Over several nights Rosalind would rise from her bed, walk into the living room as if in a trance, and deliver a number of communications from the dead. There were words from a great many deceased relatives, some of them very distant ones, and then came urgent messages that had, said Rosalind, to be written down and sent to various people in the town (sadly the content of these notes was never documented). The following night she announced that two of the messages had not been delivered – which was true – and, following a hasty delivery of the notes, on 31 August the trancified Rosalind stated that the spirits were pleased that the requests had been fulfilled. After this date there were no further events, and check-ups in further years showed that Rosalind had had no recurrence of any symptoms.

Sources
Mrs D. and Rosalind were under the care of Dr Margaret Dewar, Consultant Psychiatrist at the Argyll & Bute Hospital. With no previous experience of the paranormal, Dr Dewar discussed the case with her colleague Dr James McHarg of Dundee. Dr Dewar's progressive blindness prevented her from writing up the case and before her death she passed the notes to Dr McHarg, who presented the case at the 1987 conference of the Society for Psychical Research. The talk was never published, but a tape of it is available from the SPR.

Context
After her acrimonious divorce, Mrs D. moved in with her mother. The two women quarrelled, and so the next move was to the council house occupied by Mrs D.'s grandmother, to whom she was close. Of Mrs D.'s three daughters, the eldest soon relocated to another relative's, leaving Rosalind, twelve, and an eight year old. At this time Mrs D. was thirty-four, and working as a shop assistant. The granny abruptly went to live with Mrs D.'s sister in Cardiff. A short while later – 17 March 1963 – the old woman died of cancer, leaving the family in Argyll distraught. Phenomena started just over three months after their bereavement. Neither Mrs D. nor Rosalind had a history of mental illness.

Interpretation
Dr Dewar talked to neighbours and the police and was convinced nothing fraudulent was in play. After the divorce

and the bereavement the stresses within the family can easily be imagined. Dr McHarg speculated that Rosalind was also physically entering puberty at the time, but this cannot be proven. Of course, it is mere supposition that Rosalind was the focus – it could have been her mother or eight-year-old sister.

If we assume Rosalind was indeed the focus, events may have proceeded like this:

a) Rosalind grieved deeply for three months, then, via the noises, unconsciously exteriorized her unhappiness.
b) Dr Dewar told her that her granny was not suffering any more.
c) Rosalind, comforted, achieved an internal reconciliation.
d) Her granny's concerns during the final months of her life – either picked up by the normal abilities of a twelve-year-old girl in a cramped house, or possibly acquired through supernormal means such as grandmother/grand-daughter telepathy – now swam into Rosalind's subconscious.
e) Rosalind's subconscious, expressed during altered mental states, sought to finalise her granny's unfinished business with her relatives and community.

On the other hand, perhaps the case supports the survival-after-death hypothesis. It's that ambiguous.

78. SANDAIG, LOCHALSH, HIGHLAND: 1964

Period
Several days in May 1964.

Phenomena
Sandaig was the remote idyll inhabited by the celebrated author Gavin Maxwell and the world's most famous otters – Mij, Edal and Teko, the stars of Maxwell's trilogy *Ring of Bright Water*, *The Rocks Remain* and *Raven Seek Thy Brother*. The house was known to millions under the fictionalised name of Camusfearna. At 10 p.m.

one May night in 1964 a marmalade jar flew off a kitchen shelf and smashed on the floor, an act witnessed by Jimmy Watt (one of the otter assistants), Maxwell's friend Richard Frere, and Maxwell himself. The latter two men looked at each other, and both said 'Poltergeist!'

The following day a glass windowpane was discovered pushed some 5ft out from its frame, leaving the putty behind. A baby's plastic bottle, used for feeding animals, shot out from a high shelf directly towards Maxwell, falling to the floor just before it hit his face. This was witnessed by Jimmy Watt, and was just one example of the polt's precision. One day Maxwell watched as a stack of LPs stored under a table spread out like a pack of cards, to form a regular fan-like arrangement on the floor.

Maxwell and Frere were convinced the psychical source of the poltergeist was one of the author's former assistants, a troubled young man who was then living about 5 miles away. Frere called him Brewster and characterised him as a former juvenile delinquent. Douglas Botting's biography *Gavin Maxwell: A Life* uses the youth's real name – Philip Alpin – and more charitably describes him as keen to get his life on track using skills acquired on a recent outdoor adventure course. When Alpin popped in and Maxwell started to tell him about the events, both heard a loud crash coming from the coatroom. Investigating, they found the laundry hamper had flown more than halfway across the room, being sufficiently agile to miss two pairs of fishermen's thighboots that were in its line of flight. After this, no more disturbances took place.

Sources

The events were described by the two eyewitnesses: Maxwell in *Raven Seek Thy Brother* (1968) and Frere in his memoir *Maxwell's Ghost: An Epilogue to Gavin Maxwell's Camusfearna* (1976).

Context

Maxwell was a notoriously challenging and difficult individual; in addition, his extensive involvement with curses, paranormal voices and other praeternatural incidents is covered in the present author's *The Guide to Mysterious Skye and Lochalsh*. The house at Sandaig burned down in 1968, and only a monument now survives. The beach is a long way from the nearest road, requiring an adventurous walk.

Interpretation

Was Alpin/Brewster, the alleged psychical instigator of the events, present somewhere near the house when the various items were moved? We don't know, but otherwise the assumption is that he was projecting his frustrations over several miles, which may stretch the credulity of the most ardent supporter of RSPK. Could it be that the source of the poltergeist was Jimmy Watt, a young man who had to put up with Maxwell's prickly personality – or even Maxwell himself?

79. CRIEFF, PERTH & KINROSS: 1960s & 1990s

Period

The 1960s, and the late 1990s.

Phenomena

Sometime in the 1960s, a hairdresser's shop on Church Street had a spate of poltergeist activity: the front door swung open on its own; tea bags and steel wool were inserted into the sink; bottles of dye and £100 of television stamps vanished, only to reappear in obvious places a few days later; and when the shop was opened up in the morning, towels were found scattered about.

Fast-forward to the 1990s. The site is now occupied by City Stores, a narrow-aisled, densely packed general shop. The heavy front door (the same one as in the 1960s) sometimes swings ajar; and at other times it is heard to noisily open, when it fact it is securely locked. In the morning, the stock is often found disturbed, with clothes and spray cans in disarray; some of these items are where the hairdresser's towel basket once sat. One spot in the shop is unnaturally cold. There are noises, too: the proprietor, John Randalls, is rattled by a loud cough right behind him while working alone late at night; he hears the electric fan running noisily in the shop next door, and voices and bangs from the upstairs flat – but both premises are unoccupied, and the empty shop does not even have a functioning electricity supply. These sounds are also heard by Hugh Mailer, the owner of the camera shop on the other side of City Stores. And in City Stores, Liz Cramb, via the CCTV camera, sees the apparition of a short, bent figure – and when a psychic visits by invitation, she too detects the presence of a hunched-over old man. Meanwhile, voices and the sound of draws opening and closing are heard coming from the empty kitchen of a flat in High Street, a short distance away.

David Cowan, a local resident with a long-term interest in ley-lines, dowsed the locations, and concluded that the flat and the City Stores/hairdresser's site were being affected by 'black spirals' of negative earth energy generated by two underground streams, with a possible connection to the old graveyard close by.

Sources
The City Stores story appeared in the *Strathearn Herald* on 10 December 1999. A full account can be found in *Ley Lines and Earth Energies*, published by David Cowan and Chris Arnold in 2004.

Context
The episodes at the hairdresser's only came to light after the City Stores investigation appeared in the local press – the owner had previously been too embarrassed to make the events public.

Interpretation
Cowan has developed an elaborate theory of earth energies, which goes far beyond the standard idea of straight ley-lines (whatever they might be). Whether or not you cleave entirely to this explanation, the notion that repeating poltergeist events, taking place at the same location but in different decades, are

generated by something in the environment is at the very least a plausible one. Note however that, according to the psychic, the disturbances were caused by the ghost of the old man.

80. GOVAN, GLASGOW: 1960s

A crucifix on a chain swung to and fro, hitting a cardboard calendar hanging from the same nail. The crucifix then spun round and round, getting faster all the time – before abruptly stopping. The event took place in a fourth-floor tenement flat at 5.30 p.m. on a Friday. The witness, Paul Anderson, wrote to author Ron Halliday, who included the episode in *Haunted Glasgow* (2008).

81. GLASGOW: 1960s

Knocks, bumps, the movement of furniture and the displacement of items forced a family from their council house. An investigating team experienced nothing during their first vigil, but on their second night they heard bangs and crashes, and witnessed a pair of iron fire-tongs 'propelled by invisible hands'. The next night they brought a medium who channelled a series of confused messages in what sounded like the croaking voice of an old woman, and which claimed to be a relative of the family. The spirit was worried about a baby, warning it had to be taken to hospital or it would die from a problem with its throat. The sceptical couple took their six-month-old child for an X-ray – which revealed a small obstruction in the baby's throat. An immediate operation prevented the infant from choking to death. The episode was passed by a correspondent to Peter Underwood, who included it in his *Gazetteer of Scottish and Irish Ghosts* (1973).

82. ROSEMOUNT, ABERDEEN: 1960s

A policeman answered a call to a disturbance at a house in the Rosemount area, and was met at the door by the sight of levitating plates. The officer told a detective colleague, who told journalist

Norman Adams, who mentioned the episode more than twenty years later in his 1998 book *Haunted Scotland*. In 2010 I contacted Norman, who could not remember why he had not followed up the story at the time, but thought it was probably for reasons of confidentiality or sensitivity. He knew his (now-deceased) source was reliable and trustworthy. In response to my Freedom of Information request, Grampian Police noted that very few records still remain from the 1960s, and those relate to serious crime only, so there is no official documentation for the case.

83. COMELY BANK ROAD, EDINBURGH: 1965

In 1965 Brian Cox – now the star of Hollywood films such as *X-Men* and *The Bourne Identity* – was a young actor at The Royal Lyceum in Edinburgh, and rented a room in a sizable house on Comely Bank Road. Lying in bed one night, he heard a tapping, and then watched as a chair started shaking, and then proceeded to glide across the floor towards him. The following morning he confirmed it was not a dream – the chair was beside the bed, and the floor bore the scuff marks of its journey from the other side of the large room. The actor moved out. The anecdote appeared in the *Daily Record* for 27 December 2004.

84. LEITH HALL, ABERDEENSHIRE: 1966-68

Period
1966-68 (two years).

Phenomena
In 1966 writers Elizabeth Byrd and Barrie Gaunt rented the fourteen rooms of the East Wing of Leith Hall, a much-extended château-like mansion originally dating from the seventeenth century. Over the next two years they and their guests experienced what seems to have been a long-term haunting, with sightings of several apparitions (a Victorian lady, children playing,

a man with a bandaged head, and a formless grey mist) and a powerful sense of being watched by some malevolent presence, a sensation which peaked in the master bedroom on the second floor. There were also occasional noises – footsteps of various gaits, childish giggles, party sounds, bagpipe music, and what sounded like a big dog padding around.

Some startling poltergeist activity also occurred. A glass moved across Gaunt's desk and broke. A tall and sturdy standing lamp was flung across the study where Gaunt was working. An ashtray was found repositioned some 8ft from its original location in his bedroom. In the kitchen, Byrd had a door slammed in her face, heard an empty sherry bottle smash and saw a heavy metal pot cover fly in an arc from its hook to the floor.

There were also a number of unusual apports, interpreted as 'gifts'. One morning Byrd found a pair of tea cosies, weighing a pound each, on her study chair. Despite extensive enquiries, she could find no human source for the items within the household, and the building was locked overnight, thus forestalling any notion of an interloper. On another occasion her husband 'received' a tooled-leather writing case, the size of a telephone book and weighing three-quarters of a pound. Within were several blotters, and a faded yellow envelope on which was written, 'I am in, please ring bell, Henrietta Leith-Hay.' The case appeared one morning in the drawer of a desk that he used every day.

Sources
Byrd's books *Ghosts in My Life* (1968) and *A Strange and Seeing Time* (1971).

Context
Leith Hall is owned by the National Trust for Scotland, and the gardens are open to the public. The interior, which could be viewed until recently, has now been converted into private accommodation, thus cutting off the once-frequent flow of visits by paranormal groups.

Interpretation

Byrd wrote extensively of her husband's psychic powers, and, although primarily a novelist, she herself was intensely interested in the supernormal. She wrote candidly of their experiences, and made a tentative link between the various apparitions and individuals from the château's colourful past. No obvious explanation was offered for the poltergeist phenomena, other than as a possible extension of the activities of the various ghosts.

85. LIVINGSTON, WEST LOTHIAN: 1968

In December 1968, within a short time of becoming the tenants of a brand-new council house in Howden, Hugh and Mary Cassels experienced anomalous bumps and thumps, saw imprints of a hand on the inside windows, witnessed their gas stove moving a couple of inches, and glimpsed the apparition of a sad-faced man sitting in a living-room chair. The couple became anxious and lost weight, and Hugh had to quit his job on a building site so he could stay with Mary, who refused to be alone in the house. The local priest, Father John Byrne, blessed the house four times, but the noises continued. The story is in Dennis Barden's 1970 book *Mysterious Worlds*.

86. THEATRE ROYAL, GLASGOW: 1970s–2007

As with many venues, the Theatre Royal has its own folklore – for time out of mind, stories have circulated among the staff of doors banging, sounds of moaning, an unpleasant atmosphere, and an overpowering 'sense of presence', all focused on the upper circle.

In the early 1970s veteran ghosthunter Peter Underwood visited the building (then a TV studio) and stated that poltergeist phenomena were present. Around 2004 a plumber stacked his tools in the basement – and when he returned, the tools were scattered across the floor. He put them back into order, but later found them once again in a mess. In 2006 or 2007 a contractor working alone in an attic space reached only by a hatch from the upper circle was hit on the back of the head with a brochure. Underwood's comment appears in his *Guide to Ghosts & Haunted Places* (1999). The other details come from personal communications with Mike Hall, who used to work at the Royal, and Gary Painter, at the stage door, both of whose contributions are given in full in my *The Guide to Mysterious Glasgow* (2009).

87. PARTICK, GLASGOW: 1970s

Period
Unknown.

Phenomena
Kenneth and his wife habitually slept in their living room, as it was the only one with a fire. One February morning in the 1970s they woke up to find every pane of glass in the room smashed, although the window frame was intact. The TV had moved to the opposite corner from its usual stance; the sideboard had been tilted against the settee; and the sideboard's contents were scattered over the floor. Most bizarre of all, every piece of china, every item of crockery and every glass ornament had been reduced to its component parts – sand. Blue and white bowls, for example, were now blue and white piles of fine sand. All of this destruction had taken place within a few feet of the sleeping couple.

The front door was still locked and bolted from the inside. The flat was on the second floor with no external access, so a burglar would have had to climb the outside wall – and anyway, the window frame was too small to allow entry. Still concerned about a robbery, Kenneth returned with his father's Alsatian. The dog refused to enter the main hall of the tenement block, never mind the flat itself. Thoroughly frightened, the couple moved out. When Kenneth returned a few days later to collect their belongings, there was no trace of the piles of fine sand.

Sources
Ron Halliday's *Haunted Glasgow* (2008).

Context
The small Partick flat had a living room, bedroom and bathroom. There are no other details about the family situation.

Interpretation
Converting crockery to sand is extreme even by poltergeist standards – the expenditure of energy must be huge – which makes this potentially one of the most intriguing cases in this book. But without further evidence, what interpretation can be offered?

88. KILMARNOCK/LANARK/MOTHERWELL/GLASGOW: 1970s

Period
Unknown.

Phenomena
In the 1970s, at a gas storage station in Kilmarnock, stones started flying through the air, bouncing off the gas tank and workers' bothy hut. There was no obvious source for the missiles, which were carefully aimed, and all the men on the small site were accounted for when the lithobolic barrage commenced. Then the keys to the station gate began to disappear, to be found hidden in cracks in the site wall. A similar fate befell other objects on the construction site, leading to fraying nerves among the workers. When a manager from the gas board visited, he was just getting out of his car when bricks hit the roof and bonnet. When the team moved to a new site in Lanark, stones appeared from nowhere to hit the storage tank. As the men walked on the metal gantry around the tank the letter 'R' appeared, scratched on the site wall, at the only spot which was just out of sight of the platform. Then the name 'Rocky' appeared, followed by another scratched word: 'freend'. Rocky was the nickname of one of the contractors on both sites: John Adams.

John started scratching questions on the wall. In the time it took him to circle the tank, a reply would appear. The mysterious messages were signed 'Jonathon', or more usually, 'JV'. At the next work site, in Motherwell, a newspaper floated out of the sky: it was marked with the initials JV. Notes started to turn up, signed with a skull and crossbones: Jonathon's tag. When John asked the question, 'Why do you follow us?' the scratched reply claimed that JV used to live at a place that the gas board had built over. JV continually asked for help, but did not explain how this help was to be delivered. Some of the team tried to communicate with the spirit using a Ouija board, although John declined to take part. As he sat outside the bothy he heard a bang and a milk bottle fell from the sky. Inside the bothy, meanwhile, a large chest of drawers rocked to and fro. On a previous occasion the bothy door had been thrown open and a pickaxe flew in, narrowly missing those inside. One day a pile of wood appeared on the path round the gantry, but by the time the men returned to same spot, the timber had disappeared. Each day as they drove back to Glasgow from Motherwell, the workers could feel a force pulling the van backwards, and one time a hard hat flew through the vehicle's interior and cut the driver across the face.

At this point the phenomena followed John back to Glasgow, including his local, the Exchequer pub in Partick. Money performed gymnastics and bounced off tables. One coin dropped into a partially drunk lager in front of John's friend Tom. The liquid foamed up and filled the glass, spilling onto the table and then the floor. A piece of paper apported out of nowhere, and when opened it read 'Rocky help JV'. Another friend, Robert, bought cigarettes from the pub's machine. When he unwrapped the packet, it contained a message from JV. A waitress shouted out that there was a telephone call for Rocky; when John went to the phone he found only strange instrumental music playing. The same thing happened thirty minutes later. On both occasions the man next to the phone said he had not heard it ring (so how did the waitress know to ask for Rocky?).

The polt also moved in with John. Curtains fluttered on a windless day, then stood out at ninety degrees from the curtain rail. The coffee table turned over, and one of its legs broke and shot across the room into a door. A lit cigarette was pulled from the fingers of John's friend Bill and tossed against a wall. An iron lifted off the kitchen sideboard and hit Bill in the face. And twice in a matter of seconds, in front of several witnesses, the polt solved the Rubik's cube puzzle as it was held behind John's back. One morning John found a whisky bottle ground into a pile of sand, although the paper label and metal top were still intact – shades of Case 87, which also took place in Partick. JV's communications became more inventive: spaghetti fell onto the table in the shape of a skull and crossbones. Peas, displaced from a kitchen worktop, created a question mark on the floor. Apports included notes with the word 'why', and, among many other objects, a pirate ship constructed of thousands of matches.

One day John heard sledgehammer-type blows start up in the rafters. They continued in a frenzy for hours; then, as suddenly as they had begun, they ceased. And from that moment on, JV was never heard from again.

Sources

The case is covered extensively in Ron Halliday's *Haunted Glasgow* (2008). Halliday met Adams several times, and described him as a solid, level-headed working-class man now in his early sixties. John claimed to have destroyed all the apports, including the notes and the pirate ship.

Context

John Adams went on to suffer another poltergeist infestation, this time in Drumchapel in the 1990s (see No.111).

Interpretation

We lack any corroborating evidence for this most extraordinary of cases. If the accounts are authentic, the obvious question is:

who/what was Jonathon/JV? (It is, of course, within the bounds of possibility that there was an unconscious psychical source of the phenomena, and that was John Adams.)

89. OSBOURNE PLACE, ABERDEEN: 1970s

Cushions, pens and other items were frequently thrown about. The owner discovered that a little girl had died in the house in the nineteenth century, so he called out using the girl's name in a 'disapproving parent' tone. The disturbances stopped. NB: just because the polt responded to the girl's name, does not mean it really was her ghost. Victims of poltergeists often feel better if they can identify their tormentor as the spirit of a specific individual, but polts are capricious, and responding to names is part of the games they play. Source: Norman Adams' *Haunted Scotland* (1998).

90. BALORNOCK, GLASGOW: 1974-75

> 'There is something strange in that house, something we cannot logically explain. You get it to materialize, and I will lock it up.'
> Police officer quoted in the *Glasgow Herald*, 17 January 1975

Period
3 November 1974-23 May 1975 (over six months), with an extension later into 1975.

Phenomena
In the red corner were David Grieve, his wife Elizabeth, her elderly mother Anne, and the two sons, Jeffrey (eleven), and Derek (fourteen, and very unhappy and lonely in the teenage manner). In the blue corner were the Keenan family: James, in his late sixties, his wife, and their thirty-year-old son Gordon (who was in poor neurological health). The Grieves lived above the Keenans in council accommodation in Northgate Quadrant, Balornock; there had been bad blood between the families

for twelve years. A few days before Bonfire Night 1974, Derek and Jeffrey created a nuisance with a bonfire in the garden; they either burned James Keenan in effigy, or pretended the Guy on the fire was the old man. This episode coincided with the opening salvo of what would prove to be one of the most extraordinary poltergeist cases of the century.

Phase One (3 November – 4 December 1974)
At 10 p.m. on Sunday 3 November, the day of the bonfire, tappings started up in the boys' bedroom. Bangs and scratchings continued until 6 a.m. Over the next few weeks the noises continued nightly, even following the boys when they slept in their parents' bedroom. The Grieves blamed the Keenans, and called the police. The officers knocked on the Keenans' door several times, warning them to cease their nonsense. When the noises persisted, the Keenans were arrested and taken to Springburn station. The noises continued, and Mrs Grieve believed Gordon Keenan had somehow escaped from the police station to carry on with the mischief. After they were released without charge, the Keenans stated they were going to sue the police for false arrest (it is not clear if they ever did so). Fisticuffs ensued, leading to Mr Grieve receiving a suspended sentence for assault on Gordon Keenan.

After a time, ornaments were thrown around and furniture shaken in the Grieves' flat, lights flickered, and the noises started beating out the rhythm of 'The Dead March'. As the knocks seemed to be responsive to questions. Elizabeth Grieve devised a system in which each letter of the alphabet was spoken out loud in order, A, B, C, D, and so on, until raps were received to 'choose' that letter. Using this easily misinterpreted code, the noises claimed to be the spirits of miners killed in a pit accident. Messages also urged the Grieves to strangle James Keenan, because, it was claimed, he had been the mine manager responsible for the explosion (it should be said that there is no evidence Mr Keenan had worked in mining when he was a younger man).

▲ Poltergeist over Scotland ▲

The Grieves fled to the house occupied by the Brouwers (Mrs Grieve's sister and her husband) – but the phenomena travelled the three-quarters of a mile with them. 'We saw an ornamental model of a whisky barrel made of wood and brass suddenly being thrown upwards and on to the floor,' wrote Mr Grieve in an account of his family's nightmare. 'Within seconds of this happening a picture, built on a swivel, revolved to show the mirrored side and shortly afterwards a basket-work box turned a half-somersault before our eyes, to show us the base of the box.' Water dripped from the dry ceiling for no reason. A priest came to bless the house. That night those sleeping in the Brouwers' lounge, woken by smoke, watched as a heavy ash-stand hit the floor. Then a Dutch musical box began to play, the sails of its windmill turning round, while the tea-trolley supporting the model wheeled across the floor. When the Grieves returned to Northgate Quadrant, they found the bathroom flooded. After a plumber fixed the fault, the taps turned themselves full on, and only a heavy wrench could close them.

By now, housing officials, councillors, workmen, the GPO, family doctors, and the local Church of Scotland minister had been called out to Northgate Quadrant, and many had witnessed the noises and other phenomena. Police and council officials standing in the downstairs flat swore the noises were coming from upstairs, while their colleagues in the upper flat said the source was below them. Natural causes were ruled out. Spiritualist séances and Christian blessings had no effect. With officers turning in reports along the lines of, 'The bed was proceeding in a northerly direction,' on 29 November the exasperated police requested the assistance of the Revd Murdo Ewan McDonald, Professor of Practical Theology at the University of Glasgow.

The minister found the family in a state of hysteria, with Mr Grieve obsessed with the dead miners (a medium had also made 'contact' with these alleged spirits). The boys' bedroom was alarmingly cold, and the Revd McDonald witnessed the tappings, a door closing of its own accord, and alarm clocks setting off at random. The following day David Grieve phoned to tell him that a coffee table had just levitated, a standing ashtray moved across the room, and a toy flown through a window into the front garden. On 4 December the minister conducted an exorcism in the house, commanding the invading spirit to depart and leave the family in peace. During the same session the Revd Max Magee, Chaplain of the University of Strathclyde, laid hands in blessing on every member of the family. Phenomena now ceased for several weeks.

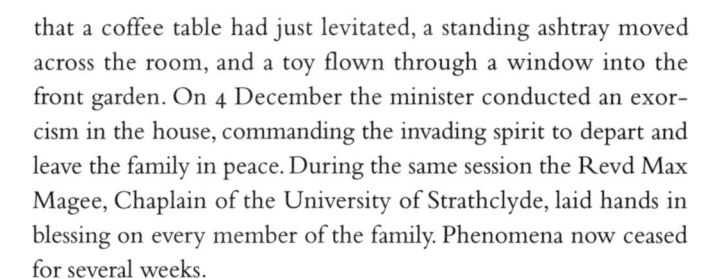

Phase Two (6-18 January 1975)
In early January the Grieves watched a television report on a Newcastle poltergeist, and, inspired, decided to tape-record their own experiences. It was as if this poked the dormant polt back into life – or perhaps it was that the school term had started, and Derek loathed school. A potato scoop and a wooden clothes-hanger flew through the air. But that was just the start. The tappings began quietly then blossomed into veritable house-quakes, as if a giant was wielding a mighty hammer, striking every few seconds for hours on end. Pictures jumped on their hooks with every bang and the walls shook, but no structural damage was ever caused. Fleeing to the Brouwers', the Grieves found no respite. There, a cushion under Derek's head rotated, and pulled away; his sleeping bag kept unzipping; a large double bed shifted to the centre of the room and then banged back against the wall; camp beds slid to and fro. When they returned home they found the house in chaos – furniture scattered, and toys smashed or stuffed down the toilet bowl. When Derek went back to the Brouwers', fuses blew when he touched electrical items, and on one occasion strange bangs started up in his father's car when he was in it; a few minutes later the vehicle's electrical system went haywire. At school a pencil danced across Jeffrey's desk, and doors closed in his face without anyone else being present. On 17 January the story made it to the *Glasgow Herald*. Over time the boys became ostracised at school, Jeffrey missed weeks of education, the phone number had to go ex-directory, and the family's collective health suffered from a combination of stress, fear and sleepless nights.

A professional medium visited and after a session announced she had released the spirits of three dead miners. Strange, then, that the phenomena continued with even more force. The Revds McDonald and Magee were also called back in. They believed the poltergeist was powered by the family situation, so they convinced the Grieves to try and maintain a calm atmosphere. Peace now reigned for two weeks, although not before one or other of the boys assaulted both their father and the Revd McDonald with abnormal strength.

Phase Three (3 February – 23 May 1975)
Without any obvious catalyst, the noises started up again with a vengeance, prompting the return of the Revd Max Magee, now accompanied by Archie Roy, Professor of Astronomy at Glasgow University and a leading light with the Scottish Society for Psychical Research. This time, however, there also seemed to be a definite and malicious attempt to 'control' Derek and Jeffrey. The boys' bodies contorted into horrible shapes and they developed involuntary limb movements, as if being tied into knots. If they hurt themselves while lashing out, the contortions paused for a minute or two, and then continued just as wildly as ever. The boys seemed to mimic the bangs by twisting round on the bed to hammer their feet on the walls. After this they would be pushed off the beds. Eleven-year-old Jeffrey, who was a small boy, kicked a large heavy wardrobe away from the wall with great strength, and overpowered his brawny (6ft 2in, 16 stone) uncle. As witnessed by Professor Roy, Jeffrey was persistently bounced from a horizontal position on the bed 2ft into the air, as if he were a rubber ball. It was impossible for him to achieve this through normal muscular exertion. On 2 May Derek temporarily demonstrated complex motor skills – dexterous card tricks that he had never done before, and which he could not perform ever again. His parents interpreted this as his being possessed by one of the dead miners.

The presence of Magee or Roy seemed to have a calming effect, so one or other of the investigators found themselves offering support to the blitzed family by spending long hours in the house, sometimes staying overnight. On one occasion Magee, irritable through lack of sleep, desperately shouted, 'This is ridiculous! Stop it!' - and the phenomena temporarily abated. Tape recordings were made of the wall-shaking bangs, but the sound quality was poor, with a high background noise level not heard at the time. The tape recorder was working fine both before and after the recording.

Other phenomena are not securely dated but occurred at some point during the infestation. One of the boys was heard to speak in a foreign language he had not learnt, and, while asleep, cried out 'Help me!' in a gruff male voice. A book nobody recognized appeared in the house, and then vanished just as suddenly. Cushions from the armchairs in the lounge were found substituted for the drawers in the sideboard, and vice versa. A mirror in the hallway passed through the closed doors of the lounge and kitchen and crashed into the bathroom. A 'gonk' doll – a very Seventies item – spun round like a cartoon character and dematerialized and materialized at will. During a period spent at a relatives' house, the bedclothes were found arranged in the shape of a body, with a polystyrene wig-head for a head.

Via the family GP, Magee and Roy now brought in Dr Peter McHarg, a consultant psychiatrist from Dundee and a distinguished contributor to the Society for Psychical Research. McHarg visited the family three times, starting on 9 May, and continuing into 1976, and found no evidence of fraud, epilepsy, neurosis, or psychosis.

About 23 May, the phenomena suddenly stopped. Around the same time, James Keenan, having been ill for a long time, passed away in hospital from bronchial carcinoma. The Grieves told McHarg that they believed Mr Keenan had died the same night as the disturbances finally ceased, and made the obvious link. As it turned out this was not the case, as the poltergeist gave up the ghost approximately forty-eight hours before the death of Mr Keenan. It was, however, a synchronicity that played strongly in the minds of all concerned. But was it actually meaningful? Around about the same time, Derek, who had been the focus of so many of the incidents, went to stay with his grandparents in the north of Scotland. And on 18 May, with the flat briefly empty (the family were at church), Magee and Roy went from room to room, performing a cleansing ceremony in each. So any one, or two, or all three, of these developments may have contributed to the cessation of the infestation. On the other hand, none of them may have had any impact. Who knows with polts?

Phase Four (later in 1975)

During Derek's holiday in north Scotland, a piece of metal struck him on the forehead, and jewellery was displaced from a drawer to elsewhere in the house. On another holiday, this one in Spain, a shaving mirror drifted through the air from its perch on a tent pole, and jets of sand spurted up around Derek as he and others were sunbathing. Now fifteen, Derek left school in the summer of 1975 but could not get a job. During this time several electrical fires broke out in the house. The central rose for the living room light burst into flames more than once. The house wiring was renewed twice in two weeks. Shortly after, he achieved his ambition of getting an apprenticeship as an electrician. And the phenomena ceased, once and for all. Over the following years the Grieves regained their interest in life, their appetite, and their peace of mind. They sent Archie Roy a Christmas card every year: 'All is well', the message read.

Sources

There is no one definitive case study, and the above summary has been pieced together from the following sources. The case first came to public light in the *Glasgow Herald*, 17 January 1975. In 1977 McHarg published his report, 'A poltergeist case from Glasgow' in the academic volume *Research in Parapsychology 1976* (McHarg stated the phenomena commenced in August or September 1974, while all other accounts gave November as the start date). Stewart

Lamont's detailed discussion in *Is Anybody There?* (1980) included extracts from David Grieve's own written account. Professor Roy wrote up the story for the *News of the World* in June 1978 ('The Case of the Council House Rowdy') and, with further extracts from David Grieve's narrative, and extensive interviews with the key participants, covered the case comprehensively in *A Sense of Something Strange* (1990). Here, for the first time, the names were pseudonymised and the location of Balornock in north Glasgow was disguised as Maxwell Park in south Glasgow. Using a different set of pseudonyms, the Revd Max Magee described his own experiences in an article for *The Christian Parapsychologist* journal in September 1991. Tapes also exist of Archie Roy speaking at the SPR, and the Revd Magee talking to the Churches' Fellowship for Psychical and Spiritual Studies. The missing piece in all these reports is any testimony from the Keenans, but the hostility of the situation meant it was impossible for them to be interviewed at the time. My Freedom of Information Request to Strathclyde Police showed that, due to the passage of time, no official records exist of the events.

Context

Northgate Quadrant's two-storey council flats were built postwar. Balornock and nearby Springburn are honeycombed with mine workings.

Interpretation

A powerfully puzzling case indeed. For the Grieves (at least initially) and the various mediums involved, this was a clear case of the intrusion of the realm of the dead into the world of the living. Yet the phenomena continued long after the 'trapped spirits' were supposedly released. The investigators could come to no conclusion, other that whatever 'it' was, it was connected to the stresses within the household, and particularly the frustrations of the two sons. Part of the case suggests the exteriorisation of internal distress, perhaps with Derek and Jeffrey as a dual focus; but Roy and Magee also suspected that the boys' mother, as well as the Brouwers' handicapped daughter, plus Gordon Keenan downstairs, may also all have been the partial focus at some points, as if the poltergeist was shifting from one person to another (remember, major disturbances took place when there was no one in the flat).

In 1977 the Enfield Poltergeist in London made worldwide headlines; many of the disturbances there were almost carbon copies of those in Balornock, as if the entity had decided to move south.

Malign, cruel, threatening, destructive, mercurial and puerile, and possibly connected to both teenage angst and terminal cancer, as well as to several different individuals and multiple locations: the Balornock poltergeist is easily one of the most baffling cases in this book.

Chapter Six

The Twentieth Century, Part III (1976-1999)

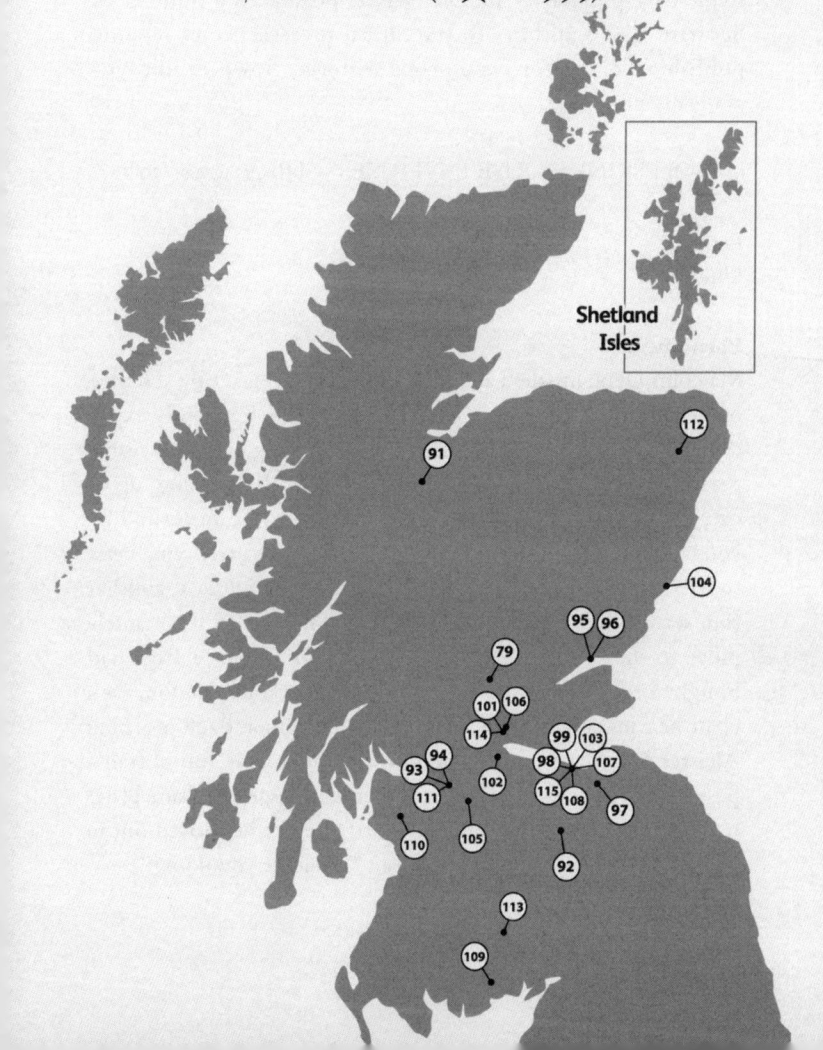

'They're here!'
It knows what scares you.

Publicity lines for the film *Poltergeist* (1982)

Cinema (*Poltergeist* I, II, and III) and television (*Ghostwatch*) helped push poltergeists into mainstream consciousness during the final quarter of the twentieth century, and almost certainly shaped interpretations of a number of cases. In the 1990s, the staggering popularity of *The X-Files* prompted a number of Scottish-based authors to start local investigations, feeding publishers' desire for paranormal material, however idiosyncratically presented.

91. BOLESKINE HOUSE, INVERNESS-SHIRE: 1970s?/1980s?

Period
Unknown.

Phenomena
Malcolm Dent, installed as a kind of live-in caretaker by absentee owner Jimmy Page of rock band Led Zeppelin, frequently experienced doors slamming all night (or all opening as if an invisible person was running through them), along with the piling up of carpets and rugs. The disturbances seemed to be instigated by construction work. One night what sounded like a terrifying beast snorted and banged outside his bedroom door, while at another time a small porcelain figure of the Devil floated off the mantelpiece to the ceiling, then smashed into the fireplace. Page had bought a set of furniture from the Café Royal in London, each chair bearing a nameplate of a famous customer. Each morning Aleister Crowley's and Marie Lloyd's chairs were found transposed – and then it was discovered that their respective nameplates had been accidentally swapped. Shortly before he moved out in 1991/2, Dent heard a voice boom out, 'What are you doing?'

The Twentieth Century, Part III: 1976-1999

Sources

Interviews with Malcolm Dent in the *Inverness Courier*, 3 November 2006, and the *Highland News*, 8 February 1997.

Context

For those interested in the occult, 'Boleskine' is a name to conjure with. Between 1899 and 1913 the large detached house on the shores of Loch Ness was home to Aleister Crowley, although the notorious magician and self-publicist was only in residence for a total of about two years during that time. In his *Confessions* Crowley goes into great detail about the demons he raised there, both accidentally and deliberately. Page, a Crowley obsessive, owned Boleskine from 1970 to 1992. Dent sometimes found himself under siege from trespassers seeking the Crowley/Page mystique. For details on the 'Great Beast', type his name into a search engine and prepare to be deluged. More on Boleskine's bizarre history can be found in the present author's *Guide to Mysterious Loch Ness*.

Interpretation

'We just used to say that was Aleister doing his thing,' said Dent of the disturbances. Crowley looms so large over Boleskine's story that alternative interpretations tend to be forced out, but quite possibly the polt wasn't Uncle Aleister or his merry demons at all.

92. PEEBLES, SCOTTISH BORDERS: 1975?-95?

Noises from empty rooms, glasses toppling, a cleaner's bucket moving; the Cross Keys Hotel may have had a typical pub ghost, a cocktail created from one part bar-room legend, one part historical notable (a former landlady), and one part the occasional uncanny incident. Sources: Norman Adams' *Haunted Scotland* (1998) and the *Daily Record*, 8 September 2007.

93. GARTLOCH HOSPITAL, GLASGOW: 1976

A student nurse in Gartloch Psychiatric Hospital was overseeing Ward 10 when she noticed the usually restless and unsettled patients were oddly quiet. She then experienced an intense and frightening sensation of 'something' behind her. At this point a stack of 45rpm records flew out of their rack and hit her arm. The following day a sister told her that odd things had happened in Ward 10 before. The witness was interviewed by Innes Smith of the Scottish Society for Psychical Research in 2008, and his report appears on the Society's website.

94. MOSSPARK, GLASGOW: 1978

Period
Several days or weeks in summer 1978.

Phenomena
'The tenant had only been in occupancy for two weeks when complaints were made about a supernatural presence in the house … although staff were naturally sceptical … it was conceded because of the obvious mental and physical effect this was having … the only answer to the problem was to rehouse this family.' Thus ran a report by Glasgow's housing management department in August 1978. Phenomena in the council house on Airth Drive included strange noises, doors opening and closing, and an apparition described as the Virgin Mary. According to an unnamed council official, the house had a history of poltergeist activity, although no further details were given. The family were relocated a short distance away at Arran Drive, also within the Mosspark housing development. When the press picked up the story in December, the former tenants vehemently denied any supernatural activity, and blamed the problems with the Airth Drive house on damp and subsidence.

The Twentieth Century, Part III: 1976-1999

Sources

The story appeared in the *Evening Times* (14 December 1978) and the *Glasgow Herald* (15 December). It came to the attention of the press because Regional Councillor James Dunnachie had compiled a dossier of unusual lets or transfers within the council house system. My Freedom of Information request failed to turn up this dossier, or any documentation relating to the episode.

Context

At one time Glasgow was the largest single owner of public housing in Western Europe, and council house disputes were common fare within the local newspapers. The house on Airth Drive had been occupied as temporary accommodation by four families over the previous eighteen months, until they were allocated tenancies elsewhere. Councillor Dunnachie went on to be the Labour MP for Glasgow Pollok, 1978-87.

Interpretation

A tough one, given the limited evidence. The reference to a vision of the Blessed Virgin Mary is intriguing, as historically, religious visionaries were often associated with poltergeist activity. However, there is no clear sense that the Virgin Mary was indeed what was seen, and the whole episode rests on shaky (or subsiding?) foundations.

95. DUNDEE: 1978

'I am a poltergeist and I have come back to haunt you!' Thus one man's torments began, the warning heard as what felt like a finger poked into his ear. Screams, screeches, scratchings on the wall, flashes of light and other phenomena followed, with such intensity that the victim asked a priest to conduct an exorcism. Later he was treated by psychiatrist Dr James McHarg, who diagnosed Temporal Lobe Epilepsy (TLE), a condition where hallucinations are created by transient electrical impulses in the temporal lobes of the brain. As TLE is not a 'florid' condition, its presence can go undetected by both the sufferer and those around them. Dr McHarg mentioned the case in 'The Paranormal and the Recognition of Personal Distress', written for the SPR's *Journal* in 1982. This is a salutary case: it shows that not every report of poltergeistic phenomena relates to objective events. Other cases in this book – particularly those with only one witness, and no corroborating evidence – may possibly be examples of neurological disruption.

96. DUNDEE: 1970s

Numerous objects moved of their own accord, and a heavy bookcase toppled over. The 'focal person' had suffered sexual abuse in childhood. Under the guidance of their GP, the family attended a clinic, and remedial social and medical solutions were implemented, at which point the phenomena ceased. Source: Dr McHarg's article cited in No.95.

97. EAST LOTHIAN: UNKNOWN

The kettle was switched on, the video recorder reset, loud bangings on the wall were heard by neighbours, apparitions were glimpsed, and two children saw a 'bad man' and a fire outside the back window. This was another of Dr McHarg's cases.

98. DUNDAS STREET, EDINBURGH: 1980s

'Lynn' was sitting in her flat drinking coffee when the mug shot out from her hand, flew through the air in a straight line and smashed against the opposite wall. Source: Ron Halliday's *Edinburgh After Dark*.

99. LEARMONTH HOTEL, EDINBURGH: 1980s

Doors: opened, closed and locked. Lights, kettles and hairdryers: switched on and off. Corridors: filled with whistling, footsteps and the passing of an invisible presence. The heyday of the hotel's ghost appears to have been the 1980s. Source: Alan Murdie's *Haunted Edinburgh* (2010).

100. CAROLE COMPTON: 1982

This case did not take place in Scotland but the focal person was Scottish and – as it is such an intriguing episode – is worth briefly considering. Carole Compton, a twenty-one year old from Ayr, worked as a nanny for two successive families in Italy. Pictures and ornaments smashed, strange scratching noises were heard – but the principal phenomena were fire-related. Labelled a witch, an Italian court found Carole guilty on two counts of arson, and one of attempted arson, but the sentence was suspended on account of the time already spent in custody and she was released. Hans Bender, a renowned poltergeist expert, visited Carole in prison and concluded she was the unconscious source, having exteriorized her unhappiness. As well as extensive press coverage at the time, Carole published a book, *Superstition: The True Story of The Nanny They Called a Witch* (1990). See No.5 for a possibly similar case of pyrokinesis.

101. SAUCHIE, CLACKMANNANSHIRE: 1986/7

Period
August(?) 1986 to February 1987 (seven months or so).

Phenomena
Here we have a unique case – three adjacent houses sharing the same phenomena. Most of the disturbances were concentrated on the central house in the block of three on Gartmorn Road, occupied by Ms H. and her eighteen-year-old daughter. To one side was Mrs P. and her family, while on the other was a third family who were not named. Over about six months the events in the main house included: a kitchen drawer opening

and a knife and fork arcing through the air to land on the floor; the TV and radio switching on and off; transient cold spots; the dog refusing to go upstairs, to the point of attempting to bite anyone trying to bring it up on the lead; the terrified animal found in an upstairs bedroom that was locked from the inside; a growling noise from a bedroom cupboard; a presence in the kitchen making a 'swishing noise'; and loud bangs – lots of them – from the loft. As these occurrences accelerated, the three families congregated for a discussion in Ms H.'s living room – only to hear wild thumping from above. The group piled into the hall, and all heard footsteps descending towards them, although the stairs were quite empty.

On the apparitional side, Mrs P.'s eight-year-old son claimed to have had several nocturnal visits from a man and a woman holding a baby; the woman often spoke to the boy, and expressed a dislike of the dog next door. And an apparent doppelganger of Ms H. was witnessed by her mother, who was staying the night: the figure walked down the stairs wearing a nightgown Ms H. did not own, silently ignored the mother's offer of a cup of tea, and then returned upstairs – all while Ms H. was asleep. There were also mimicked voices – the boyfriend of the eighteen-year-old heard her voice calling him from upstairs, although the teenage girl was actually asleep in the living room; and Ms H. heard the voice of her twenty-one-year-old son, even though she knew he was not at home. Next door, Mrs P.'s television developed a mind of its own, and she saw a man's face reflected in the glass door of the stereo unit. We are not told what occurred in the third house.

Local group Scottish Paranormal Investigations (SPI) got involved on 8 February 1987, and spent a night in the house without experiencing anything. They took the H. family to the Alloa Christian Spiritualist Church, and during the meeting, loud banging and other noises erupted from the locked and empty room above: the phenomena had followed the family. On 16 February SPI and the Spiritualists visited the house; Ms H.

was pushed off a wooden bench in the living room by invisible hands, and a few minutes later Mrs P., the neighbour, seemed to become 'possessed', chanting out a semi-nonsensical message from what seemed to be a dead woman. SPI's psychic encouraged the trapped spirits to 'move into the light'; but all three families moved away soon after, so it was not clear if the phenomena ceased at this point.

Sources
Two of the SPI investigators wrote up the case: Ron Halliday in *Evil Scotland* (2003), and Malcolm Robinson in *Paranormal Case Files of Britain* (2010). There are also mentions by Halliday in the *Evening Times* (10 March 2001) and the *Daily Record* (23 October 2003). The accounts use a plethora of variant pseudonyms for the participants, so I have tried to simplify the names in the case.

Context
The houses were built in 1937.

Interpretation
SPI investigations favoured Spiritualist/mediumistic interpretations, with an emphasis on the spirits of the dead. This view rather swamps other alternatives. I wonder, however, whether the phenomena actually centred on the eighteen-year-old daughter, who may have been the unconscious poltergeist agent. But we do not know whether she was present for most or all of the disturbances, and the details we have do not allow us to make this presumption.

102. FALKIRK: 1988-90

Six years after moving into her small council flat in Bainsford, thirty-something Ms L. had the bathroom upgraded. This may possibly have instigated a range of phenomena: luminous effects (moving red lights, a kind of 'film' of a ballerina projected onto a wall); apports (brilliant-coloured balls floating in the air); physical effects (ornaments displaced, curtains billowing with no wind); smells (perfume); noxious substances (something like blood on a door handle); touches from invisible fingers; apparitions (a male figure, and white fog or smoke); and writing appearing on the bedroom wall (the numbers 32 and 57, the letters E and D, and, in a childish scrawl, the words 'You are…'). The SPI investigation in October 1990 identified several spirits, including a two-year-old boy who had drowned in the bath, and after the medium had 'sent them into the light' the disturbances ceased. See Halliday's *Evil Scotland* and Robinson's *Paranormal Case Files of Britain*.

103. OUTER LIMITS CLUB, EDINBURGH: 1989

Period

Several weeks around January–February 1989.

Phenomena

The locus was the Outer Limits club venue in Tollcross, particularly the top storey, the Barbados Suite. Most of the events were standard polt-pub fare: glasses were found smashed on the floor below where they had been stacked overnight; bottles of whisky, cleaning liquids and cloths were displaced; doors opened and closed without reason; pools of water formed on the floor. But one morning a heavy industrial vacuum cleaner moved round the floor by itself. And it wasn't plugged in. This event was made even more spectacular by the coloured lights in the ceiling flashing on and off, without a controlling human agency.

Cleaning staff heard scratching sounds during the day, and female screams echoed round the empty building. One morning several cleaners taking a cigarette break in the Bermuda Triangle area of the club on the first floor saw a male figure enter through the door from the bar, appear clearly in the wall-mirrors – and then vanish.

Sources
Ron Halliday was called in by the club during February 2009 and wrote the case up for *Edinburgh After Dark* (2010).

Context
The owners were concerned about their staff's experiences and not seeking to create a 'haunted club' vibe for commercial purposes.

Interpretation
A member of staff psychically identified the ghost as a young woman who was killed on the premises, while, from the line-up of spirit suspects, a medium picked out a twenty-year-old man who had died from a fire in a previous building on the site. Which just goes to show that you picks your psychic and you takes your choice. No other options were apparently considered.

104. JOHNSHAVEN, ABERDEENSHIRE: 1990s

Period
Unknown.

Phenomena
Let's start with the usual. We have the fire alarm and the cooker going on and off; objects disappearing, only to be returned after several days; sounds of footsteps, voices, children playing and a dog padding up the stairs; and doors slamming shut and locking. Now move up a step. A girl is pushed off her bed and scratched; a black blanket-like haze appears; the apparition of a little girl manifests in the lounge and stairway; ghostly visitors force the children to play games at night; and a carpet of mist approaches the house, creeps in through the living room window and thickens into a cloud in which can be discerned the shapes of people. Finally, the climax: you pop out to the shop for fifteen minutes, and return to find your kitchen crawling with maggots.

Sources
The report is in Ron Halliday's 2003 *Evil Scotland*.

Context
The end-terrace house was a new build overlooking the sea. The family consisted of grandmother, mother and at least two children. The events started about a month after they moved in.

Interpretation
The mother seemed to blame the events on her use of a Ouija board, but the details are scant.

105. MOTHERWELL, NORTH LANARKSHIRE: 1990s?

Toiletries, ornaments and library books went missing without explanation in Brian Mackenzie's house. Footsteps were heard on the stairs late at night. But most bizarrely, a 6in envelope leapt off a table in the living room, landed flat on the floor, and then rose on its end and spun round like a top for thirty seconds. Source: Ron Halliday's *Evil Scotland*.

106. TILLICOULTRY, CLACKMANNANSHIRE: 1990s?

Gel and toothpaste smeared across bathroom walls; ornaments relocated from the mantelpiece to the kitchen floor; running footsteps on bare boards at night; a dark shadow passing through a wall. A medium told the flat-owner that the disturbances were caused by the spirit of a child who drowned in a well in the mill grounds. Which is the kind of thing that mediums tend to diagnose rather a lot (he said cynically). From Ron Halliday's *Evil Scotland*.

107. THE NEW TOWN, EDINBURGH: 1992-97

Paul Haig, former lead singer with post-punk group Josef K, lived with a poltergeist for five years in his large New Town flat. Phenomena included the television switching itself on, the attic hatch high up on the bathroom ceiling being pushed open, chills in the hallway, and a hazy presence following his girlfriend out of the bedroom. Source: an interview in the *Sunday Times*, 18 October 2009.

108. SOUTH BRIDGE/NIDDRY STREET VAULTS, EDINBURGH: 1994-96

> 'Be Warned!! The vaults are dark and often damp. Also, the South Bridge Poltergeist has been known to attack. People genuinely experience health problems and stress within the haunted vault. You enter at your own risk.'
>
> Auld Reekie Tours website

Welcome to the latest development in the wonderful and frightening world of the paranormal – the poltergeist as commercial attraction.

Period
December 1994 to 1996-ish (two years, or maybe longer).

Phenomena
Moving down the shop-lined, traffic-clogged thoroughfare of Edinburgh's South Bridge, you have no sense whatsoever that you are on a bridge – except at one point, where a gap in the buildings allows you to gaze down on Cowgate several storeys below. The urban architecture completely obscures the fact that you are crossing a valley between two low hills. South Bridge was completed in 1785-88, one of five major bridges constructed between 1765 and 1833 to link the medieval Old Town on Edinburgh Rock with the expanding city being built on the surrounding hills. Other than the Cowgate underpass, all the twenty giant arches of the viaduct are invisible behind buildings, some of which are nine storeys high here. These arches were infilled with vaults and chambers, initially used for storage by merchants and shopkeepers. Then small tradesmen set

up shop in the windowless spaces. But these more-or-less respectable citizens were driven out by the cold and damp, and the vaults degenerated into a noisome, filthy rookery: a subterranean slum. Late nineteenth-century social reforms eventually saw the lightless vaults evacuated and sealed off. In the 1980s they were 'rediscovered', and several used for practice by rock bands, or cellar storage for pubs. Other businesses took an interest, and in 1994 the first tours started – not as 'ghost tours', but as an extension of the ever-popular historical walking tours. And then things started to go polt-shaped.

The dense mass of buildings that rises out of the valley of Cowgate, Niddry Street and South Niddry Street to tower above the hidden viaduct of South Bridge has long had a series of minor poltergeistery. A spirit nicknamed 'the imp' was blamed for the hiding or relocation of objects in various premises, from pub cellars to shops and backpacker hostels. In December 1994, at Whistle Binkies, a pub recently opened up in the converted chambers, a barmaid left an orange on the bar, turned her back for a few seconds – only to find the fruit had been peeled and segmented during that time. The pub clock persistently stopped at 4.15 a.m. In February 1995 a barmaid found herself trapped in the cellar; after ten minutes the inexplicably stuck door swung open by itself. Shuffling and other frightening noises were reported from the same cellar over the next couple of months. From April 1995 it seemed as if the imp was active in the vaults as well. Torches were the main target, flickering, failing, or dimming in certain chambers then regaining their power in the next room. On one tour every single torch in a group of twelve went out. As the torch-pranks faded out after three months, they started to be replaced with light-based phenomena – green glows, cross-shaped lights, and bright luminescence.

In July 1995 the phenomena escalated. A woman was grabbed by something. A backpacker had his rucksack emptied as he was wearing it. The following month an eleven-year-old boy was scratched on his arm. Come November, the polt was amusing itself by switching off a workman's radio. Cold spots were now being detected, and individuals started collapsing on the tour. Through 1996 there were aggressive but invisible attacks on visitors and tour guides alike, and one vault was now dubbed the Haunted Chamber (initial capitals compulsory). A large wooden barrier was tipped over, narrowly missing a tour group. People reported 'freezing spots', where the temperature dropped so low it was painful.

In February 1996, with permission, a coven of white witches built a pagan temple in one of the vaults. The leader, George Cameron, spent a night alone in the lightless chamber and was convinced something evil was trying to get into the circle of low stones. Other people identified a mirror set up in the temple as a portal through which a demonic force was gaining entry. From August to October the circle was mysteriously flooded; when the circle was moved to another vault, the inundation ceased.

Events slowed to a trickle from 1997, although occasional encounters are still reported (as of 2012). The vast majority of episodes in recent years have actually been of apparitions, rather than poltergeist activities. The apparitional events have been dubbed the 'South Bridge Entity'.

Sources
The key text is Jan-Andrew Henderson's *The Town Below the Ground: Edinburgh's Legendary Underground City* (1999), with the same author's *Edinburgh: City of the Dead* (2004) providing an update on the South Bridge Entity. More information can be found in Gordon Rutter's *Paranormal Edinburgh* (2009).

Context
Three rival tour companies provide visits to different sections of the vaults. Is it a coincidence that people pay good money for a ghost tour, and then claim to experience something strange? Could expectation, heightened anxiety, group-think and collective social pressures account for many of the reported events? Gosh, could it even be the case that exaggeration creeps into the narrative? For commercial gain? Surely not.

Interpretation

The physical environment of the vaults is purpose-built for the employment of adjectives such as 'creepy', 'scary' and 'eerie'. And indeed an experiment conducted by parapsychologists in the South Niddry vaults during the 2001 Edinburgh International Science Festival showed that many participants were predisposed to interpret elements in the environment – such as a slight draft, or an especially darkened area – as paranormal in nature (see 'An investigation into alleged "Hauntings"' by Richard Wiseman *et al* in *The British Journal of Psychology*, 2003). In the end, events at the South Bridge vaults are experienced through the lens of both commercial activity and the excitement of a tourist-friendly space in central Edinburgh where there is the possibility of encountering repeating phenomena. Does this mean everything is fake? No. Does it mean everything is real? Probably not.

109. DALBEATTIE, DUMFRIES & GALLOWAY: 1995

As is often the case, this episode in a clothes shop started with minor incidents: lights switched on, locked doors opened. One November morning stock was scattered over the floor. The following day hanks of wool were displaced to other parts of the shop, while the floor was carpeted with baby clothing. On the third day it was the turn of the wedding gowns to go walkabout. Staff and police confirmed that nothing had been stolen, the money was still in the till, and there was no sign of forced entry. Owner Linda Williamson brought in Canon Kevin Conway, whose ministrations dispelled the polt. The report was in the *Glasgow Herald*, 27 November 1995.

110. DALRY, NORTH AYRSHIRE: 1990s?

When the owners of Woodside's Ironmongers shop opened up, they found some of the stock scattered over the floor, wire baskets in the aisles, and shoes displaced. This happened over several mornings, and there was no sign of burglary or forced entry. A relative told author Dane Love, who included it in his *Scottish Spectres* (2001). For another 1990s shop polt, see No.79 (Crieff).

III. DRUMCHAPEL, GLASGOW: 1995

In this very strange episode we return to John Adams, the subject of No.88 from the 1970s.

Period
Weeks or months.

Phenomena
From October 1995 a poltergeist entered John Adams' life once more; this, however, was not the (relatively) benign entity that called itself 'Jonathon', but something much more malevolent; something that claimed it was a demon.

The entity announced its presence by banging on the furniture and roof, after which John was pulled out of bed and thrown around the room. Objects were cast off bedroom tables onto the floor, doors were slammed, carpets moved, and lamps and furniture shifted around. Phenomena increased in violence, and John felt something was hovering over him trying to invade his body and mind. One time his face was pressed into a cushion as if suffocation was intended. He tried communicating with the entity, first picking out letters arrayed below a pendulum, and then via automatic writing, where his hand was guided by an unseen scribe. Hundreds of messages came through from dozens of spirits, including self-proclaimed demons with names such as Jinfer, Ceber, Volfufnah and Ruster. The messages were often gibberish, but the coherent ones included:

'In December 1992 I got involved in a fight with [deleted] in Drumchapel and he killed me. I am [deleted] from Balornock and I'm being held in your body by demons.'

'I will get out of your body now. You must believe that I'm going to leave you. And you must be brave as you will feel groggy and you will be sick.'

'I will not be flesh much longer as I am getting weaker and I won't be getting any more power as you have found a believer who is praying for you. You are fading and I won't be able to possess you anymore after tonight.'

'I am going in half an hour. I must leave your body before I go and you will have to go to bed before then. And you must take the crosses off and be brave.'

Even stranger, several communications were from extraterrestrials, one of which concerned a UFO crash in Arizona in 1961. Apparitions included a figure formed from twisted strands of red and blue electrical discharge, and something like an orang-utan with a human face. One demon – by name Ibeza, supposedly an angel – made the link with John's previous poltergeist. 'I am going to catch Jonathon for you,' it said, and told John that Jonathan, aka 'JV', was responsible for the ongoing torture.

Sources
Ron Halliday met John Adams several times and wrote up the case in *Haunted Glasgow* (2008). Other than the victim's direct testimony, the degree of any supporting evidence is ambiguous.

Context
At the time of the events, John Adams was in his early sixties, and living alone in Drumchapel.

Interpretation
John sought assistance from Christian groups and mediums. He was utterly convinced of the reality of the demons, although he did not believe any of their communications. I think this is the kind of case that would have benefited from the insights of someone such as the late Dr McHarg (see Nos 90, 95 and 96).

The Twentieth Century, Part III: 1976-1999

112. METHLICK, ABERDEENSHIRE: 1996

Period

1996.

Phenomena

Several members of a family reported a 'bad atmosphere' in part of their croft and within the cab of their lorry. They saw objects move, glimpsed a moving shape, felt that a malign presence was watching them, and became fearful at one particular spot in the garden. Headaches and anxiety became their daily experience. The local authority checked if radon emission or electrical fields were responsible. Assistance was then sought from both the local dowser and the Revd Angus Haddow of Methlick parish church. No one other than the family witnessed the object movements, but the minister had the sensation that one of the rooms had an unpleasant feel to it. He brought the family together in prayer and blessed the 'evil' rooms. Meanwhile two dowsers found an unusual grid-like pattern of 'lines of force' around the croft. The family did not get in touch again, so presumably the problems ceased.

Sources

The Revd Haddow's unpublished book *Dowsing for Patterns of the Past* is available online at http://historyandmysterytours.blogspot.co.uk. Several details, such as the exact date, and the nature of the household, were clarified through personal communication with the now-retired minister in April 2012.

Context

The buildings were isolated and at a distance from other crofts, so it is unlikely the family were being persecuted by a malicious neighbour. The clergyman noted that the family were troubled by a (unspecified) domestic dispute, and that at some time earlier a young man had committed suicide in the house.

Interpretation
The dowser diagnosed the lines of force as severe geopathic stress, connected to underground water channels; the very centre of these invisible forces was the room of the house with the bad atmosphere. Haddow noticed that the family's headaches became worse during the waxing moon, while they reduced in intensity in wet weather. The conclusion seemed to be that the already disturbed psychological situation within the household was exacerbated by energies generated by the geology. Frustratingly, we have no descriptions of the movement of objects.

113. AULDGIRTH, DUMFRIES & GALLOWAY: 1993 & 1997

In 1993 a family living in a cottage on the Blackwood Estate near Auldgirth were plagued by the slamming of heavy doors, cries as if of a child in pain, the noise of furniture shifting in the empty kitchen (without the chairs physically being moved), touches and grabs by invisible fingers, footsteps, a chiming noise unlike that of a clock, and several apparitions. In September 1997 the cottage was back in the news. A second set of tenants quit, citing locked doors opening by themselves then slamming shut, lights turning on and off, a stench of rotten meat with no source, swarms of flies, and sightings of an apparition. As of March 1998, the company leasing the cottage was obliged to inform prospective tenants of the haunting. Source: the *Sunday Mail*, 14 September 1997 and 22 March 1998.

114. SAUCHIE, CLACKMANNANSHIRE: 1999-2000

Period
Summer(?) 1999-June 2000 (twelve months?).

Phenomena
Around two weeks after moving into their council house in 1999, James and Mandy Maxwell experienced various phenomena: a

baby crying, a nailed-shut cupboard door repeatedly flying open, doors slamming, lightbulbs exploding, bangs, a sense of presence, rustling sounds from an empty carrier bag, object displacement, and sightings of a dark figure that rippled like water. Mandy had been pinned to the wall and thrown across the bedroom. The parents and children were sleeping in the same room, and James had festooned the house with crucifixes. Brian Allan of Strange Phenomena Investigations visited the house and detected nothing. The disturbances ceased to be reported, so perhaps they stopped.

Sources
The story broke in *The Wee County News* in June 2000, in which it was erroneously stated that the house was the very one which had hosted the famous 1960 Sauchie Poltergeist (No.76). In reality, the house was merely on the same street as the Virginia Campbell case. A further story appeared in *The Scotsman* on 20 July 2000. Allan's report was included in Malcolm Robinson's *Paranormal Case Files of Great Britain* (2010). A few other details are in Ron Halliday's *Evil Scotland* (2003).

Context
The location was a fairly typical semi-detached council house.

Interpretation
Allan's report is ambiguous, and can be interpreted as (a) the poltergeist agent was one of the children, or (b) there was no poltergeist, merely a circle of fear, in which the frightened adults were infecting the children with their anxieties, which then made things worse.

115. GREYFRIARS KIRKYARD, EDINBURGH: 1999-2012?

'Is this graveyard the home of Edinburgh's scariest poltergeist?'
Headline in the *Edinburgh Evening News*, 3 July 1999

Period
January 1999-2012? (thirteen years?).

Phenomena
A tabloid journalist once told me that for a murder to penetrate public consciousness, it has to have a title – the Acid Bath Killer, the Lady in the Lake, the Moors Murders, and so on. This identity – which is often invented by the media – becomes the murder's 'brand name', if you will. And here we have a poltergeist with a brand name. The Mackenzie Poltergeist is, arguably, one of the most famous supernatural entities in the world, its fame spread by media and the thousands of visitors who have taken the City of the Dead graveyard tour, during which, as of 2012, over 450 incidents have taken place across thirteen years. The events are documented, and many appear to be genuine. The brand works its magic; but the name's about as authentic as a politician's election promise.

The narrative of events commences in late December 1998, with a homeless man seeking shelter by worming his way into the Mackenzie Tomb in Greyfriars Cemetery. The structure is an impressive if dour-looking cylinder with a bell-shaped roof. The circular space on the ground floor was empty, but contained a grille set into the floor. Lifting this, the vagrant descended a flight of stairs into a crypt filled with several elaborate coffins. Attempting to break into one of the coffins – in the hope that there might have been something worth stealing inside – the man fell through a weak area of the floor and landed face down in a sub-crypt overflowing with graveyard dirt and mouldering skeletons. His terrified exit was witnessed by a late-night dog-walker, who called the police; they investigated, found nothing had been damaged, and closed the case. About a week later, a woman peering through the small viewing window set in the front of the monument was pushed onto her back by what she said was a blast of frozen air from within. A month later various visitors pottering round one of the tombs a few dozen yards away reported bittersweet smells, a sensation of intense cold or nausea, and laughing noises. Interested parties made the link that something had been disturbed in the Mackenzie Tomb, had exited, and had relocated a stone's throw away in an entirely unrelated mausoleum. This was 'obviously' the spirit of 'Bluidy' George Mackenzie, lawyer, politician and, from one point of view, seventeenth-century mass murderer.

But a moment's reflection will show that this identification is utterly bogus. Let us grant for the moment that the tramp's intrusion did disturb something supernatural (although bones have been dug up and redistributed in the vastly overcrowded graveyard for two centuries, without the aggrieved owners of the bones complaining about it). And let us stretch credulity to the point that this phantasm gathers its strength for a week before taking flight at the very moment that a tourist is peeking through the viewing window. And then let us assume that this now homeless spirit blithely takes up residence in an entirely different tomb, one which – unlike many of its neighbours – happens to still retain its roof, thus making for a dark, claustrophobic space, coincidentally the perfect location to generate uneasy feelings in visiting humans. Even if all this is allowed to pass, there is the slight issue of identification: there are dozens of bodies in the Mackenzie tomb, some of which were deposited well after George Mackenzie died in 1691, and any one of them could provide the source for the putative ghost. And the skeleton of George Mackenzie is still at rest in one of the fancy coffins, while the nameless bodies in the sub-crypt are the ones that were desecrated.

But there's the rub. Unnamed corpses of long-forgotten nobodies do not a brand name make. But Sir George Mackenzie – well, if you want a famous historical figure, and a pantomime villain to boot, here you go. Mackenzie started as a liberal-minded lawyer who supported the Covenant, the grouping of Presbyterians who opposed Charles I's attempts to impose English-style Anglican Church worship on Scotland. In later life, as King's Lord Advocate under Charles II, Mackenzie persecuted

Poltergeist over Scotland

the Covenanters, and sent thousands to their doom. Several hundred Covenanters were imprisoned in part of Greyfriars Kirkyard, in a walled enclosure open to the skies, suffering the Edinburgh winter while armed guards patrolled outside what was effectively a concentration camp. This locus of death and suffering was later called the Covenanters' Prison, and later still the long rectangular enclosure became lined with the tombs of Edinburgh's well-heeled. And it was in one of these mausolea that visitors were reporting strange events. The irony of having Mackenzie's uneasy spirit active in the prison where many of his victims died was too delicious to ignore. And so the events in the Covenanters' Prison were now well and truly established as instigated by the poltergeist of 'Bluidy' George Mackenzie, even though there is no link whatsoever. One more tweak to the story was required, however: the haunted location needed a better name than just 'that stone tomb on the left in the Covenanters' Prison with the roof and the iron gate, no, not that one, the other one'. And so the name of the Black Mausoleum was born. The Mackenzie Poltergeist and the Black Mausoleum are now Scotland's leading supernatural brand names: marketing genius.

And while we are on the subject of spurious namings, in 1999 it was claimed that the Mackenzie Poltergeist of Greyfriars Kirkyard was the same as the attacking entity that sporadically manifested several hundred yards away in the South Bridge/Niddry Street Vaults from 1994 to 1996 (see No. 108). Other than the allegedly similar *modus operandi*, the link was based on the utterly amazing fact that 1) Mackenzie was buried in Greyfriars and 2) he lived not far from Niddry Street. Gosh, I'm convinced, aren't you? It makes perfect sense when you see it explained like that. According to both Jan-Andrew Henderson's book on the Mackenzie Poltergeist, *The Ghost that Haunted Itself*, and the *Edinburgh Evening News* for 3 July 1999, the link with the Niddry Street events was suggested by a visiting American parapsychologist, R.D. Slaither. I have searched the paranormal literature in vain for any articles by, or mentions of, Mr Slaither; if he is out there, please get in touch.

The Twentieth Century, Part III: 1976-1999

Putting aside the role of how a good brand name helps ensure commercial success, what about the events themselves? In March 1999 Jan-Andrew Henderson formed City of the Dead tours, with exclusive access to the walled Covenanters' Prison, which, having been long open to all, was now locked up. At this stage the tours were historical in nature, with stories of ghosts and ghouls added in for entertainment. The few earlier reports of odd goings-on in the newly christened Black Mausoleum had not yet reached a wider audience. On 17 June 1999 eleven-year-old Megan Bilingsly from Leeds emerged from the Covenanters' Prison to find blood on her arm; she had been gouged with four strokes. Two days later a woman collapsed in the Black Mausoleum after complaining of freezing cold. On 25 June another woman reported something had pulled her hair. On 1 July several in the group heard a rumbling noise from the dark rear of the structure. A woman collapsed on 8 July. Two days later a twelve-year-old boy felt something touching his hair and emerged with cuts on his forehead. 15 August brought more thumping, and a massive temperature drop. On 20 August another visitor fainted.

And so it went on. That first summer was the start of many years of astral assaults, many involving visible scratches, burns, cuts and bruises. To date (2012), around 140 people have collapsed or had to be helped from the tomb. Others have reported being pushed, punched or pulled. Rumblings and thumps have been heard inside the mausoleum, and cold spots and smells reported. These experiences are gathered by the tour company, and include witness statements, photographs and video footage. The attacks certainly do not take place on every visit, and vary in frequency over the years. It has to be said that incidents have declined in number since 2005.

It is obvious that in many ways this, as poltergeists go, is hardly typical. Even more curiously, in January 2000 poltergeistery started to be reported in some of the flats overlooking the graveyard from Candlemaker Row. Gail Baird returned from shopping to find her entire collection of fluffy animal toys had been built into a pyramid on her bed. At 2.30 a.m. she and her boyfriend came home to a flat where all the pictures had been removed from their wall-hooks and stacked in a neat pile in the middle of the floor. At other times the shower room door opened of itself, and items were displaced from the living-room to the kitchen. Claire Valentine found a pair of shoes (including one that she had lost) lined up neatly on her bed. Glasses and toothbrushes were displaced from room to room. Doors opened and closed. Multiple voices were heard, as well as sounds of giggling or breathing. Minor electrical disturbances took place, even when the item (such as a bedside light) was disconnected from the mains. Of three glasses standing upright on Wilson Chapel's draining board, one smashed into pieces, a second was cut in half, and the third disappeared; it was found in its original position the following morning. And in Jan-Andrew Henderson's flat, the bead curtain at the bathroom door swished again and again, as if someone kept running to the loo.

Sources
Testimony from many dozens of witnesses, including all those mentioned above, are in Henderson's *The Ghost That Haunted Itself* (2001) and *Edinburgh: City of the Dead* (2004), both of which have much more from an insider's point of view. NB: tour guide 'Ben Scott', the main character in the first book, is Henderson himself. The website for Henderson's company Black Hart Entertainment hosts numerous photographs of injuries suffered by visitors on the tours, as well as excerpts from the American TV series *The World's Scariest Places* – if you can overlook the risible script and presentation, the programme's witness interviews are of interest. For a sampling of media coverage, try: *Edinburgh Evening News* (3 July 1999; 6 and 15 November 1999; 6 January, 5 May and 20 and 31 October 2000; 25 January; 17 September and 31 October 2001; and 8 November 2004); *The Big Issue* (September 1999); *Daily Record* (7 January 2000; 24 February 2001; and 30 October 2006); *The Scotsman* (29 January,

6 March and 24 July 2000); *Sunday Telegraph* (23 April 2000); *Daily Mirror* (24 July 2000).

In 2000 Canadian folklorist Joy Fraser studied the way City of the Dead used the 'fear factor' as a means of attracting business. Her resulting MA thesis, *Never Give Up the Ghost: An Analysis of Three Edinburgh Ghost Tour Companies* (2005) can be inspected at the School of Scottish Studies. Ron Halliday's *Edinburgh After Dark* includes an episode in which medium Gary Gray said the graveyard was 'jumping with spirits', but that the area of the Covenanters' Prison was entirely free of ghostly activity.

Context

In the summer, office workers sunbathe on the graveslabs; in the winter, shadows, mists and rain can turn Greyfriars into every horror movie cliché going. The Covenanters' Prison is a walled rectangle about 100 yards long in the south of the cemetery; even if you do not take the tour, you can peer through the padlocked gates, while the Mackenzie Tomb 40 yards away is a popular stop.

Interpretation

I'm sure many readers will be thinking, 'heightened expectation and a fearful build-up equals psychosomatic behaviour'. The guide asks anyone who is pregnant, claustrophobic or prone to panic attacks to stay outside, theatrically unlocks the gates, ushers up to thirty or forty people into a dark, almost pitch-black stone-walled tomb, and starts telling stories about what happened to previous tour groups. The fear factor is palpable. Strangers clutch each other. Everyone is on high alert for the slightest noise. Other complex emotions are also in play. Everyone present knows about the poltergeist, and most (openly or secretly) want the poltergeist to attack; they would just rather it didn't attack them.

It is entirely possible that the interesting events mentioned in the four flats have mundane explanations. On the other hand, I can't think of any normal circumstances, short of an intruder with OCD, that can explain the arrangement of cuddly toys into a pyramid, or a missing shoe placed neatly with its partner onto a bed. It seems to me that the Candlemaker Row disturbances might well be an entirely different set of phenomena to the so-called Mackenzie Poltergeist, with no causal connection: just an accident of geography. There again, perhaps the entity has read *Dr Jekyll and Mr Hyde* by Edinburgh's own Robert Louis Stevenson, and is nice to the flat-owners and nasty to the tourists.

In terms of any kind of focus, the visitors are obviously different each night, and the events do not 'favour' any one particular guide over another. Perhaps the 'attacking entity' draws its energy (or whatever it is that poltergeists utilise) from group emotions. Or perhaps not. Jan-Andrew Henderson toys with several hypotheses in his books – discarnate intelligence, ghost, human pheromones, electro-magnetic forces, human 'inductors' (focal persons) – but admits he has no idea what the Mackenzie Poltergeist actually is. And neither do I.

Chapter Seven

The Twenty-First Century (to 2012)

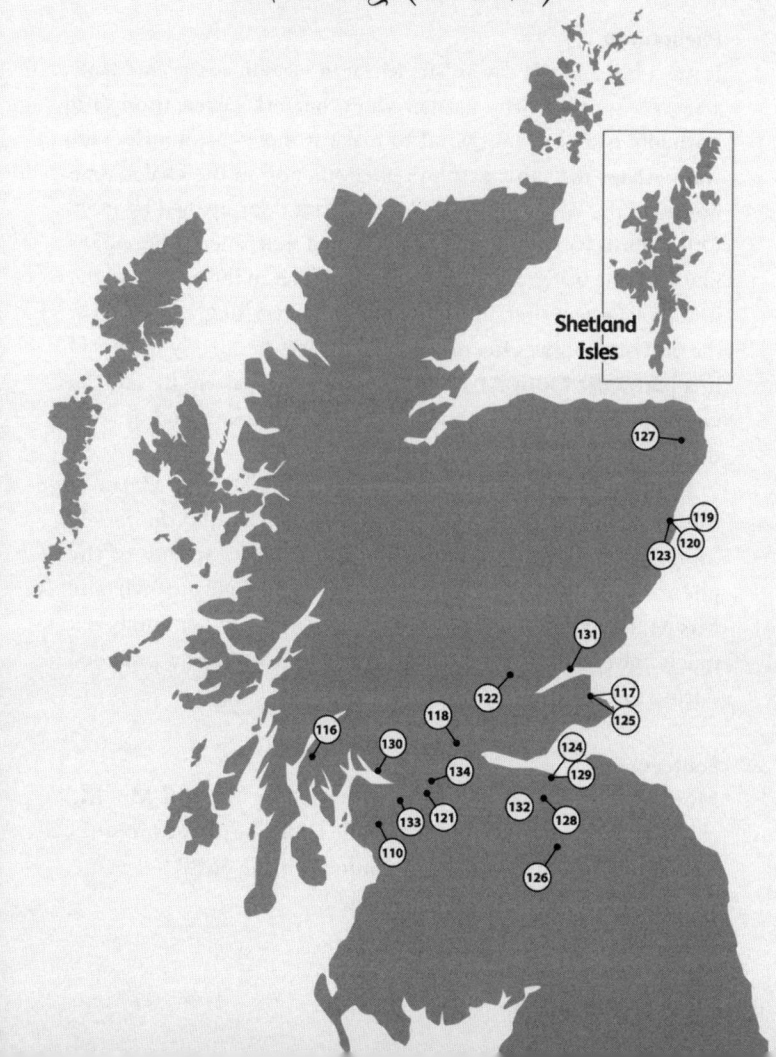

'The antics of aliens and poltergeists, when all is said and done, are often less interesting than those of the people who see them.'
Jeremy Harte, *Alternative Approaches to Folklore*, 1996

116. WEST OF SCOTLAND: 2000

Period
Two or three weeks in September 2000.

Phenomena
It was a hot and still day as Mrs M. sat in her sun-room. Suddenly a seesaw swing in the garden went 'berserk', even though it normally took a strong wind to make it move just a little. This was perhaps the most extreme phenomenon in the chalet-type house on the West Coast. The locked front door opened by itself. Other doors banged, rattled and slammed shut. There were noises like dripping water, heavy footsteps, bangings in the eaves, and the sound of a typewriter, including the distinctive 'ting' of the bell at the end of the line. One of the two cats was frequently distressed in a particular room. At 3 a.m. one morning, passers-by saw the entire house lit up, even though everyone was asleep and, as far as they knew, all the lights had been switched off.

Daphne Plowman, John Plowman and Catriona Malan of the Scottish Society for Psychical Research visited the family on 9 September 2000. The team did not witness any of the phenomena, but were convinced by the veracity of Mr and Mrs M. The following day Mrs M. phoned to say her family felt much better about the situation after the reassurances provided during the visit.

Sources
Most of the phenomena were witnessed by Mr and Mrs M., either singly or together, but the whole family heard the footsteps. The anonymised report was published on the SSPR's website; some confidential material was omitted.

The Twenty-First Century

Context

There were two sons (nine and thirteen) and a seven-year-old daughter. All three suffered health problems and the two youngest had learning difficulties.

Interpretation

The investigators recognised the stress caused by the children's medical conditions and wondered whether the teenage boy was a poltergeist focus. An alternative possibility centred on a mound of stones in the back garden, which Mrs M. had considered turning into a rockery. This may have been an ancient burial mound (at this point film fans, familiar with the plot device in the *Poltergeist* movie of the disturbed Indian burial ground, will be pleased to hear that the rockery idea was abandoned).

117. ST ANDREWS, FIFE: 2000

After living in her house for eight years, 'Sophie' converted her attic into a bedroom for her youngest daughter. Once the teenager moved in, her television turned itself on and off and the volume increased or decreased at random, the iron switched on, items were displaced and footsteps heard. On 25 October 2000 Sophie wrote to Katie Coutts, the resident psychic on *The Sun*, who suggested the disturbances were focused on a large doll in the corner of the attic, and recommended throwing it out immediately.

118. STIRLING TOLBOOTH: 2000-02

Period

Occasionally during 2000-2002.

Phenomena

Extensive renovations at the Tolbooth, Stirling's former centre of justice and administration, uncovered a pine coffin containing a skeleton. The body was identified as Allan Mair, the last person to be hanged in Stirling. The building already had a low-level history of apparitions; when it re-opened as the new arts centre in 2000, the occasional visible ghosts were augmented by more frequent poltergeist disturbances. Wine glasses flew off tables. Door handles turned by themselves. The doors of a spirits cabinet in the cellars shook violently, and bottles tumbled out to smash on the floor. The gas tap in the cellar kept turning on. Noises as if of a body being dragged across the floor were heard, and staff found part of the structure 'creepy'. In May 2002 an exorcism was suggested, but I do not think this actually took place.

Sources
The story is in Roddy Martine's *Supernatural Scotland* (2003). In 2010 I toured the building and could find no staff who had experienced anything unusual.

Context
Allan Mair was hanged outside the Tolbooth on 4 October 1843 for bludgeoning his partner Mary Fletcher to death. After his trial he spent his last weeks in the Tolbooth's condemned cell, and was buried beneath the original pend that ran below the courthouse from Jail Wynd into the prison courtyard. Eighty-four years old and possessed of a foul character, Mair attained a posthumous fame by becoming a fixture in the commercial ghost tours run in the town during the 1990s – before the skeleton was uncovered.

Interpretation
It's all too easy to assume that, because Allan Mair's bones were disturbed in 2000, his spirit decided to start infesting the fancy new arts centre and restaurant. Pfft! Here we should note three things: 1) polts often have a connection with renovations; 2) the Tolbooth has a dark past, and staff cannot fail to be aware that they were working where jail cells and prison workspaces once stood; and 3) the present building still has spaces that can spook the imagination late at night. The events may well have been evidence of

genuine poltergeist activity, or they could be our old friends the Three Misses: misperception, misinterpretation and misattribution.

119. THE OLD KING'S HIGHWAY PUB, ABERDEEN: 2000?–08?

This is an aquaphile polt: a sink in the First Floor Bar flooded, even through its tap had no water source, and elsewhere mysterious puddles appeared on the floor with no obvious source. Airborne objects included a pot of paper clips and a fork. A customer's mobile received a call from the bar landline – which no one was using, as confirmed by the customer, who had the phone in plain sight at the time. A member of staff heard their name called from the empty cellar. Strange shadows were glimpsed in the mirrors of the First Floor Bar. Male and female apparitions were reported looking outside the ground-floor windows. The experiences of staff and customers were collected by East of Scotland Paranormal before an investigation on 28 July 2008, and published on their website www.esparanormal.org.uk. A summary is in my *Guide to Mysterious Aberdeen* (2010). Note: pub polts are often calendrically vague; the dates 2000 to 2008 are approximate.

120. ABERDEEN AREA: 2002?

Period
Unknown – probably 2001/2002.

Phenomena
Bangs, footsteps, voices, and furniture movement were alarming enough, but when their eight-year-old daughter woke with scratches on her leg, the twenty-something couple called in psychic Tom Rannachan. Rannachan spent a terrifying night alone in the property, experiencing everything from noises (crashes, thumps, doors slamming shut upstairs, footsteps on the staircase, draggings, heavy breathing, and smashing glass) to electrical disturbances (lights fusing

time after time, the TV coming on at full volume) and disgusting smells (vomit and overpowering body odour). The handle of the toilet door turned as Tom watched, and the kitchen door handle rattled as if someone was trying to enter. In the darkness, the psychic's new torch battery failed, so he was forced to operate by candlelight. At some point he acquired four deep scratches on his neck.

Rannachan felt persecuted by two ghosts, male and female, both of which he could see and hear. The very tall man in particular 'hunted' the psychic, creating pandemonium as he rampaged through the property and shouting 'Thomas'. After an intense confrontation in which Rannachan prayed out loud at the predatory phantom, the house became quiet.

Sources
The episode is recounted at length in Rannachan's *Psychic Scotland* (2007). No independent corroboration exists.

Context
The location was a converted nineteenth-century gatehouse within 20 miles of Aberdeen.

Interpretation
Rannachan has a lifelong history of communication with the spirit world, and so obviously approaches cases from this perspective.

121. GLASGOW: 2000s?

Building workers were quitting because they were suffering slaps and kicks from an unseen agency, so the developer called in psychic Tom Rannachan. That night, several nails were thrown at both men, and a deep voice shouted 'Get out!' The developer fled, leaving Tom alone to deal with several abusive and violent ghosts. A heavy object was thrown at the psychic, who had a shouting match with the spirits before storming off. After that the disturbances stopped. Source: Tom Rannachan, *Psychic Scotland* (2007).

▲ The Twenty-First Century ◢

122. A MEDICAL CENTRE, PERTH & KINROSS: 2001-2002

Period
October 2001-July 2002 (nine months).

Phenomena
In October 2001 cleaners at a medical practice started finding the staff name cards removed from their rota pockets and spread in a fan-like shape on the floor below. This typically occurred between the practice being locked at 6.30 p.m. and the cleaners working in the area between 7 p.m. and 8.30 p.m. Magazines from the waiting room were also fanned across the floor, sometimes behind the backs of the cleaners. Twice on the same night the practice manager, working late, found a line of pamphlets arranged like stepping stones, marking her route to and from the reception area. A few minutes after a cleaner passed through the reception, a pot plant was displaced (safely) from the desk onto the middle of the floor. On one occasion, the sound of a crying child was heard.

After a few months of similar disturbances by the 'Practice Ghost', staff started to log the events. On 5 and 12 March 2002 light switches were seen to move. Around the same time a child's chair in the play area rocked to and fro. On 22 March the words 'I love you Mum' appeared chalked on the kids' blackboard. 5 April saw a dish tipped over in the dental area and the rota cards fanned out again. In May a blanket on an examination couch was disturbed. On 3 July two coats were displaced off hooks into a sink of water.

On 23 July psychic investigator Archie Lawrie visited with a medium, who made contact with the spirit of a four-year-old boy from a tinker family; he had been killed by his drunken father in 1918 and buried close by. The spirit did not want to 'go into the light' but the investigators were confident that the phenomena would die down now the restless spirit had been given a voice.

Sources
Lawrie included the case in his *Psychic Investigators Casebook, Volume 1* (2003).

Context
The centre was about thirty years old and stood on the edge of a greenfield site on the edge of a small Perthshire town.

Interpretation
As with cases 126 and 128 below, Lawrie's viewpoint almost always favours the presence of 'spirit' as the source of poltergeist events.

123. MOORINGS BAR, ABERDEEN: 2002-05

Period
Summer 2002–Summer 2005 (three years).

Phenomena
The typical pub poltergeist tends to throw glasses off shelves, slam doors, turn off beer pump taps in the cellar, and make noises. All these phenomena were intermittently present and correct at the Moorings Bar on Trinity Quay between 2002 and 2005. But after hours one summer night in 2002, a four-wheeled mop bucket slid off a plinth behind the bar, rotated 90°, rolled across the bar floor for perhaps 2ft, turned 90° again, moved through the hatch beneath the bar, took the step, wheeled across the floor, and then tipped onto its side. This was witnessed by owner Craig Adams and duty manager Doug Rumbles. On another occasion, at 3 a.m. in the empty pub, a breadknife flew through the gap above a partition wall at the top of the steps to the cellar, and landed in front of Craig. Staff and customers in the gents' toilet reported sneezes or taps on the shoulder from invisible companions. A clock flew off its hook and landed on a woman's head. Microphone cables twitched of their own accord. Bartender Frank Benzie watched smoke rise out of the floor, form into a vague shape, and then sink back again.

Phenomena seemed to favour the early hours, after closing time. Sometime between 2 a.m. and 3 a.m. in summer 2005 Craig Adams was working in the cellar office. Something crashed, the temperature plummeted, and he felt frightened. A passport photograph fluttered down from the ceiling. It was of a woman, a regular at the bar who had not been seen for several weeks. The word 'Anne' and a date from the 1970s were written on the back. Craig felt sick and faint, as if the air pressure had increased, and fled the building, terrified. It later transpired that the woman, an alcoholic, had died in Aberdeen Royal Infirmary in May 2005.

Mark Thomas, the bar's sound engineer who looked after the visiting bands, attempted to record electronic voice phenomena (EVP) using various microphones. Several members of staff separately interpreted one recording as a voice saying, 'Leave the price list in the cellar'. A 1970s-era price list, which was about to be thrown out along with other debris, was promptly rescued and pinned to the office wall, where it remains to this day. On another occasion, by using a laborious method of raps – 'If the answer to our question is 'yes', please make a noise, if 'no' please remain silent' – the 'spirit' claimed to be the ghost of a regular whose funeral the staff had attended that day. Another time a communication was received from a spirit claiming to be Ted, a former barman, and a glimpsed apparition also fitted Ted's description. Since 2005 phenomena has been restricted to the occasional bout of footsteps or noises, again in the empty bar after hours.

Sources
The story first appeared in Graeme Milne's *The Haunted North* (2008). For *Haunted Aberdeen* (2010) I interviewed Craig Adams, Mark Thomas and Doug Rumbles, and included the photo of Anne.

Context
The claustrophobic cellar used to be part of a coaching inn. The Moorings itself has been a waterfront pub since the 1930s; the dimly-lit bar now hosts rock bands.

Interpretation
For some staff, the phenomena were related to several inhabiting spirits; once the EVP gave them the opportunity to express their concerns, the spirits either departed or calmed down. Although some of the events may have a pub-related mundane explanation, is there a suggestion of a discarnate intelligence in the episode with the 1970s photograph?

124. BARNTON, EDINBURGH: 2000s

Period
Unknown, but several months.

Phenomena
A few months after she moved in, Ann heard glass breaking, ran through to the sitting room, and was amazed to see a leg pulling back through the broken window-pane: a leg that was apparently not attached to a body. The police found no footprints in the garden, nor any sign of an intruder. The next day, Ann's young daughter saw a 'strange man' dressed in black staring through the glass in the front door. Once again, the police were called, but only came up with truly bizarre evidence: splashes of blood on the door's woodwork, and also in Ann's bedroom.

It is possible these events had a mundane (if criminal) origin. But a few months later poltergeist activity began. Lying in bed, Ann was hit on the head by a flying phone handset, the blow leaving a bruise. Loud footsteps and distressed female voices were heard from empty rooms. The bedroom door swung open. A tall dark figure moved round the bedroom. One evening a few months later Ann and several of her guests at a small party all heard the back door open, followed by an odd scratching noise. One guest entered the kitchen to investigate and found a young red-haired man scratching the radiator. By the time she had fetched the others the figure had vanished, and the back door was locked from the inside, as it had been all along.

Sources
Ann's experiences appear in Ron Halliday's *Edinburgh After Dark* (2010).

Context
The two-storey house in the Barnton area was quite old, with modern additions. Soon after Ann and her children moved in, they all sensed an unhappy atmosphere.

Interpretation
Without further detail, this is very hard to interpret. Is it a mix of 'normal' and supernormal events? Or entirely one or the other? Is there a family or psychological context we should know about?

125. 'QUEEN MARY'S HOUSE', ST ANDREWS, FIFE: 2003?

Period
Unknown.

Phenomena
The locus here was the library of St Leonard's School, where light bulbs were unscrewed from their sockets and displaced, doors opened of their own accord, footsteps sounded, newspapers scattered about overnight, smells of antique perfumes or old wines pervaded the aisles, and a wall clock – which persistently stopped at 9.45 p.m. – was thrown to the floor despite being bolted to the wall. Staff felt that the phenomena got worse when anyone in the building was in a bad mood. The incidents ceased at an unknown date.

Sources
Carolyn Hilles, a visiting academic from Rhode Island, interviewed then librarian Rona Wishart and assistant Stephanie Nicholson, and wrote an article for the January 2004 issue

of *Library Connection*, the newsletter of the Association of Independent School Librarians.

Context

Part of the library dates to the sixteenth century.

Interpretation

My book *Haunted St Andrews* (2012) sets out the building's extensive history of apparitions and strange noises, culminating in an exorcism in the 1920s by Bishop Plumb, the chairman of the school's council. Is there a connection between the ghosts of the pre-war era and the more recent poltergeistery? Who can say?

126. INNERLEITHEN, SCOTTISH BORDERS: 2005-09

Period

2005-2009? (five years?).

Phenomena

This polt became active in the forecourt shop of a garage, and specialised in playing with food: Mars Bars, eggs, rice, barley, and other elements of the stock were thrown around. In some cases the numbers of individual items was staggering – hundreds of coins, or tsunamis of Smarties. Water appeared in mid-air, to be poured over someone's head, while puddles – square puddles – formed on the floor. Bizarre animal noises brayed round the forecourt, the radio switched on and off, a heavy car battery jumped off and back on a shelf, and laughter was often heard, both inside the shop and within customers' cars. The polt frequently spoke in an articulate child-like voice, and then over the years learned to master communication via telephone, mobile, text and e-mail.

Sources
There is a brief mention in Archibald Lawrie's *The Psychic Investigators Casebook, Volume 3* (2007). His promised book on the case will, it is claimed, cite sixty witnesses, fifteen hours of taped audio conversation with the poltergeist, and large amounts of video and photographic evidence. My thanks to Archibald Lawrie for the personal communications.

Context
The phenomena appeared to have ceased when the garage was demolished.

Interpretation
As noted above (No. 122), Lawrie is an adherent of the 'survival hypothesis'. In this case he identifies the polt as the spirit of a five-year-old girl, Beth.

127. MINTLAW, ABERDEENSHIRE: 2006

The Aberdeenshire Heritage Museum Store is a modern state-of-the-art depot in which are kept items that are not on display in the county's museums. In 2006 a member of staff at reception heard two great crashes from the adjacent but empty and darkened staff room. When the lights were switched on, all the papers from the notice board had moved to the other side of the room, although the pins were still in the board. The wall clock had also travelled across the room, but the size of the clock was far too small to have made the loud crashes. On other occasions staff found waste bins upended, lights being turned off, and peculiar smells wafting through the building. One bizarre episode involved the photographic studio: waste paper was found spread out in a perfect circle around the rubbish bin. Some episodes are in Graeme Milne's *The Haunted North* (2008). In 2009 I visited the location and spoke to staff, writing this up in *The Guide to Mysterious Aberdeenshire*.

128. PENICUIK, MIDLOTHIAN: 2006

Period

22-24 April 2006 (three days).

Phenomena

Aerial acrobatics performed by a vacuum cleaner, a games table, ornaments, clothing, duvets, CDs, kitchen utensils, food, and dozens of other items – a whirlwind of chaos that sounds akin to the famous scene of a roomful of flying objects in the film *Poltergeist*. A pair of glass candleholders, placed in a drawer as protection from the orgy of destruction, almost instantly appeared tumbling down the stairs, although the drawer was still closed. A mobile phone was displaced from a trouser pocket in the lounge, and thrown down from the top of the stairs. The items were hot to the touch. The initials 'J.C.' (or 'J.E.') were scrawled in dust. Pieces of a large jigsaw puzzle were scattered in a trail throughout the house – and then vanished again.

The events started on the Saturday, and ceased during the night when everyone was asleep, only to continue during the daytime. On Sunday investigator Archibald Lawrie arrived, returning the next day with a medium who identified two spirits within the house: a little boy who had worked in dreadful conditions in a mine nearby in the 1700s, and an old man, the previous occupant, who died in the house. According to the medium the latter admitted to throwing the CDs around, because the teenage lad in the family kept playing awful music. The rest of the disturbances were down to the 'little git', as the old man called the ghost boy. The medium persuaded this boy – who gave his name as 'James Edwards' (J.E.) – to 'go into the light', and the disturbances ceased.

Sources

Lawrie wrote up the case in *The Psychic Investigators Casebook, Volume 3* (2007). He did not witness any of the phenomena himself, but the first panicked phone call from the family was soundtracked by the sounds of a household in poltergeist overdrive, and he photographed much of the aftermath of the mayhem.

Context

The three-storey house had been extensively renovated by Mr Macrae (pseudonym), who a few years earlier had conducted regular conversations with the spirit of the old man. Relations between Mr Macrae and his wife then broke down to the extent that he was forced to leave the house, and at the time of the events he was engaged in legal action to have her evicted. Also in the house were the grandmother, Mrs Macrae's sixteen-year-old son Derrick, and at least one younger child. When Derrick was sent to the shops on the Saturday the disturbances temporarily subsided.

Interpretation

Lawrie's investigations almost always centre on the dead manifesting, as revealed through a medium. Other interpretations are of course available.

129. EDINBURGH (PROBABLY): 2006

Period

November–December 2006 (two months?).

Phenomena

The location: a mews flat, probably in Edinburgh. The witness: a twenty-something forensic pathologist, Alice (pseudonym). The phenomena: calls to Alice's father's phone when (a) the flat when was empty and (b) the calls did not appear on the phone company's system; books and credit cards displaced from the kitchen table into the oven or fridge; a vase of flowers sliding across the draining board into the sink, with the flowers then all being perfectly arranged within the sink's plughole; and a strange smell, resistant to disinfectant and deodorant. On one occasion Alice, the last to leave the mortuary at the end of the working day, emerged from the work shower to find every window on the premises wide open, even though all but one in the empty building had been closed a few moments earlier.

Sources
Archibald Lawrie's *The Psychic Investigators Casebook, Volume 3* (2007).

Context
The pathologist's partner had just moved out after they split up, and she was studying hard for her next qualification.

Interpretation
Alice contacted Lawrie on 1 December because she was now concerned that, as she spent her days performing post-mortems on children, she had 'brought something home with her'. On 13 December Lawrie and a medium visited the flat and assured her that this could not happen, as the soul has long departed by the time the body turns up on a pathologist's slab. Instead, the medium contacted the spirit of a small boy who had lived in the house on the spot before the nineteenth-century mews were built. Having promised to stop the smell – which was the psychic residue of the privy – the spirit was allowed to remain in the flat.

130. CARDROSS, ARGYLL & BUTE: 2008

Period
2008 and possibly to 2011.

Phenomena
'Every evening we clean up, straighten everything, put the alarm on and we go. The next day the Kit-Kats are all in the wrong order and the place is in disarray.' So said Laura McKirdy,

proprietor of Laura's Café on Cardross' Main Street. The bijou establishment had 'suffered' – if that is the word – the attentions of a poltergeist since opening in April 2008. Usually the sweets were disturbed during closing hours, but on one occasion lollies that had been accidentally spilled on the floor by Laura at locking-up time were found the next morning – tidied up in their jar. Other phenomena including pictures falling off walls, crumbs appearing on tables that had just been wiped, and the occasional sounds of feet moving under the café tables.

Sources
The *Lennox Herald* (the local paper) broke the story on 5 December 2008. The *Daily Record* for 25 June 2011 – two and a half years later – carried a very similar report, which makes me wonder whether there was some recycling going on, or whether the phenomena had indeed continued into 2011.

Context
The café was bounded by shops on either side, with two storeys of flats above, all in a block 110 years old. Intriguingly, in 1896 a house somewhere in the village suffered unexplained knockings for two months.

Interpretation
Laura was convinced the 'spirit' was a friendly old woman, possibly someone who used to work in the women's clothing shop that preceded the café. This narrative seems to have been suggested or reinforced by a friend who said the local Spiritualist group had recently made contact with 'an old lady who loved to touch sweets'.

131. DUNDEE: 2008

Forty-something Tony was thrown against the kitchen units by the invisible force, pushed down the stairs, and 'punched' in the face.

Things calmed down after the local Catholic priest blessed the council house in Mid Craigie, but around ten days later a pair of ceramic pigs were found displaced onto the stairs – and then the malevolence kicked in. The phrase 'You must go' was scrawled on a wall, and 'Gonna hurt you' appeared on a notepad. Bedclothes, posters, T-shirts, towels and a bedroom carpet were slashed with what looked like knife marks. A cradle started to rock for no reason, and the baby's clothes were scattered over the floor. The ten-week-old infant was transported from its parents' double bed to close by the bathroom door – and on his chest was one of the ceramic pigs that had previously been relocated within the house. When the baby's young parents moved away out of fear, the older members of the household found a Bible at the foot of the cradle – and in the cot was an 8in carving knife. Some time afterwards Tony and his partner Rose also fled. The story was in *The Sun* on 14 November 2008.

132. THE LOTHIANS: 2008

A family moved into a new suburban house somewhere in Edinburgh and the Lothians; within a short time strange noises and object movement were reported. Clinical psychologist Thomas Rabeyron interviewed the family and found the woman hated the house and was deeply unhappy about the move. As she discussed the poltergeist experiences with him, Rabeyron heard seven very loud noises coming from the room above, as if someone was banging on the ceiling. Source: interview with Thomas Rabeyron, the *Evening News*, 17 December 2008.

133. ELDERSLIE, RENFREWSHIRE: 2009

Crime novelist Caro Ramsay happily shared her home with a gentle poltergeist dubbed Agnes, whose speciality was removing the keys from locks – once trapping the writer in the house for three hours. Items vanished, music played, doors closed and footsteps proceeded up and down the stairs. A previous owner experienced levitating TV remote controls, items flying about, and faces emerging from walls. Sources: interviews with Ramsay in the *Daily Record* (13 May 2009 and 28 September 2010) and the *Paisley Daily Express* (17 March 2012).

134. KIRKINTILLOCH, EAST DUNBARTONSHIRE: 2011-12

Period
Unclear – probably 2011 into early February 2012.

Phenomena
'It's just like living in a horror movie – I fear for our safety.' So claimed Ashley Summers after fleeing her first-floor council flat on Friars Croft. The catalogue of horror movie-style persecution encompassed: physical disruption (airborne shoes and mobile phones, pots and pans scattered over the floor, doors slammed, cupboard doors banging, bedclothes pulled); noises (voices, 'death rattles'); electrical disturbances (flickering lights); destruction (damage to a photograph); and displacement (a crucifix vanishing).

After calling on a Catholic priest (who was unable to quieten the phenomena), Ashley turned to a pair of Spiritualists, who advised her to spread flour in the kitchen to see if the spirit would communicate. She did so, and left the flat. On her return she found the latter 'D' in the flour. This seemed to confirm her fear that the phenomena were concentrated on her four-year-old son David. David had conversed with a bald man marked by an injured eye, who said he would not hurt the boy – just everyone else. Ashley had dismissed the tale as a typical child's imaginary friend, but later this ghost supposedly told David to cover a lightbulb so a fire would start.

One report stated the problems had commenced in a minor way three years' previously, but the disturbances appear to have escalated in late 2011. Ashley claimed the previous tenant had also experienced similar problems in the flat, seven years earlier. She herself moved into a privately-let flat at double her former rent.

Sources

The *Kirkintilloch Herald* (8 February 2012), followed in quick succession by the *Daily Record* (9, 10 and 11 February).

Context

The household was Ashley (twenty-six), David (four) and another son (eight).

Interpretation

Discarnate intelligence? Ghost? Child or adult RSPK? In terms of our understanding of cases like this, we may as well be back in the seventeenth century...

Bibliography

BOOKS AND MAGAZINES

Anon., *A History of the Witches of Renfrewshire who were burned on the Gallowgreen of Paisley* (Alexander Gardner; Paisley, 1877)

Aberdeen Buchan Association Magazine No. 10 (Nov. 1913) and No. 11 (Jan. 1914)

Adams, Norman, *Haunted Valley: Ghost Stories, Mysteries and Legends of Royal Deeside* (Tolbooth Books; Banchory, 1994)

Adams, Norman, *Haunted Scotland* (Mainstream Publishing; Edinburgh, 1998)

Agnew, Andrew, *The Hereditary Sheriffs of Galloway* (David Douglas; Edinburgh, 1893)

Allan, Brian, *Revenants: Haunted People & Haunted Places* (11th Dimension Publishing/Healings of Atlantis; Hayes, 2010)

Anderson, Robert, *Aberdeen in Byegone Days* (Aberdeen Daily Journal Office; Aberdeen, 1910)

Anderson, William, *Guide to the Formantine and Buchan Railway* (W.L. Taylor; Peterhead / A. Brown & Co.; Aberdeen, 1862)

'An old residenter' [Charles Ogg], *Banchory-Ternan 60 years ago: Reminiscences of Bygone Days* (Free Press Office; Aberdeen, 1870)

Back In The Day No. 4, March/April 2006

Baillie, Robert, *The letters and journals of Robert Baillie … M.DC.XXXVII-M.DC.LXII* (The Bannatyne Club; Edinburgh, 1842)

Barbour, Margaret Frazer, *Memoir of Mrs. Stewart Sandeman of Bonskeid and Springland, by Her Daughter* (James Nisbet & Co.; London, 1892)

Barden, Dennis, *Mysterious Worlds* (W.H. Allen; London, 1970)

Baxter, Richard, *The Certainty of the World of Spirits Fully Evinced* (H. Howell; London, 1840 – originally published 1691)

Black, G.F. (ed. Northcote W. Thomas), *County Folk-Lore Vol. III. Examples of Printed Folk-Lore Concerning the Orkney & Shetland Islands* (The Folklore Society/David Nutt; London, 1903)

Botting, Douglas, *Gavin Maxwell: A Life* (HarperCollins; London, 1993)

Brownlie, Niall M. *Bailtean is Ath-Ghairmean, Townships and Echoes* (Argyll Publishing; Glendaruel, 1995)

Byrd, Elizabeth, *Ghosts in My Life* (Ballantine Books; New York, 1968)

Byrd, Elizabeth, *A Strange and Seeing Time* (Robert Hale; London, 1971)

Campbell, John Gregerson (ed. Ronald Black), *The Gaelic Otherworld [Superstitions of the Highlands & Islands of Scotland, and Witchcraft & Second Sight in the Highlands & Islands]* (Birlinn; Edinburgh, 2005 – first published 1900 & 1902)

Campbell, John L. and Trevor H. Hall, *Strange Things: The Story of Fr Allan McDonald, Ada Goodrich Freer, and the Society of Psychical Research's Enquiry into Highland Second Sight* (Birlinn; Edinburgh, 2006 – first published 1968)

Chambers, Robert, *The Picture of Scotland* (William Tait; Edinburgh, 1827)

Colman, George, *Random Records* (Henry Colburn & Richard Bentley; London, 1830)

Compton, Carole (with Gerald Cole), *Superstition. The True Story of the Nanny They called a Witch* (Ebury Press; London, 1990)

Cowan, David and Chris Arnold, *Ley Lines and Earth Energies* (Adventures Unlimited Press; Illinois, 2004)

Crowe, Catherine, *The Night-Side of Nature, or, Ghosts and Ghost-Seers* (T.C. Newby; London, 1848)

Davies, Owen, *The Haunted: A Social History of Ghosts* (Palgrave MacMillan; Basingstoke and New York, 2007)

Dick, C.H., *Highways and Byways in Galloway and Carrick* (Macmillan & Co.; London, 1916)

Dingwall, E.J. and Trevor H. Hall, *Four Modern Ghosts* (Duckworth; London, 1958)

Donaldson, Andrew, *Guide to Kirkmaiden* (J. Maxwell; Dumfries, 1908)

Eyre-Todd, George, *History Of Glasgow* (Jackson, Wylie & Co.; Glasgow, 1934)

Floyd, Thomas, *Cairntable Rhymes* (The Muirkirk Advertiser; Muirkirk, 1929)

Fort, Charles, *The Book of the Damned* (John Brown Publishing; London, New Ed. 1995 – first published 1919)

Fort, Charles, *Lo!* (John Brown Publishing; London, New Ed. 1997 – first published 1931)

Fort, Charles, *Wild Talents* (John Brown Publishing; London, 1998 – first published 1932)

Frere, Richard, *Maxwell's Ghost: An Epilogue to Gavin Maxwell's Camusfearna* (Birlinn; Edinburgh, 1999 - first published 1976)

Gammie, Alexander, *The Churches of Aberdeen: Historical and Descriptive* (Aberdeen Daily Journal Office; Aberdeen, 1909)

Gibson, Isobel, 'The Haunting at Auchencairn' in *The Scots Magazine* Vol. 135, No.1, April 1991

Goldstein, Diane E., Sylvia Ann Grider & Jeannie Banks Thomas, *Haunting Experiences: Ghosts in Contemporary Folklore* (Utah State University Press; Logan, Utah; 2007)

Goodare, Julian (ed.), *The Scottish Witch-Hunt in Context* (Manchester University Press; Manchester & New York, 2002)

Bibliography

Goodrich-Freer, A. (Miss X) and John, Marquess of Bute, *The Alleged Haunting Of B---- House* (George Redway; London, 1899)

Goss, Michael, *Poltergeists: An Annotated Bibliography of Works in English, circa 1880-1975* (The Scarecrow Press; New Jersey & London, 1979)

Grant, James Shaw, *The Gaelic Vikings* (James Thin; Edinburgh, 1984)

Halliday, Ron, *Evil Scotland* (Fort Publishing; Ayr, 2003)

Halliday, Ron, *Haunted Glasgow* (Fort Publishing; Ayr, 2008)

Halliday, Ron, *Edinburgh After Dark* (Black & White Publishing; Edinburgh, 2010)

Hassan, Selim, *Excavations at Gîza 7: 1935-1936. The Mastabas of the Seventh Season and their Description* (Government Press; Cairo, 1953)

Henderson, Jan-Andrew, *The Town Below the Ground: Edinburgh's Legendary Underground City* (Mainstream; Edinburgh & London, 1999)

Henderson, Jan-Andrew, *The Ghost That Haunted Itself: The Story of the McKenzie Poltergeist* (Mainstream; Edinburgh & London, 2001)

Henderson, Jan-Andrew, *Edinburgh: City of the Dead* (Black & White Publishing; Edinburgh, 2004)

Holder, Geoff, *The Guide to Mysterious Perthshire* (Tempus; Stroud, 2006)

Holder, Geoff, *The Guide to Mysterious Glasgow* (The History Press; Stroud, 2008)

Holder, Geoff, *The Guide to Mysterious Aberdeenshire* (The History Press; Stroud, 2009)

Holder, Geoff, *Haunted Aberdeen & District* (The History Press; Stroud, 2011)

Holder, Geoff, *Haunted Dundee* (The History Press; Stroud, 2012)

Holder, Geoff, *Haunted St Andrews* (The History Press; Stroud, 2012)

Jánosi, Peter, 'Wo waren Chephrens Töchter bestattet?' in '*Zur Zierde gereicht...' Festschrift Bettina Schmitz zum GO* (Verlag Gebrüder Gerstenberg; Hlldeshelm, 2008)

Johnstone, C.L., *History of the Johnstones 1191-1909, with descriptions of Border life* (W. & A.K. Johnstone; Edinburgh and London, 1909)

Kirk, Robert, *The Secret Commonwealth of Elves, Fauns and Fairies* (Eneas Mackay; Stirling, 1933)

Lamb, John Alexander (ed.), *Fasti Ecclesiae Scoticanae: The Succession of Ministers in The Church of Scotland from The Reformation. Volume 9 – from the Union of the Churches 2 October 1929, to 31 December 1954* (Oliver & Boyd; Edinburgh, 1961)

Lamont, Stewart, *Is Anybody There?* (Mainstream Publishing; Edinburgh, 1980)

Law, Robert (ed. Charles Kirkpatrick Sharpe), *Memorialls, or the memorable things that fell out within this island of Britain from 1638-1684* (Archibald Constable & Co.; Edinburgh, 1818)

Lawrie, Archibald A., *The Psychic Investigators Casebook Volume 1* (1st Books; Bloomington, Indiana, 2003)

Lawrie, Archibald A., *The Psychic Investigators Casebook Volume 3* (Archibald A. Lawrie; Scotland, 2007)

Lecouteux, Claude, *The Secret History of Poltergeists and Haunted Houses* (Inner Traditions, Rochester, Vermont, 2012 – published 2007 as *La maison hantée: Histoire des Poltergeists*)

Lee, Frederick George, *A Statement of Facts with regard to his resignation of the incumbency of St John's, Aberdeen* (A. Brown & Co.; Aberdeen, 1861)

Lee, Frederick George, *Glimpses of the Supernatural: Being Facts, Records and Traditions Relating to Dreams, Omens, Miraculous Occurrences, Apparitions, Wraiths, Warnings,*

Second-Sight, Witchcraft, Necromancy, etc. (H.S. King & Co.; London, 1875)

Lockhart, John Gibson, *Memoirs of the life of Sir Walter Scott, bart* Volume 4 (Carey, Lea, & Blanchard; Philadelphia, 1838)

London Dialectical Society, *Report on Spiritualism of the Committee of the London Dialectical Society* (Longmans, Green, Reader & Dyer; London, 1871)

Love, Dane, *Scottish Spectres* (Robert Hale; London, 2001)

McHarg, J.F., 'A poltergeist case from Glasgow' in J.D. Morris, W.G. Roll & R.L. Morris (eds.), *Research in Parapsychology 1976* (Scarecrow; Metuchen, N.J., 1977)

Macintyre, Lorn, *Pitmilly House: 'Poltergeist Manor'* (Priormuir Press; St Andrews, 2011)

Mackay, Charles, *Memoirs of Extraordinary Popular Delusions and the Madness of Crowds* (Office of The National Illustrated Library; London, 1852)

McLachlan, Hugh (ed.), *The Kirk, Satan and Salem: a history of the witches of Renfrewshire* (Grimsay Press; Glasgow, 2006)

McLachlan, Hugh V. and Kim Swales, 'The bewitchment of Christian Shaw: a reassessment of the famous Paisley witchcraft case of 1697' in Yvonne Galloway Brown and Rona Ferguson (eds.), *Twisted Sisters: Women, Crime and Deviance in Scotland since 1400* (Tuckwell; East Linton, 2002)

MacLean, Donald, *Duthil, Past and Present* (The Northern Newspaper and Printing and Publishing Company; Inverness, 1910)

McPherson, J. M., *Primitive Beliefs in the North-East of Scotland* (Longmans, Green & Co.; London, 1929)

Maidment, James (ed.), *Analecta Scotica: Collections Illustrative of the Civil, Ecclesiastical, and Literary History of Scotland* (Thomas G. Stevenson; Edinburgh, 1834)

Marchbank, Agnes, *Upper Annandale: Its History and Traditions* (J. & R. Parlane; Paisley / John Menzies & Co.; Edinburgh and Glasgow, 1901)

Martine, Roddy, *Supernatural Scotland* (Robert Hale; London, 2003)

Masson, David, *The Life of John Milton* (MacMillan & Co.; London, 1877)

Maxwell, Gavin, *Raven Seek Thy Brother* (Longman; London, 1968)

Maxwell-Stuart, P.G., *Ghosts: A History of Phantoms, Ghouls and other Spirits of the Dead* (Tempus; Stroud, 2006)

Maxwell-Stuart, P.G., *The Great Scottish Witch-Hunt* (Tempus; Stroud, 2007)

Maxwell-Stuart, P.G., *Poltergeists: A History of Violent Ghostly Phenomena* (Amberley; Stroud, 2011)

Milne, Graeme, *The Haunted North: Paranormal Tales from Aberdeen and the North East* (Cauliay Publishing; Aberdeen, 2008)

Mitchell, Arthur, *The Past In The Present: What Is Civilization?* (Harper & Brothers New York, 1881)

Mitchell, J. and J. Dickie, *The Philosophy of Witchcraft* (Murray & Stewart; Paisley, et al, 1839)

Mordle-Barnes, Mollie, 'Merry Pranks in a Scottish Rectory' in *True Ghost Stories Of The British Isles* (Bounty Books; London, 2005)

Murdie, Alan, *Haunted Edinburgh* (The History Press; Stroud, 2010)

Notes and Queries, October, November & December 1889

Owen, A.R.G., *Can We Explain The Poltergeist?* (Helix Press; New York, 1964)

Owen, Robert Dale, *Footfalls on the Boundary of Another World* (J.B. Lipponcott & Co.; Philadelphia, 1860)

Bibliography

Parsons, Coleman O., *Witchcraft and Demonology in Scott's Fiction* (Oliver & Boyd; Edinburgh & London, 1964)

Penny, George, *Traditions of Perth* (Dewar, Sidey, Morison, Peat and Drummond, Perth, 1836 – reprinted Wm Culross & Son, Coupar Angus, 1986)

Powicke, Frederick J. (ed.), *Eleven Letters of John, Second Earl of Lauderdale (and First Duke), 1616-1682, to the Rev. Richard Baxter (1615-1691)* (Manchester University Press; Manchester, 1922)

Rannachan, Tom, *Psychic Scotland* (Black & White Publishing; Edinburgh, 2007)

Robertson, James, *Scottish Ghost Stories* (Warner Books; London, 1996)

Robertson, R. Macdonald, *Selected Highland Folktales* (Oliver & Boyd; Edinburgh & London, 1961)

Robinson, Malcolm, *Paranormal Case Files of Great Britain Volume 1* (11th Dimension Publishing/Healings of Atlantis; Hayes, 2010)

Rogo, D. Scott, *The Poltergeist Experience* (The Aquarian Press; Wellingborough, 1990)

Roy, Archie, *A Sense of Something Strange* (Dog & Bone Press; Glasgow, 1990)

Rutter, Gordon, *Paranormal Edinburgh* (The History Press; Stroud, 2009)

Scott, Hew et al, *Fasti Ecclesiae Scoticanae: The Succession of Ministers in The Church of Scotland from The Reformation* (Oliver & Boyd; Edinburgh, 8 Vols, New Edition 1915-1928)

Scott, Sir Walter, *Letters on Demonology and Witchcraft* (Wordsworth/The Folklore Society; Ware & London, 2001 – first published 1830)

Sharpe, Charles Kirkpatrick, *A Historical Account of the Belief in Witchcraft in Scotland* (Hamilton, Adams; London / Thomas D Morison; Glasgow, 1884)

Sharpe, James, *Instruments of Darkness: Witchcraft in England 1550-1750* (Hamish Hamilton; London, 1996)

Sinclair, Sir John (ed.), *The Statistical Account of Scotland: Volume 15 County of Orkney* (EP Publishing; Wakefield, 1983 – originally published 1791-1799)

Skene, William Forbes, *East Neuk Chronicles* (Aberdeen Journal Office; Aberdeen, 1905)

Smith, David Crawford, *The Historians of Perth and Other Local and Topographical Writers* (John Christie; Perth, 1906)

Smith, Robert, *Grampian Curiosities* (Birlinn; Edinburgh, 2005)

Spicer, Henry, *Facts and Fantasies: A Sequel to Sights and Sounds; The Mystery of the Day* (Thomas Bosworth, London, 1853)

Spicer, Henry, *Sights and Sounds: The Mystery of the Day: Comprising an Entire History of the American 'Spirit' Manifestations* (Thomas Bosworth; London, 1853)

Stevenson, Robert Louis, *Edinburgh: Picturesque Notes* (Seeley, Jackson, and Halliday; London, 1878)

Stuart, John (ed.), *Extracts from The Presbytery Book of Strathbogie* (The Spalding Club; Aberdeen, 1843)

Symonds, Richard, (ed. Charles Edward Long), *Diary of the Marches of the Royal Army during the Great Civil War* (The Camden Society; London, 1859)

Temperley, Alan, *Tales of Galloway* (Skilton & Shaw; London, 1979)

Underwood, Peter, *A Gazetteer of Scottish and Irish Ghosts* (Souvenir Press; London, 1973)

Underwood, Peter, *Gazetteer of Scottish Ghosts* (Fontana/Collins; Glasgow, 1975)

Underwood, Peter, *Guide to Ghosts & Haunted Places* (Piatkus; London, 1999)

Walker, William, *The De'il at Baldarroch, and other poems, in the Scottish Dialect* (printed for the author; Aberdeen, 1839)

Walker, William, *The Bards of Bon-Accord, 1375-1860* (Edmond & Spark; Aberdeen, 1887)

Walker, William, *'Boodie Brae': A Longside Legend* (Milne & Stephen; Aberdeen, 1913)

Watt, Archibald, *Highways and Byways Round Kincardine* (Gourdas House; Aberdeen, 1985)

Westwood, Jennifer and Sophia Kingshill, *The Lore of Scotland* (Random House; London, 2009)

Wilson, Alan, Dan Brogan & Fran Hollinrake, *Hidden and Haunted: Underground Edinburgh* (Mercat Tours; Edinburgh, 1999)

Wilson, Colin, *Poltergeist! A Study in Destructive Haunting* (New English Library, Sevenoaks, 1981)

Wilson, Ian, *Worlds Beyond* (Weidenfield and Nicolson; London, 1986)

Wodrow, Robert, *Analecta, Or, Materials for a History of Remarkable Providences; Mostly Relating to Scottish Ministers and Christians* (Maitland Club; Edinburgh, 1842-43)

Wood, J. Maxwell, *Witchcraft and Superstitious Record in the South Western District of Scotland* (J. Maxwell & Son; Dumfries, 1911)

Wyness, Fenton, *Royal Valley: The story of the Aberdeenshire Dee* (Alex P. Reid & Son; Aberdeen, 1968)

JOURNALS

[JSPR = Journal of the Society for Psychical Research]

Alvarado, Carlos S. and Nancy L. Zingrone, 'Characteristics of Hauntings with and without Apparitions: An Analysis of Published Cases' in *JSPR* Vol. 60 (1994-1995)

Bath, Jo and John Newton, '"Sensible Proof of Spirits': Ghost Belief during the Later Seventeenth Century' in *Folklore* Vol. 117, No. 1 (April, 2006)

Colvin, Barrie, 'The Acoustic Properties of Unexplained Rapping Sounds' in *JSPR* Vol. 73 (2010)

Cornell, A.D. and Alan Gauld, 'The Geophysical Theory of Poltergeists' in *JSPR* Vol. 41 (1961-1962)

Craigie, W A., 'Donald Bán and the Bócan' in *Folklore* Vol. 6, No. 4 (Dec., 1895)

Henderson, Lizanne, 'The survival of witchcraft prosecutions and witch belief in South West Scotland' in *Scottish Historical Review* Vol. 85, No. 216 (2006)

Houran, James and Rense Lange, 'Diary Of Events in a Thoroughly Unhaunted House' in *Perceptual and Motor Skills* Vol. 83, Issue 2 (Oct. 1996)

Houran, James and Rense Lange, 'A Rasch hierarchy of haunt and poltergeist experiences' in *Journal of Parapsychology* No. 65 (2001)

Journal of the American Society for Psychical Research No. 41 (Oct. 1947)

JSPR Vol. 2 (1885-1886)

JSPR Vol. 8 (1897-1898)

JSPR Vol. 13 (1907-1908)

JSPR Vol. 20 (1921-1922)

Keyworth, G. David, 'Was the Vampire of the Eighteenth Century a unique type of Undead-corpse?' in *Folklore* Vol. 117, No. 3 (Dec., 2006)

Bibliography

Lambert, G.W., 'Poltergeists: Some Simple Experiments and Tests' in *JSPR* Vol. 38 No. 687 (March 1956)

Lambert, G.W., 'Scottish Haunts and Poltergeists: A Regional Study' in *JSPR* Vol. 40 (1962) and Vol. 42 (1964)

Lambert, G.W., 'Stranger Things: Some Reflections on Reading "Strange Things"' By John L. Campbell and Trevor H. Hall' in *JSPR* Vol. 45 (1969-1970)

McCue, Peter A., 'Theories of Haunting: A Critical Overview' in *JSPR* Vol. 661, No. 866 (Jan. 2002)

McCue, Peter A., 'Recurrent Spontaneous Phenomena and UFO Sightings: A Case Report' in *The Paranormal Review*, 28 (Oct. 2003)

McDonald, S.W., A. Thom, and A. Thom, 'The Bargarran Witchcraft Trial: A Psychiatric Re-assessment' in *The Scottish Medical Journal* Vol. 14 (1996)

McHarg, James F., 'The Paranormal and the Recognition of Personal Distress' in *JSPR* Vol. 51 No. 790 (Feb. 1982)

Matheson, Norman, 'The Apparitions and Ghosts of the Isle of Skye' in *Transactions of the Gaelic Society of Inverness*, Vol. 18 (1891-92)

Mitchell, Arthur, 'The Miracle Stone of the Spey, Vacation Notes in Cromar and Strathspey' in *Proceedings of the Society of Antiquaries of Scotland* Vol. 4 (1875)

Podmore, Frank, 'Clairvoyance and Poltergeists' in *JSPR* Vol. 9 (June 1899)

Wiseman, Richard, 'The Haunted Brain' in *Skeptical Enquirer* Vol. 35.5 (Sept/Oct 2011)

Wiseman, Richard, Caroline Watt, Paul Stevens, Emma Greening, and Ciarán O'Keeffe, 'An investigation into alleged "Hauntings"' in *British Journal of Psychology* Vol. 94 (2003)

WEBSITES

Auld Reekie Tours: www.auldreekietours.com
Black Hart Entertainment: www.blackhart.uk.com
East of Scotland Paranormal: www.esparanormal.org.uk,
Haddow, Angus H., *Dowsing for Patterns of the Past - The Stone Circles of Aberdeenshire*: http://historyandmysterytours.blogspot.co.uk
The House of Seton of Scotland: www2.thesetonfamily.com
Scottish Society for Psychical Research: www.sspr.co.uk
Tiree Place Names: www.tireeplacenames.org
Tobar an Dualchais: www.tobarandualchais.co.uk

RECORDINGS OF TALKS

McHarg, James, 'An Argyll Poltergeist' (Society for Psychical Research, 1987)

Magee, Max, 'Dealing with a Poltergeist' (The Churches' Fellowship for Psychical and Spiritual Studies, 1991)

Roy, Archie, 'The House at Maxwell Park. Poltergeist, Possession or…?' (Society for Psychical Research)

UNPUBLISHED ITEMS

Anon., 'Black Ert', manuscript (Shetland Archives D18/446/1)
Circuit Court Books JC10/1 and JC10/4 (National Records of Scotland)
Edinburgh Sheriff Court Advising Books SC39/3/32 (National Records of Scotland)
Privy Council PC1/51 (National Records of Scotland)
Process Notes JC26/26 (National Records of Scotland)
Williamson, Joan, Transcript of interview on 15 December 1982 (Shetland Archives SA3/1/95)

Index

Abbotsford 60-61
Aberdeen 57, 77-80,
  108-110, 150-151, 158,
  199-200, 202-204
Aberdeenshire 15-17, 58,
  65-67, 70-73, 96-97,
  106, 151-153, 177-178,
  185-186, 207
Alloa 142, 174
Angus 107-108
Ardachie Lodge 130
Argyll & Bute 64,
  74-75, 93-95, 110-111,
  144-146, 210-211
Auchencairn 31
Auchterarder 68
Auldgirth 186
Ayr 173
Badenoch 63
Baldarroch 70-73
Ballechin House 97-101
Banchory 70-72
Banshee 108
Bargarran 40-45, 54, 77
Baxter, Richard 14-15, 17
Benbecula 89-90
Berneray 107
Blessed Virgin Mary
  170-171
Boat of Garten 63,
  85-87

Boleskine House
  168-169
Bócan 55-57, 92
Bonskeid 62-64
Botary 15-17
Caithness 73
Cardross 210-211
Charles II 17, 189
Civil Wars, The 12, 14,
  17, 23
Clackmannanshire
  140-144, 173-175, 178
Compton, Carole 25,
  173
Covenanters 12, 14,
  45-48, 51, 189-191,
  193
Crieff 148-150, 183
Crowley, Aleister
  168-169
Dalbeattie 31, 182
Dalry 182-183
Demons/The Devil 6-7,
  9, 13, 15, 18-25, 27-30,
  36, 38-39, 40-41, 44,
  50, 52, 54, 60, 64, 66,
  73, 80-81, 91, 96-97,
  168, 169, 181, 183-84
Dumfries 57
Dumfries & Galloway
  17-25, 31-40, 45-48,

  50-52, 57, 182, 186
Dundee 68, 133, 145,
  163, 171-172, 211-212
Dunstaffnage Castle 64
Dunnottar 58
East Ayrshire 47, 83-85,
  128
East Dunbartonshire
  213-214
East Lothian 29-31,
  76-77, 111, 172
East Renfrewshire
  40-45
Edinburgh 12-15, 27, 37,
  47, 68-70, 77, 80-81,
  87-88, 111-112, 113,
  116-124, 130-133,
  137-138, 141, 151,
  172-173, 176-177,
  178-182, 187-194,
  204-205, 209-210, 212
Elderslie 212-213
Ellon 96-97, 106
Eriskay 88, 89-90
Exorcism 68, 137, 171,
  198, 206
'Fairies' etc. 6, 8, 9, 56,
  60, 64-65, 92, 95-96,
  132-133
Fairmilehead 137-138
Falkirk 175-176

223

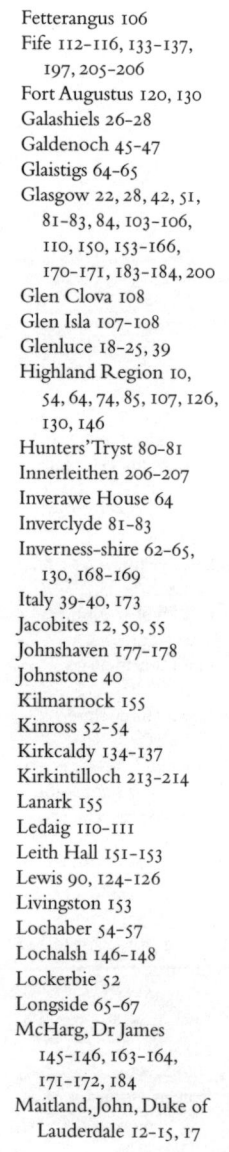

Fetterangus 106
Fife 112-116, 133-137, 197, 205-206
Fort Augustus 120, 130
Galashiels 26-28
Galdenoch 45-47
Glaistigs 64-65
Glasgow 22, 28, 42, 51, 81-83, 84, 103-106, 110, 150, 153-166, 170-171, 183-184, 200
Glen Clova 108
Glen Isla 107-108
Glenluce 18-25, 39
Highland Region 10, 54, 64, 74, 85, 107, 126, 130, 146
Hunters' Tryst 80-81
Innerleithen 206-207
Inverawe House 64
Inverclyde 81-83
Inverness-shire 62-65, 130, 168-169
Italy 39-40, 173
Jacobites 12, 50, 55
Johnshaven 177-178
Johnstone 40
Kilmarnock 155
Kinross 52-54
Kirkcaldy 134-137
Kirkintilloch 213-214
Lanark 155
Ledaig 110-111
Leith Hall 151-153
Lewis 90, 124-126
Livingston 153
Lochaber 54-57
Lochalsh 146-148
Lockerbie 52
Longside 65-67
McHarg, Dr James 145-146, 163-164, 171-172, 184
Maitland, John, Duke of Lauderdale 12-15, 17

Maxwell, Gavin 146-148
Mellantae 50-52, 77
Methlick 185-186
Midlothian 208-209
Mintlaw 207
Moffat 17-18
Monessie 54-57
Motherwell 155-156, 178
Muirkirk 83-85, 128
Mull 64
Naples 39
Nesting 95-96
North Ayrshire 182-183
North Lanarkshire 155-156, 178
Ollaberry 90-93
Orkney 58
Ormiston 29-31
Paisley 41, 42, 44
Peaston 76-77
Peebles 169
Penicuik 208-209
Perth 58
Perth & Kinross 52-54, 58, 62-64, 68, 97-101, 148-150, 201-202
Peterhead 67
Pitlochry 62
Pitmilly House 112-116
Port Appin 74-75
Port Glasgow 81-83
'Possession' 10, 40-45, 130, 144-145
Rerrick 31-40, 43
Ross & Cromarty 126-127
St Andrews 115, 133-134, 197, 205-206
Salem 43
Sandaig 146-148
Sandwood Bay 132
Satan *see* Demons/The Devil
Sauchie 140-144, 173-175, 186-187

Scott, Sir Walter 58, 60-61
Scottish Borders 26-28, 60-61, 107, 169, 206-207
Shetland 90-93, 95-96
Skye 74, 107
Society for Psychical Research 7, 60, 88, 98, 99-100, 101, 105, 110-111, 113, 114, 115, 130, 133, 143, 145, 162, 163, 165, 170, 172, 196
South Lanarkshire 47, 155
South Uist 88-90
Spiritualism 6, 57, 60, 76, 82-83, 103, 109-110, 111, 113, 135, 136, 142, 160, 174, 175, 211, 213
Stevenson, Robert Louis 80-81, 194
Stirling 25-26, 197-199
Stonehaven 71, 72
Stranraer 18, 45
Strathglass 64-65
Strathspey 85-87
Stronsay 58
Sutherland 132
Tain 126-127
Temporal Lobe Epilepsy 171
Tillicoultry 178
Tiree 74-76, 93-95
Tolsta Chaolais 124-126
Trow/Trowie 92
West Lothian 153
Western Isles 88-90, 107, 124-126
Witchcraft & magic 7, 9, 12, 15-17, 20, 23-24, 25-26, 27, 33, 35, 39-44, 47-48, 50, 54, 60, 67, 77, 91-93, 95-95, 107, 169, 173, 181

Visit our website and discover thousands of other History Press books.
www.thehistorypress.co.uk

The History Press